W9-CEZ-515

TANZANIA: JOURNEY TO REPUBLIC

To Susan, who bore the heat and burden of the day.

DATE DUE

MAY 0 9 2002

DEC 1 1 2002

JUL 1 5 2005

AUG 2 9 2005

MAR 2 0 2006

JUL 2 0 2008

Printed
in USA

Contents

Contents

Illustrations

Colour plates

Black and white plates

Acknowledgements

This book, started many years ago, would never have been finished without the great help and encouragement of Professor Miriam Chaiken of the University of Indiana, Pennsylvania, and one of her students, Tara Lufy, who managed to decipher my handwriting and type most of the initial text.

My friend and neighbour, Natasha de Woronin, expertly completed the task helped by her African background.

Most of the photographs were taken by my old friend, Bernard Kunicki, who also gave constant support and encouragement; the remainder were presented to me by the Tanganyika Government Public Relations Department.

Last, but not least, my children Lucy and Gerald spurred me on and refreshed my memory.

Foreword by Julius K. Nyerere

Randal Sadleir, whom I have known for over four decades, has tried to convey in this book his personal impressions of the last years of colonial rule in the then Tanganyika, and the first years of independence in Tanzania. He writes from the viewpoint of an unusually individualistic Irish district officer, whose ill-concealed sympathy for the nationalist cause before *uhuru* in 1961 was only matched by his forthright opinions after it.

I knew him best through the critical years of the independence struggle from 1955–61, when his better knowledge of Kiswahili among the colonial officers led him to the Public Relations Department in charge of the colonial government's press and radio, with personal responsibility for liaison with TANU (... *kutawaliwa ni fedheha*: colonialism is a disgrace) put him in trouble with his masters; his accurate translation of my speech, on another occasion, spared them some possible troubles with TANU supporters.

He was among a number of colonial officials who gladly accepted my invitation to serve my government after independence. He served the new government with equal loyalty, playing a key role in the cooperative movement, the training of African officers overseas, and the success of the Tanzanian pavilion at Expo 70 in Japan. As the last expatriate district officer to leave the country in 1973, for which he was nicknamed '*mkoloni wa mwisho*', he has a unique tale to tell.

I commend this book to all wishing to understand something of the background to the dramatic events surrounding the birth of Tanzania, as seen through the eyes of a detached, yet sympathetic, foreign, participant.

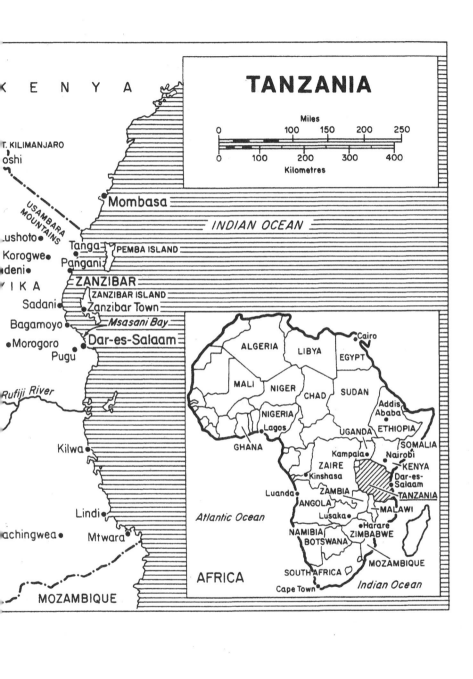

TANZANIA

Miles

0   100   150   200   250

0   100   200   300   400

Kilometres

KENYA

T. KILIMANJARO
oshi

USAMBARA MOUNTAINS

ushoto •

Korogwe •

deni •

IKA

Sadani •

Bagamoyo •

• Morogoro

Pugu

Rufiji River

Kilwa •

Lindi •

achingwea •   Mtwara •

MOZAMBIQUE

Mombasa

INDIAN OCEAN

Tanga   PEMBA ISLAND

Pangani

ZANZIBAR

ZANZIBAR ISLAND

Zanzibar Town

Msasani Bay

Dar-es-Salaam

AFRICA

ALGERIA   LIBYA   EGYPT   Cairo

MALI   NIGER   CHAD   SUDAN

NIGERIA   Addis Ababa

GHANA   Lagos   UGANDA   ETHIOPIA

SOMALIA

Kampala   Nairobi

ZAIRE   KENYA

Kinshasa   Dar-es-Salaam

Luanda   ZAMBIA   TANZANIA

ANGOLA   MALAWI

Lusaka

Atlantic Ocean   Harare

NAMIBIA   ZIMBABWE

BOTSWANA   MOZAMBIQUE

SOUTH AFRICA

Cape Town   Indian Ocean

1

A Childhood Dream,
1924–42

I was born in spring in an old mill house with a beautiful garden on the banks of the River Liffey. The big pink cherry blossom tree by the millrace was in full bloom. It was 1924 — the year Lenin died and two years after the creation of the Irish Free State. My brother and I had an enchanted childhood playing in the garden, swimming in the river and browsing among the books in the house. My father Tom seemed old, fierce and very scholarly, my mother Norma young, gentle and pretty. Indeed, so literary was the atmosphere that I am told that the first word I uttered was 'book'.

But it was the garden, girt by the river and pierced by the tranquil waters of the millrace, that we loved the most. I have never ceased to dream of it since, with its orchard and paddock, tennis court, kitchen garden, rock garden, water garden and weir, great copper beech trees, sycamores, maples, silver birches, larches, a monkey puzzle and thickets of bamboo. Tulips, forget-me-nots, primroses, polyanthus, primulas and daffodils in spring, roses everywhere in summer: roses on trellises over the millrace, rose beds cut in grassy banks, roses of all colours, roses with odd names.

Then, in autumn there would be falling leaves and games of conkers with chestnuts, fading gradually to winter with blue smoke from turf fires, bare branches and raucous rooks, snow drifts, snowmen and logs for the fire.

Christmas was a thrilling winter pageant for the children of Celbridge — church bells and carols, parties, plays and services,

1

and richer children surrendering teddy bears and dolls to poorer children. I was richer, so my bear Benjamin was duly handed over at the altar rails to the rector Canon Fletcher. I felt sad, but proud. A smaller bear Frankie remained to comfort me, while Tiger Tim also did his best on the walls of the night nursery. We lacked for nothing, but went on long country walks between meals, sometimes supplementing our ample rations with a farthing's worth of bullseyes from Miss Coyle's little shop in the main street.

We knew everyone and everyone knew us. Some had known my grandfather and even my great-grandfather, which gave one a wonderful feeling of warmth and security. Horse-drawn vehicles were still common on the unpaved country lanes, from the traps and dogcarts of the prosperous to the carts and bogeys of the peasants. Occasionally, our elderly neighbour Miss Alice Kirkpatrick would pick us up on the road and take us for a drive in her carriage — the last in County Kildare.

Thus the precious days of early childhood passed easily, broken only by a round of children's parties in the neighbours' houses, fancy dress balls, dancing classes, hunt-the-slipper in the winter, paper chases, rounders and sports in the summer. Most exciting of all, a visit to the pantomime in the winter and a trip to the seaside at Portmarnock or Donabate, with a rare visit to the zoo in the Phoenix Park, and tiny pots of strawberry jam. In the autumn, my grandmother joined us for the annual blackberry-picking expedition on Boston Hill, one of the highest points in Ireland's flattest County Kildare, home of the Curragh Camp where my father was born, and the bog of Allan.

There was always the river, Ana Livia (Mother Liffey), on the margin of our lives. Sometimes it was a raging brown torrent flecked with foam like soap suds, flooding its banks, flooding the villages and roads, once even flooding our basements, sweeping all before it, muddy and murderous. At other times, it was a clear rippling stream, with rocks and stepping stones exposed as miniature waterfalls and rapids here and there, mossily murmuring.

The road to Dublin — 12 miles distant — follows the river through Lucan and Chapelizod before entering the city at Parkgate to an unforgettable aroma of roasting coffee, soon to be succeeded by the pungent smell of Guinness whose barges and barrels had ruled the Liffey for centuries.

We usually drove along the south bank of the Quays to the clatter of horses' hooves on the cobblestones, the cry of seagulls, · and the chiming of church bells. Spanned by eight graceful bridges, the river was now nobly escorted to the sea by the pink and silver elegance of brick and granite Georgian buildings, crowned at the North Wall by Gandon's stately Custom House.

Indeed, the deep sense of history and beauty always aroused by these quaint quays — the very heart of the city — has never left me and returning to Ireland the day after my birthday after my longest ever absence of seven years moved me to write the following haiku:

> Two Birthdays
> Like A Persian King
> Weep Silently
> And Sing
> Without Tears.

Mountains surrounded the bay where the river ran into the sea. The mystery of the waters meeting was heightened by the mists, which floated up the river and veiled the city in a luminous haze. At night, the glare of the street lamps reached for the stars until the great copper domes and slender grey spires danced across the sky, fleecy clouds flecked with gold.

Dublin, the epitome of the Anglo–Irish cultural achievement, in its eighteenth-century Georgian heyday the fourth city in Europe after London, Paris and Vienna, has always made me acutely aware of the contradictions in my blood. Father, stern scion of the Cromwellian invader, the colonial conqueror; Mother, brown eyed Celtic beauty, a Kenny from Killeshandra set deep in the lakes and hills of faraway Cavan, wild and rarely visited. We were Irish and not Irish; sometimes unkindly called West Britons, yet certainly never English, British perhaps, Protestant certainly, though often present at the weddings and funerals of Catholic relations.

I longed to identify myself with the romantic image of Ireland, land of saints and scholars, and spent hours reading every Irish history book I could find, learning Yeats's poetry by heart, singing

3

Moore's immortal melodies and promenading at the National Gallery and National Museum. In Dublin, as in Athens and Rome, a boy could pace the streets and gaze on the statues of his heroes — Parnell, O'Connell, Grattan and Burke — within the space of half-an-hour. The gentry in general and the Protestant gentry in particular had played a surprisingly prominent part in Ireland's 700-year struggle for independence. Lord Edward Fitzgerald and Wolfe Tone in the 1798 rising, Daniel O'Connell who had led the fight for Catholic Emancipation finally obtained in 1829 and Charles Stewart Parnell the Home Rule leader were all Protestant landlords with the sole exception of Daniel O'Connell, who was a Catholic one. Sir Roger Casement and Erskine Childers carried on the tradition to still greater lengths in the First World War, their executions turning them into English traitors and Irish martyrs. It should not be forgotten that the Irish Republic's first president was the venerable Gaelic scholar and Protestant Douglas Hyde.

From the same Protestant ascendancy came Wellington and Montgomery, Alexander, Alanbrooke, French and Gort, Beatty and Cunningham, Lawrence of Arabia and a hundred lesser martial heroes whose fortunes lay in loyalty to the British crown. Even St Patrick himself was an English slave, while the name of the great patriot de Valera betrays his Spanish origins. Perhaps to be Irish is more an idea than an ethnic reality — to be everything contrary (in their own idiom) to the English — to be wild, impulsive, generous, imaginative, pugnacious and talkative rather than orderly, calm, cautious, dull, peace-loving and reserved. It is to be for God but agin the government (including one's own).

My family had lived in Ireland for 300 years. My ancestor Colonel Thomas Sadleir had gone there in 1649 in command of a foot regiment after joining the parliamentary army in 1643. He subsequently became adjutant general in Cromwell's army in Ireland and governor of Galway and Wexford. He was also MP for Carlow, Kilkenny and Wexford in Cromwell's parliament (1654–58), MP for Galway and Mayo (1658–59), MP for County Tipperary (after the restoration of the monarchy from 1661 to 1664), and High Sheriff in 1666.

He obtained large grants of land in Tipperary and Galway,

including Kilnelagh Castle in Lower Ormond, which he renamed Sopwell Hall after his English home in Hertfordshire. He was awarded a 'gold medal and chain worth £50 for faithful service by Order in Council of 18 September 1655'.

A succession of soldiers, sailors, clerics and scholars followed him, 22 of whom were educated at Trinity College Dublin from 1727 onwards, one of them my great-great-grandfather, Franc Sadleir, was provost from 1837 to 1851.

Perhaps the most distinguished soldier, Major George Forster Sadleir of the forty-seventh regiment, made the first crossing of the Arabian Desert by a European in 1819. He served in India, Burma, South America and Persia (where he trained the army of the Shah, who awarded him a sword — the Sadleir scimitar — in gratitude) before becoming Sheriff of Cork in 1837 and dying in New Zealand in 1859 at the age of 70.

One of my first cousins, the provost's namesake Major Franc Sadleir of the Devon regiment, was killed in action in Normandy in June 1944 after being awarded a Military Cross for bravery. Admiral Sir David Beatty — First World War hero of Jutland, and later Commander-in-Chief of the Grand Fleet, whose mother was a Sadleir, was a distant relation. In one way or another, after 300 years, we were related to many of the people we met socially in Ireland from the old Anglo-Irish 'ascendancy'. Indeed, in such a closed community, even if we didn't know the families personally, we knew exactly who they were and all about them.

It has been well said that the English invaders became 'more Irish than the Irish themselves'. Certainly, the terms Protestant or Anglo-Irish ascendancy were to some extent misnomers. The term came to include not only Catholic peers like Lord Fingall and Lord Killanin, but also native Irish princes, Catholic and Protestant alike. They had romantic titles such as the Macgillycuddy of the Reeks, the Macdermot-Prince of Coolavin, the O'Conor Don and the two FitzGerald princes, one Catholic (the Knight of Kerry) and the other Protestant (the Knight of Glin) — a distant kinsman of mine. Their wives, reflecting French influence, took the quaint titles of 'Madam', thus the 'Knight of Glin and Madam FitzGerald'.

It is small wonder then that thoughtful Irishmen of all persuasions are torn apart by the myriad historical contradictions inherent in the term 'ascendancy' whose members used to be so charmingly described by the peasantry as 'the quality'.

My father had few doubts. For 27 years, he worked in the office-of-arms in the upper castle yard in Dublin castle, from which British viceroys had ruled Ireland for centuries. When the British government finally abolished his anachronistic office in 1943, he was proud of having been the last British servant — deputy Ulster King-of-Arms — to serve in the Irish Free State. Furthermore, when Mr de Valera paid him a second visit and offered him the post of genealogical officer at twice his previous salary, he quixotically declined the honour on the grounds that 'only sovereigns could grant arms'. At any rate, after the war his grateful sovereign, King George VI, granted him a civil list pension of £250 per annum 'for services to scholarship', which my father claimed was the highest awarded to anyone since Dr Johnson. He saw himself as essentially an English settler, visited London every summer and paid regular pilgrimages to the little Hertfordshire village of Standon where his forebears had lived for a century before their Irish colonial adventure began. He seldom mentioned that one of his mother's Burke ancestors had been executed at Galway in the late seventeenth century for fighting against the English.

His life centred on the cloistered world of the castle, Trinity College, St Patrick's Cathedral and the Kildare Street Club, where Yeats and Dunsany were fellow members. He was a member of the Royal Irish Academy, the Athenaeum and the Friendly Brothers. Among other members of the Celtic twilight set, he knew A. E. Russell, Bernard Shaw, Percy French, Lady Gregory, Oliver St John Goganty and Dr Douglas Hyde (who became the first president of Eire and a Protestant one at that). He was a great disciple and admirer of the provost of Trinity College, Dublin, Dr J. P. Mahaffy. He brought out two monumental books under his aegis, Georgian Mansions in Ireland and Alumni Dublinenses — a two-volume register of Trinity College Dublin students from 1593 to the end of the nineteenth century. Though financially disastrous to him at the time, they are now ironically collectors' items, rare and expensive, seldom seen in private libraries.

A *Childhood Dream*, 1924–42

Cross-channel authors, scholars, poets and heralds came to stay frequently in the sunny days before the Second World War. Some were already distinguished, like Philip Guedalla who had entrusted my father with all the Irish research for his famous biography of the Duke of Wellington, The Iron Duke, and Alan Houghton Brodrick the traveller, and Christopher Hussey, the editor of *Country Life*. Other young men in their twenties were later celebrated. Anthony Wagner, then Portcullis Pursuivant but later Garter King-at-Arms; Harford Hyde, then private secretary to Lord Londonderry became a distinguished historian and biographer and coincidentally wrote a sympathetic appreciation of my father in *The Times* after his death on 21 December 1957. There were also Michael Maclagan, Philip Magnus (the biographer of Kitchener) and our cousin Terence Prittie, who introduced many of them to our home in successive horse show weeks.

This flow of interesting visitors ceased abruptly on the outbreak of war, though a young cultural attaché in the British embassy in Dublin, John Betjeman and his wife Penelope often came down for the day to talk and be shown around the garden. Well I remember their visits so full of brilliant conversation punctuated by peals of laughter. My father was immensely impressed with his ability and sense of humour, normally considered a rare quality in an Englishman in Ireland.

Meeting him again at a very large formal luncheon over which he presided at a London hotel 35 years later, I ventured to enquire — when introduced — if he remembered my father Tom Sadleir. He didn't hesitate as his eyes lit up with fond recollection as he said, 'Of course, at Celbridge with a lovely garden — the deputy Ulster King-of-Arms.'

Later, as I said goodbye to him, he recalled those halcyon days. He also mentioned our neighbours next door at Celbridge Abbey, the Gregorys, especially the lovely Anne whose golden hair was immortalized in a famous short poem by Yeats, whereupon the Poet Laureate proceeded to my delight to recite it by heart. He then waved goodbye, declaiming 'Oh, to be Deputy Ulster'. I felt my father could have wished for no more fitting epitaph.

Why should one wish to abandon such an idyllic existence?

When our house seemed full of lovely books and paintings and our garden full of flowers, birds, trees, bees, honey, not to speak of milk in the shape of Dolly the Friesian cow.

True, we could not afford to hunt and had to pursue the pleasures of the chase vicariously. We followed the 'Killing Kildares' on foot, gazing with admiration upon the pink-coated, top-hatted chivalry, superbly mounted on their fine thoroughbreds. Then, they would set off from their Georgian mansions to gallop and leap across each other's broad demesnes to the haunting notes of the hunting horn and the music of the hounds. Later, at children's parties and dances in the evenings, the horse and the fox dominated the conversation to the exclusion of all else. I can still recall the pangs of envy and sense of 'not belonging' to the inner circle of the mounted élite, which one suffered on these occasions. To a child I don't know which was worse, the relative 'poverty' that precluded hunting or perhaps the greater shame of being well enough off to hunt but actually being unwilling to do so.

Hunting was not so much a sport as a traditional tribal custom closely kin to war, where accidents were commonplace and even death itself not too rare. The military affinity was strengthened by the diverse, gorgeous evening coats of the bacchanalian hunt balls, with the ancient dances and songs of the British Isles interspersed with blasts on the horn. Generals claimed that the hunting field gave soldiers an 'eye for country', which no other training could equal and the cavalry regiments often gave their officers 'hunting leave' at Christmas.

The gates seemed closed to glory and adventure at home and from an early age I was consumed by a great desire to travel and a burning curiosity about the outside world. For hours I lay on my bed poring over the pages of an atlas, reciting the magic names of distant places and dreaming of exciting journeys. My imagination was further fired by a book called *Heroic Deeds of Great Men*, which started with Philip Sidney, the hero of Zutphen, ended with Lawrence of Arabia and included such paladins as Drake, Raleigh, Nelson and Wellington, Havelock, Roberts and Gordon — above all Gordon. He was the pasha who knew no fear, in his blue and gold uniform and scarlet fez superbly mounted on his racing camel in the Sudan desert. He was the earlier leader of the ever-victorious army in China, the founder of the Ragged Boys School in Gravesend and doomed to die on the steps of the Residency in Khartoum. What a hero he was for any boy — in the best tradition of my earlier Arthurian heroes Lancelot and Galahad — *sans peur et sans reproche*. An old Victorian coloured print in the nursery entitled 'Last Shot in the Sudan' reinforced this image.

Soon after going to my preparatory school near Conway Castle in North Wales, an attack of asthma led to my being taken away from school for the spring term in 1934 and sent instead with my mother to recuperate on the Riviera. Such was the enchantment of my first trip abroad that the asthma vanished forever and the earlier fantasies were succeeded by a gradual determination to travel, to master foreign languages and, if possible, to join the diplomatic, colonial or consular service, or the Indian Army.

From the moment we landed at Calais — looking for *porteur numéro quarante-quatre* amid the excited crowd of passengers on the quay — I tasted the thrill of foreign travel — of arriving for the first time in a strange place, a thrill that to a lesser degree has never left me. Then we took the Blue Train, which sped to the sunny south. We passed through Lyons, Avignon and Orange to the sunlit sea, to the spring glory on the Riviera, to the Villa Delfina at Bordighera and the Villa Lumas at Menton. There were walks through the foothills of the Alpes Maritimes, unfamiliar wayside shrines, peasants singing in the fields, terraced gardens and the warm blue sea.

There were the domestic delights of forbidden water — replaced by wine mixed with water in the fashion of the Roman nobility — of croissants and honey for breakfast, veal for lunch and supper, French windows and mosquito nets. This was a new world of senses, of strange sights, sounds and smells.

Above all, it was a world of flowers. We watched the Battle of Flowers at Bordighera on Easter Day. Float after float of gaily bedecked cars manned by the fairest young women, bombarded the populace with carnations and other flowers, which were duly fired back at the radiant targets to the delight of all. I have never before or since seen such prodigal use of such rare and lovely ammunition.

Mussolini was in his heyday. There were already statues of him in Bordighera and San Remo. He had lined the coastal roads with trees and flowers, was said to have arranged for trains to run on time and had abolished tipping. I was impressed by the crack Italian *bersaglieri* in their green uniforms, with pheasants' feathers in their hats, and by the sky-blue uniformed French *chasseurs alpins* watching each other warily across the frontier at Ventimiglia.

All too soon, this blissful glimpse of gentle southern skies came to an end leaving me permanently entranced by travel in general and by France in particular. It set the seal on childhood aspirations and confirmed my decision to live and work abroad if possible. I was strengthened in this resolve by a gift for languages and a love of history and geography; from then on all my reading, all my interests were directed to the study of foreign affairs. Thus, I found myself avidly attending French and German church services in Dublin, going to foreign films and later as a student at Trinity College, even acting in a German play.

My parents had sent me to a preparatory school in North Wales in September 1933. My younger brother Digby followed a year later. It was an excellent school near a small village called Deganwy a mile away from Conway Castle and a few miles from the seaside town of Llandudno. It was called Woodlands and most of the 60 or so boys came from Lancashire or Cheshire with a dozen or so from Ireland.

'Ascendancy' children were usually sent to school in England or Wales where it was thought the education was better, and to avoid learning Irish — now compulsory in schools in the Irish Free State. Captain Clifford Lloyd and his wife Millicent ran Woodlands extremely well, assisted by a few young Oxbridge graduates, a lady matron Miss Penny, and music and art teacher Miss Fanny Ward. After my dramatic recovery from asthma, my brother and I were very happy there and made many friends. We were also fairly successful playing cricket, football and rugby for the school and passing the common entrance exam with flying colours, as well as being made prefects.

I was pleased when the school magazine described me as 'rather a rustic-looking batsman who often makes runs by sheer determination'. There were sweet moments of triumph when I scored a hat trick playing centre forward against Oriel House St Asaphs, and of disaster when I dropped an easy catch at point from their cricket captain Hearle, when he had made 44.

We were seldom allowed out during term time in those days, which was just as well as my parents never visited us at school, except for my father when he brought me there for my first term, leaving me quite cheerful with the other new boys in the 'train room'. However, a kind Irish cousin, Belle Johnston, married to a genial Welsh solicitor 'Uncle Barlow', collected us at half terms. On occasional Sundays, they would take us home for lunch followed by a drive around local beauty spots, which, if we were lucky, ended with bumper boats and ginger beer on the pier. They had no children of their own and I hope enjoyed having us — I can never forget their great kindness.

Highlights of the period included the death of the much-loved old King George V, the abdication of King Edward VIII and the coronation of King George VI. These events were marked by special issues of new stamps, which fuelled the current philatelic craze and accounted for most of our modest pocket money, the balance buying tea, acid drops, bullseyes and (very expensive) nougat on sale in the tuck shop. Although the food was good, we seemed to be always hungry and much appreciated our aptly named bedtime stodge of hot cocoa in enormous jugs, doughnuts and currant buns doled out by the matron who was up early next morning to supervise our naked plunge into a cold bath.

In 1938, aged 14, it was time to leave Woodlands and move on to public school. It had been intended to send me to Westminster, but war clouds were gathering and my parents, fearful of the expected air raids on London, U-boats in the Irish Sea and food shortages, sent me instead to Portora Royal School at Enniskillen in Northern Ireland. It was beautifully situated on a hill overlooking Lough Erne just outside the historic city of Enniskillen (Inniskilling). This was where the siege in 1689 had led to the formation of the Fifth Royal Inniskilling Dragoon Guards, and the Royal Inniskilling Fusiliers (27th Foot) into which I was to be commissioned five years later. Founded by James I in 1608, it was one of the leading Irish schools at that time, though little known out-side Ireland.

It catered for the relatively less well-off members of the Protes-tant Anglo-Irish, especially sons of the clergy who could not afford to send their children to England; the fees were only £90 a year. The majority of the boys went on in turn to join the Church, the services and banks, or to return to their family businesses or farms. Oscar Wilde and Samuel Beckett were notable exceptions.

It was a celebrated rugby school that had produced many inter-national players, including Dicky Lloyd, one of the greatest Irish fly halves of all time, who had captained the great team of 1908-9 five of whom were capped for Ireland, two while still at school. Indeed, the long defunct *Sporting and Dramatic News*, which I read at Woodlands in about 1936, described them 'as one of the greatest school teams of all time.' I was proud to play for the First XV in 1940 and score a try against the Sherwood Foresters, who had returned a few months earlier from the disastrous campaign in Norway.

The Second World War started on Sunday 3 September 1939, and my brother Digby joined me at Portora for the beginning of the Christmas term a couple of weeks or so later. The school was small with four boarding houses called after the provinces Ulster, Munster, Leinster and Connaught, with about 40 boys in each plus about 40 dayboys, around 200 in all. Three of the four housemasters were English graduates of Oxford or Cambridge, though the young 39-year-old headmaster Ian Stuart was a graduate of Trinity College Dublin and an Irish rugby international who had been a master at Harrow. Digby and I were in Leinster House with Major Gerald Butler — 'The Man', our housemaster — a greatly loved and respected veteran of the First World War who came from the Lake District, taught history brilliantly and rarely raised his voice. The school was spartan with a cold dip every morning, and even shaving — when old enough — in cold water; a hot bath once a week and winter heating minimal. With 20 boys in big open dormitories, it was fairly democratic — no studies and no fagging, though school prefects shared a small common room in the daytime.

A Childhood Dream, 1924–42

The war inevitably reduced the scale of my father's genealogical work and his income was halved. I was therefore taken away from school in early 1941 and sent to Trinity College Dublin instead to read modern languages until I was old enough to join up. It was a big saving for my family, for the tuition fees alone were only about £20 per annum and I could live at home (12 miles away), go to and fro by bus and get a very cheap lunch in the college dining hall for 5d. Before leaving Portora, I had passed the school certificate, but had not had time to take the higher certificate. I therefore passed the university matriculation exam instead, which had not changed much in 100 years. An 80-year-old mathematics professor called Cotter dispensed with my viva voce and passed me on the spot because 'he had taught my Uncle Ralph 56 years earlier'. It was small wonder I felt at home in such an admirably quaint institution.

I loved the new freedom, played for the Rugby Second XV and explored the museums and art galleries of Dublin. I duly passed my first year's exams in the Honours School of English, French and German and set sail for England in January 1942 to join the army as a volunteer.

Since Ireland was an independent state and had declared itself neutral, there was no need for me to go at all, and there was some talk at home of 'getting my degree' first. Strange as it may seem now, it seemed inconceivable to me then not to join up as soon as possible, since all my friends and relations were there, and some had already been killed or wounded. Quite apart from family traditions and loyalty to the Crown, it seemed obvious that if England lost the war, the Germans would soon occupy Ireland too and the dark ages would return.

2

Imperial Might, Majesty, Dominion and Power, 1942–44

On arrival in England, however, I was still a few months too young to go straight into the army, for my eighteenth birthday was not until 6 May 1942. My cousin, Sir Gerald Burke, now a retired Irish Guards officer and adjutant of the Henley-on-Thames home guard, kindly kept me in his home Rupert Place on the banks of the Thames until the Irish Guards called me up. He suggested that meanwhile I could join his home guard unit and get valuable training there. At 17, I was thrilled to be guarding Henley Bridge at midnight against a still possible German parachute attack; I was a teenager in 'Dad's Army'.

In the meantime, I learned enough Russian to qualify as an army interpreter in that language. I added French and German in the following year while I was an infantry officer-cadet at the RMC OCTU at Aldershot. Three months after being commissioned as a second lieutenant in the Royal Inniskilling Fusiliers on 2 July 1943, I was posted overseas 'to native troops', sailing from Gourock on MV *Tegelberg* on 23 October to an unknown tropical destination. I was going abroad now with a vengeance and my dreams of foreign travel were soon to be fulfilled though hardly in a manner that one would have chosen.

Our convoy of 30 assorted troopships sailed down the river to the cheers of thousands of shipbuilders, escorted by a dozen sleek grey destroyers into the cold green seas and gloomy skies of the western approaches. The 40 officers of Draft RNLVV drawn from diverse

14

infantry regiments had little to do save attend PT classes and life-boat drills, leaving plenty of time for interminable sessions of bridge.

As we sailed south towards the sun scattered over miles of sea slowly zigzagging hither and thither — speculation on our immediate future increased. Somewhat to our surprise, one evening we turned due east and sailed defiantly through the Straits of Gibraltar and into the Mediterranean Sea, which I had last seen ten years before. To the north stood the massive Rock of Gibraltar, where my father had spent his summer holidays at the end of the last century when my grandfather had been stationed there as an army chaplain, and to the south lay the mountains of Africa.

We were said to be the second largest troop convoy to enter the Mediterranean since it had been reopened to Allied shipping after the capture of Sicily in the summer had pushed the Luftwaffe bases back to the Italian mainland. Naples had just been captured, and many of the ships in our convoy put in at Syracuse where thousands of reinforcements disembarked. Earlier, German aircraft, using the new magnetic bombs, had attacked the convoy in the dusk off Phillipeville on the Algerian coast. Three ships were sunk, including one carrying an ENSA concert party, and three German aeroplanes were destroyed before the enemy was driven off as darkness fell. Our own ship suffered some casualties from machine-gun fire. A destroyer, hit in the boiler room, blew up and sank in flames to our stern; no one stopped to pick up survivors. Those who had died were buried at sea the next day. We slept in our uniforms and carried life jackets the whole time.

We soon saw Crete in the distance and soon the spicy desert breezes of Egypt blew upon us, and land birds with wild cries flew out to greet us. At dawn one day, we arrived safely at Port Said, our senses pleasantly assailed by the unique pungent smell of the Middle East — a sensuous blend of seas and sand, of jasmine and oleander, of hubble-bubble, camel dung and the incense from a hundred mosques.

Dozens of the bumboats, laden with bargains swarmed against the portside of the *Tegelberg*, while lighters manned by brown-skinned coolies clad in loincloths, supervised by military police also came alongside. Suddenly, some kind of scuffle started on one of the lighters and an English sergeant seized one of the young coolies and savagely kicked him overboard into the sea.

How rudely shattered were my dreams of imperial ideals. I felt quite sick with anger and shock and inwardly resolved there and then that, if I survived the war, I would devote my life to protecting the interests of the poor and defenceless. It was small matter that the boy was rescued by his friends, or that for all I know he had probably been pilfering war department property, or had been insolent, or both — I knew that such a thing could never happen at an English dockside.

'The bloody wog had deserved it' was not an uncommon view on board our ship. 'All Egyptians were wogs' ('wily oriental gentlemen'), they averred while the more insular spirits declared wittily that 'The wogs begin at Calais' — an expression scarcely calculated to endear us to our Common Market partners.

My views were reinforced a few weeks later when sailing south from Suez to Mombasa on board SS *Salween*, and a group captain who had lived in Rhodesia lectured us on 'How to deal with the natives'. He said his motto in Africa was 'I boot the blacks, and the blacks black my boots!' He added that one should never permit servants to speak English or to wear shoes in one's presence and that one should never do any form of manual labour whatsoever in Africa for fear of forfeiting the respect of the natives. I later learned that, at that time, the vast majority of whites living in Africa shared his views, with the disastrous results subsequent events sadly have revealed.

We spent some weeks in a tented camp at Aqaba near Suez waiting for a ship to take us to East Africa or India. Our arrival at camp was inauspicious. Alighting ravenously hungry from the Port Said train at 4.00 a.m. in the bright desert moonlight, we were greeted with the news that the expected meal was not ready because 'The cook's *maleesh*!' The cook — a Pole — was apparently suffering from the Arabic equivalent of the wartime RAF English 'browned-off'.

Our stay in the tented camp in the dunes was uneventful and typical of the dull ennui of wartime transit camps: weary monotony, a sense of isolation, an absence of duties, a spate of rumours.

16

The 8000-ton SS *Salween* had originally plied between ports in the Gulf of Bengal and she had a Lascar crew with British officers. She was somewhat overcrowded and we slept naked in hammocks slung between decks in the stifling heat of the dreaded Red Sea.

It was nearly two months since we had sailed from embattled Britain; it was high time we landed somewhere and settled down on dry land, if only for a few weeks. How we longed to go ashore — to get mail from home, a glass of beer, a glimpse of a young woman.

We were not disappointed. On the morning of 12 December we sailed slowly up the bright creek lined with palm trees and mangrove swamps, past Mombasa island to Kilindini (the place of deep waters). It was an unforgettable sight, 50 or 60 warships of the East Indies Fleet, gay with the ensigns and pennants of half-a-dozen Allied navies, visibly expressed imperial might, majesty, dominion and power in an unsurpassed Kiplingesque setting. Here, a great grey British battleship rode proudly at anchor, surrounded by sloops and destroyers — a Royal Marine band played sea shanties under a white canopy on her deck. There, a free French cruiser lay next to a Dutch destroyer and a Polish submarine; decks were alive with the scarlet pompoms on her sailors' hats. It was an extraordinary spectacle — like some great tropical Spithead review coming literally out of the blue at such a time and in such a place; it set the seal on our hopes of certain victory.

This splendid naval pageant was a noble prelude to our arrival at the quayside and disembarkation (in military parlance) in the cool of the late afternoon. As I stepped ashore into the brilliant light and vivid colours of Africa and met for the first time the amazing warmth and friendliness of its people, I was conscious of falling into a delightful dream from which I have never since wholly emerged. I instantly felt completely at home and utterly relaxed, at ease with myself and with everyone else.

I found that Africa, far from being the 'dark continent' was a 'fair continent' indeed, bathed in bright sunlight by day and bright moonlight by night, whose long horizons made sunrise and sunset daily dramas, whose brilliant tropical colours dazzled the eye of the beholder. Perhaps, the sheer mass of purple bougainvillaea and the avenues of scarlet acacia trees overwhelmed me at first by the scale of their splendour, dominating as they did, the dark green coast — studded with red-tiled roofs of European bungalows, as it swept down to the golden margin of the shore.

At about 6.00 p.m., our train pulled out of the station, crossed the causeway in the mangroves from Mombasa island to the mainland and chugged slowly inland, at about 20 m.p.h. burning firewood, towards Nairobi. As we steamed slowly past coastal villages set amid coconut palms and flooded fields of rice and sugar cane, the entire population came out to greet us. Led by enchanting children who had never known a toy, they would reach alongside the carriage shouting *Jambo* (How do you do?) — the first Swahili word I had ever heard, which, resembling 'Jumbo', seemed altogether delightful and appropriate.

Their fathers wore long white cotton robes and embroidered hats; their mothers the black gowns (*khanikis*) of the poor occasionally enlivened by bright red, yellow, green and blue cotton pieces (*khangas*). They themselves were naked save for ragged shorts, their shining skins more brown than black, reflecting centuries of Portuguese, Arab and Shirazi descents upon the coast; their perfect white teeth and mischievous brown eyes illuminating proud and intelligent faces, often creased by a great grin stretching from ear to ear. They did not, I suspect, know much about the white man's war.

For the first time we experienced that abrupt transition of day into night that is the tropical dusk and sunset — for half an hour the light faded fast; by 7 o'clock it was pitch dark, only the noise of distant drums and faint flickers of candlelight marked the villages now. In the carriage it grew cooler as we began our slow climb into the Kenya Highlands. Soon after dawn the following morning, we awoke to find ourselves in the legendary world of wide open spaces, crossing the famous Athi Plains, east of Nairobi, where thousands of wild animals roamed as far as the eye could see in a scene reminiscent of the Garden of Eden.

Soon, the train arrived to a bustling welcome at Nairobi station. A few minutes later, we were in the back of a three-ton lorry travelling along the roads — savouring the cool air of the Kenya

Highlands *en route* to Langata camp on the outskirts of the city. There we were shown the strange wooden grass thatched *bandas* that were to be our temporary quarters for the next few days. Then came the mail — read with excitement — and we saw for the first time the new airgraphs (photostat messages) then considered the most marvellous invention and the fastest form of mail hitherto known. It was almost two months since we had left home and for nearly all of us, far and away the longest period in which we had no news whatsoever from anyone. This gave one a strange sense of suspended reality, heightened by the knowledge that no one had the faintest idea where we were, save perhaps those shadowy figures in the War Office who presumably plotted our comings and goings with such meticulous precision.

The next day we were addressed by General Sir William Platt — victor of Keren, Commander-in-Chief EA Command — who compared our position as leaders of African troops with that of Polish officers leading British troops. He asked, 'How would you like to be led into battle by Poles who didn't even speak a word of English?' Fittingly enough, we were sent the next day to the Jeanes School Kabete, a dozen or so miles from Nairobi, for a three-week 'crash course' in Swahili. And taught Swahili we were — for seven hours a day by British majors and captains in the Army Education Corps, and African sergeants and corporals who took us for long walks in the afternoon for Swahili conversation and maddeningly pretended that they could not understand English. The instruction was based on a splendid army manual, which began with the imperative tense of various verbs, starting with '*simama*' — meaning stand still, stand up or halt.

Nevertheless, learning Swahili by numbers laid the foundation of a lifelong love of this beautiful language — the leading language of Africa and perhaps the twelfth language of the world, spoken from the Cape to Cairo, from Zanzibar to the Congo. A blend of Arabic with Bantu vernacular language, hence its name Swahili (from the Arabic adjective for coastal).

Bantu idiomatic genius produced such pure concepts as *ndege* (bird, also aeroplane), *kifaru* (rhino, also army tank), and loveliest of all *mwana hewa* (child of the air or airman). Shades of Homer's

19

'wine-dark sea' and the classical simplicity of Ancient Greek were forged in a not altogether dissimilar environment.

Bantu vagueness and tactful lack of precision also produced a grammatical identity of time and place, reminiscent of Donne or Einstein, so that only the context could tell one whether a sentence meant 'where he died' or 'when he died'. A situation further exemplified by the common Swahili word for 'yes' (*ndio*) which merely means 'that's it' — has led many a frustrated foreigner down the wrong road, aided by the innate African desire to please (and perhaps get rid of the intruder). Few language enthusiasts could have entered such an idyllic academy, a fairy tale language, lending novelty and enchantment to every hour, set amid the flamboyant scarlet acacias and purple jacarandas of Jeanes School Kabete.

On Sundays we went to Nairobi — the place of cold waters, in the Masai language, Hamitic and harsher than the Bantu tongues — then small and intimate like a small English country town. It seemed to have only two real main streets in the sense that they were tarred with the then rare tarmac — Delamere Avenue and Government Road, which met in a T-junction in the heart of the city. Nearly all the hotels, restaurants, shops, banks and offices were to be found here, or in the adjoining streets.

After the essential preliminary of a visit to the army pay office to draw £10 or so, which would keep us going for days, we gravitated to one of the only four hotels. These were the sedate and Edwardian Norfolk, on the outskirts under the pungent scented blue-green eucalyptus trees, and in the centre the old New Stanley, Torrs and the Avenue. They were strung along Delamere Avenue, in the middle of which stood a statue of the great Lord Delamere himself — aristocratic pioneer settler and in his heyday uncrowned king of the White Highlands. His statue has since been replaced by one of President Kenyatta, who has also taken over the name of the street and changed it from Irish 'Avenue' to English 'Drive'.

Early in January 1944, I passed out of the language class and was posted to the 9th (Tanganyika) Battalion of the King's African Rifles (KAR) as a platoon commander. The battalion, together with the 16th (Kenya) Battalion of the KAR and the 4th

20

Battalion of the Northern Rhodesia Regiment (NRR), made up the thirty-first (East Africa) infantry brigade. It was already on its way north to Ethiopia to take its turn for a year as the British garrison in the somewhat turbulent 'reserved areas' of Ethiopia adjoining the frontiers of British Somaliland and the recently conquered Italian Somaliland. *Shifta* bandits in the area — a perennial source of trouble — thrived on the unsettled conditions following the collapse of the Italian Empire, and enjoyed themselves stealing cattle from the tribes on the British Somaliland side of the border. The Rer Malingur tribe from the 'yellow hell of Ogaden' in particular inspired respect, since they were notorious for their 'debollocking' operations.

3

'From Birr to Bareilly':
The King's African Rifles,
1944–45

The twenty-ninth East African Infantry Brigade, which we were to relieve in Ethiopia, began moving south as we moved north and, indeed, a 'mock battle' called 'exercise exchange' was arranged at the small town of Iscia Baidoa, midway between the Juba river to the south of Italian Somaliland and the capital Mogadishu on the Indian Ocean. When I joined the brigade at Yatta, north of Nairobi, I found that my battalion had already left and so I was temporarily attached to 16 KAR, until we could catch up with the Tanganyikans at Iscia Baidoa — a week or so later.

At dawn next morning, we set off north along the now familiar, narrow red murram road — the only road — from Cape Town to Ethiopia. I sat in the front cab of one of hundreds of three-ton lorries, trying out my newly acquired knowledge of Swahili to the driver who responded to my importunities with infinite patience and good humour. We moved slowly — at dust distance — hour after hour, stopping in the afternoon to establish camp behind a big thorn *zariba* and to prepare the evening meal of maize-flour porridge and tea.

At night, we slept in the open under the stars, the officers on camp beds; the *askari*s in a circle round them on grass sleeping mats on the ground. *Askari*, the Swahili word for soldier or policeman, was derived from the Arabic *uskar*. The Turkish military title *effendi*, a survival from the early days of the KAR, was used to address officers. At that time, the KAR's native noncommissioned officers (NCOs) were largely Sudanese or Nubians, brought up in the traditions of the Ottoman Empire when the Sublime Porte held sway over most of Arabia and the Middle East.

Apart from the regular soldiers of the KAR's six permanent battalions — two Kenyan, two from Nyasaland, one Ugandan and one Tanganyikan — and the Northern Rhodesian Regiment's first battalion (1 NRR), all of whom were volunteers, mainly NCOs, by 1944 the *askaris* were largely conscripts. District commissioners with the cooperation of local chiefs and headmen recruited them. They seemed to be pretty willing recruits, however, with the prospect of foreign travel, free food, uniforms and the princely pay of 28 shillings a month. The gratuity at the end of the war would also provide sufficient money to build a house and get married.

His uniform in East Africa consisted of a light khaki tunic and 'long shorts' (to keep out thorns), a khaki slouch hat, with the battalion number on it in Arabic numerals, and boots, the latter just introduced and worn unwillingly on the parade ground only. Heads were closely shaved against lice. With the exception of a few warrant officers, education instructors, signalmen and medical orderlies, the entire army was illiterate. One result of this was that there were two complete sets of senior NCOs, from the regimental sergeant major (RSM) downwards. A battalion parade was much like a chessboard with black and white sergeants shouting orders in English and Swahili to the black ranks, while the thin white line of officers paced to and fro waiting their turn to march onto the board. Another was that the white platoon commander spent several hours every Sunday writing letters home, dictated in Swahili, for his men. They followed a formal pattern:

Greetings,
  Your letter has reached me safely. I am well; my only fear is for you. How are you? And the cattle and the farm and the crops? Greet my mother, my brothers, my sisters. I have no more news.

Your faithful son,
Madulu Bundala

This pattern seldom varied but could be extended slightly to include appropriate comments on a birth, death or marriage. It was fortunate that the writer's limited knowledge of the language was only matched by the simple nature of the message.

It would have been exciting enough to be in East Africa with British troops. To serve with African troops made life doubly interesting in that one had the unique opportunity to learn the language and study the peoples themselves as represented by the flower of their manhood, at the same time as one was engaged in the usual military duties.

I first met Tanganyikans — with whom in one way or another I was to spend the best part of my life — late one evening in a tropical rainstorm outside Iscia Baidoa. 'C' company HQ, consisting of Major Gerry Hughes (a Sandhurst-trained regular, aged 21, fair-haired, blue-eyed, married, of the Queen's Own Royal West Kents) and Captain 'Brad' Bradbury, his second in command, was established in the back of a three-ton lorry in the flickering light of a Tilley lamp. They gave me a warm welcome and we celebrated by drinking a variety of strange drinks until I crawled away to sleep in the back of another lorry, snug in my valise, to the lullaby of the rain pattering on the tarpaulin roof.

After a few days of lively manoeuvres, during which 'the enemy' on one occasion opened fire on us with live ammunition by mistake, we moved into Mogadishu for a weekend's rest. It was built and laid out in the grandiose style of Mussolini's latter-day Roman Empire, complete with triumphal arches, pretentious palaces and statues of Il Duce himself.

At dawn the next day, we set off north along the magnificent *strada imperiale* in the finest tradition of metalled Roman roads, which ran for hundreds of miles to the Ethiopian frontier town of Fer Fer. At that time, it must have been one of the finest roads in Africa; it was infinitely superior to anything in British East Africa. On and on we went, along the dusty roads through Hargeisa, the seat of government of British Somaliland, to our destination at Aubarre, a former Italian district headquarters in the now 'reserved areas' of Ethiopia. It looked a broken down sort of place, dry and dusty. The battalion headquarters moved into the administration office blocks, the colonel into his house and the rest of us into the surrounding bush. Towards sunset, my tent was pitched under a euphorbia tree; the *askari* warned me to beware of the white sap, which if it got into one's eyes would make one blind. There was a sit-down supper in the big mess tent waited on by Mwangi Kamau (a typical Kikuyu name) and cooked by our Chagga cook, Sifa Eli ('praise God' as I later learned in his tribal language). This was of the familiar menu, which consisted of bully beef, biscuits, baked beans and tins of grapefruit, sometimes varied by ghastly soya link sausages, local vegetables and fruit, corn on the cob being especially delicious.

So began a fascinating year in Abyssinia, as we then called it. From the military viewpoint, it was a complete backwater from where the tides of war had receded, leaving only the murky pools of intertribal strife and the *shifta* bandits and cattle thieves who thrived on the vacuum resulting from the breakdown of the Italian administration.

The strange spectacle of white men killing white men boded ill for the future of white rule in Africa. For us, the life seemed fairly reminiscent of my old friend Henty's Through Three Campaigns or similar tales of the North-West Frontier of India at the close of the Victorian era. We experienced constant hardship, occasional danger, camaraderie, much fun and excitement, sunshine, physical fitness and the thrill of yet another strange land. We also experienced virtual isolation from civilization, from civilian life, from women, elders, children, churches, buses, trains and houses, from fields and hedgerows, streams and gardens, from tennis courts and cocktail parties, newspapers and accurate maps.

Instead, there were endless dusty plains, empty *tug*s (watercourses), thick acacia thorn bushes and great gaunt rocky outcrops like Jifu Meider. Some miserable millet grew where the Aubarre road joined the main Hargeisa–Giggiga road at Tug Wajale, by a lone tree and distant blue mountains. There the road climbed up the Marda Pass to the Ethiopian Highlands beyond the town. Somali nomads' camels, mosques and markets, the pungent smell of camel-dung smoke and unapproachable dusky beauties had replaced the familiar trappings of western Europe.

Brigade headquarters were in the sand-coloured, Beau Geste style Italian fort at Giggiga. Gigigga, whose onomatopoeic name coincides with the word for a common activity, brought roars of mirth from the brutal and licentious soldiery. This was the provincial town whose denizens provided relief to the troops from their isolation. It was where my cheerful orderly Magesa Matiku from Musoma went for the day on the ration truck pleading that 'his body ached for a woman'. On his return in the evening, grinning all over, he announced proudly: 'Three women fought over me in the brothel *bwana*, so strong and handsome was I.'

Faithful Magesa, whose friends said he spoke as if he had potatoes in his mouth, never left my side. He slept at the door of my tent, poured the hot water into the canvas bath, which he then presided over, holding up the towel, discoursing the while of the maize and the cattle in his village near Lake Victoria. He advised me one hot afternoon to take a greatcoat on night patrol, warning me that it would be needed, advice I foolishly disregarded. Later, trying to sleep for a few hours under a tree on a bitterly cold night, I awoke at dawn refreshed and snug, to find that he had covered me with his own coat. Such was our community — black soldiers from a hundred tribes, white officers and NCOs from many infantry regiments, living among the slim Somali nomads and the Abyssinian border tribes known to the troops as Habash.

I learned Swahili all day long and the *askari* were the most patient and good-humoured instructors, correcting my mistakes politely and taking part in the most bizarre conversational practice at any time. By the end of March, I had been awarded £10 for passing the army lower standard Swahili test. A few months later I got £20 for passing the higher standard test, a comparatively rare feat in the KAR, which led to my being appointed battalion intelligence officer and later brigade intelligence officer. These fascinating jobs gave one rather more responsibility and scope than platoon commander.

One of my duties was to liaise with the colonial administration in nearby British Somaliland and with the military government in the reserved areas of Ethiopia. As a result, I often visited the local district commissioner (DC) at Borama, Major Moggeridge, whose famous garden supplied our mess with vegetables and whose home — where he and his wife once had me to stay the night — was a real oasis in the desert.

I was frankly disappointed the first time I met him. He was concerned about a butchers' strike, which seemed a mundane matter for the holder of such a romantic office — how little I knew. However, the next day he took me on safari in the grand manner and I was immensely impressed. We rode mules along rocky paths in the hills for 20 miles or so, escorted by a dozen *ilalo* (the DC's tribal police) and preceded by a veritable baggage train of camels. All the time, he regaled me with the most interesting conversation about the customs of the Somali tribes, their religion, language, their camels, cattle and crops, the climate and the state of the roads. He seemed to know the names of every kind of tree encountered on our route and demonstrated an encyclopaedic knowledge of everything pertaining to the Borama district.

The camels had arrived before us and had already been unloaded and the camp established. The central feature was a mobile flagpole, painted white from which the Union Jack proudly flew over the hundreds of assembled tribesmen from the Habr Awal and Rer Yunis tribes. Next to the flagpole were a trestle table and two chairs. Behind the two chairs was a vast well furnished tent with a table and tablecloth laid for dinner, complete with good glass, silver and napkins, the customary camp beds, baths and washstands and, to my amazement, a fine Persian carpet on the floor.

A series of lesser tents pitched in the vicinity housed our retinue in the scented acacia glade as camels and mules were watered, firewood cut and campfires prepared. Meanwhile, the DC spoke briefly to the crowd through his Somali interpreter. He heard a few appeal cases from local courts and listened patiently to a number of complaints about water holes and taxes before dismissing his *baraza* (a meeting, originally held on or from a veranda) and settling down to a bath, a drink and a five-course dinner.

Such was my first experience of Pax Britannica in action in a far-flung corner of empire. The apparent effortless authority of one British officer struck me in this harsh and alien environment. Military power doubtless buttressed his role as part ruler, part oracle and nearly always friend, but to a far lesser extent than the centurions of other empires.

At the end of September, I was posted to brigade headquarters in the fort at Gigigga as brigade intelligence officer and promoted to acting captain. I was sorry to leave 9 KAR, where I had spent such a happy time and first met the spirit of Tanganyika, which was to become my home from home for the best years of my life. I felt then, and have never ceased to feel, a strange affinity with Africans. Their sensitive natures, wonderful sense of humour, lively intelligence, sympathy and exquisite manners endear them to me. They have an unrivalled capacity for enjoyment, a prodigal extravagance, and an innate fatalism bred of centuries of war, slavery, witchcraft, poverty, ignorance and disease. They are lovers of leisure, dancing, music and poetry, 'lifeists' and slap-happy bowsies of the most beguiling kind, admirers of plain speech, yet devious when necessary. Often scorned for their failure to produce the three essential prerequisites of 'civilization' — the wheel, the bridge and writing — it is perhaps enough in all the circumstances that they survived.

I was lucky, I had the privilege to grow up with my own age group, to live with them, march with them, sing with them, laugh with them and learn from them. 'Where are they now?' as the old saying has it. Where is buck-toothed Platoon Sergeant Ogutu, a Luo from north Mara on the Kenya border, black as coal, tall and stern? Where is Corporal Nyangaila, the small, wiry section leader with a brown face, mischievous smile and twinkling eyes? Where are thin, brown, quiet Wambura and fat, lazy, clever Dionnes? He was a yo-yo NCO, always being busted, his rifle stolen by the shifta Hanga, humping an anti-tank rifle, tall, thin, less stupid than he looked, with filed teeth like most of his *watende* (circumcised) compatriots? Where are the two comics Chacha Mwita and Mwita Chacha, with one ear up and one ear down on a day off? Where is round-faced fat boy Marwa, always smiling, also from Lake Victoria's eastern shore? Where are friendly solid Shaibu, the horseman from the deep south, and Ali the fisherman from Lindi, with a great grin from ear to ear? Where are all the members of C company's ninth platoon who, like 'my uncle down in Texas', couldn't write their names?

At battalion headquarters, however, the intelligentsia was concentrated mainly in the signals and intelligence sections led by the only fluent English speaker, the education sergeant, Joseph Salim from Ulanga district. Salim's slow-speaking, diffident manner and warm, shy smile concealed surprising determination and authority, which stood him in good stead in his later career as a middle school headmaster. Corporal Mwakambaya (Bad Year), with a distinctive egg-shaped head, was a Hehe warrior from Iringa; and Sergeant Alfred Musa, the 'I' sergeant, big and pleased with himself, was an Mchagga from Mount Kilimanjaro. A special favourite was tiny 18-year-old signaller Matthew Ndugumchana (brother of the day), whose lovely daughter Catherine worked in our ministry in Dar es Salaam nearly 30 years later — just after her father had died after long faithful service in the forest department.

Other poetic names were *Rohoyamungu* (Spirit of God) and *Shauri ya Tanga* (the Tanga Affair). The latter was a reference to the crushing of an attempted British landing in Tanga in 1914 by General von Lettow-Vorbeck, in which his father, a German *askari*, had probably participated. More prosaic, we also had a Sergeant Motokaa.

These were my friends and I did not realize how much they had come to mean to me until the time came to say goodbye — when I suddenly felt overcome with emotion and with difficulty choked back my tears on the dusty corner of the parade ground. I can still hear them singing their famous marching song:

Tu Funge Safari	Let's prepare for the journey
Tu Funge Safari	Let's prepare for the journey
Amri Ya Nani?	Whose are the orders?
Amri Ya Bwana Kapteni	The captain's orders
Amri Ya Keyaa KAR	The orders of the KAR

To combat the high incidence of VD among troops, the Royal Army Medical Corps (RAMC) organized a brigade brothel. An attempt to distribute hundreds of thousands of captured 'Italian letters' among the *askari* was less successful. As one of them cheekily put it: 'Do Europeans like wearing shoes in the bath?'

29

As for the officers, any form of friendship leave alone intimacy with a 'native' woman, was virtually unthinkable in the KAR of 1944, so they were left with their dreams and such earthy practical advice as our medical officer, Sandy Pringle, tendered from time to time. Martial exhilaration, physical exhaustion and drink were the traditional substitutes, gently bound together by those visible and invisible threads of discipline, tradition and good manners, which go to make up esprit de corps.

In such a place, everyone was waiting. They were waiting for some minor action or excitement. They were waiting to join the East African division now fighting in the Kabaw valley, in Burma, or the 22nd or 28th brigades in the Arakan (Burma); waiting for leave or waiting to go home; we were all waiting for the war to end. Some of the older officers had already spent years away from wives and children and only wanted to return to their homes and jobs; several of them lived on farms in Kenya, tantalizingly near and yet so far. They were commissioned either into the KAR reserve of officers or the Kenya Regiment and, paradoxically, referred to us from Britain as 'imperials'. One such person was Major Charles Corbett from Thompson's Falls, Kenya, a veteran of the 3rd (Kenya) KAR's historic stand at Moyale on the northern frontier when the Italian army unsuccessfully attempted to invade Kenya in 1940. Others were William Polhill, our quartermaster from Kinangop, and my fellow subaltern in 'C' company David West from Kitale. Of the 'imperials', 'A' company commander 'Stretch' Collins, nicknamed Bwana Chupa (bottle), lived up to his name. He was ably assisted by John Tyler, Flash Hardick and my own company commander Gerry Hughes — all veterans of the battalion's earlier somewhat hilarious tour of duty in Mogadishu. Of the more recent arrivals, Noel Shepherdson of the Buffs, very old at 29, was the adjutant and only fellow member of draft RNLVV, where I had got to know him well through a shared interest in literature.

Even more serious minded was a Scot — Major Fraser Murray, King's Own Scottish Borderers (KOSB). He commanded 'B' company after an earlier spell as adjutant and had his right hand blown off by a 36 grenade in my presence during an assault course exercise in the bush. It happened while he was gallantly waiting for one of his men to leave the 'bomb explosion area' into which he had strayed by mistake. Far from being commended for his action, he was subjected to a tedious 'inquiry' at his hospital bed in Hargeisa, at which I was a witness, and later ironically censured for 'failing to observe adequate safety precautions'.

He proved the truth of the old Arab proverb, 'those who drink the waters of Africa will return to drink them again and again' by joining the colonial legal service in Tanganyika soon after the war as a Crown counsel. He later set up in private practice in Dar es Salaam, becoming one of the most successful advocates in East Africa and the first legal adviser to the Tanganyika African National Union (TANU) and its young president, Julius Nyerere, when it was formed on 7 July 1954.

So, I duly moved off to the Italian fort at Gigigga, in the plains below the Marda Pass 50 miles further into Abyssinia on the high road to Harar, where I found congenial quarters in a disused loft, snug within the outer walls of the fortress.

* * *

Soon after I arrived, Brigadier R. A. F. Thorp of the Life Guards was replaced by Brigadier R. W. H. Fryer of the Northumberland Fusiliers, who had just been 'bowler-hatted' — along with many others — by General Montgomery in Normandy for failing to advance fast enough. With a DSO and MC, he had obviously been gallant enough in his youth, but like many other commanders was not ruthless enough in risking the lives of his men, though quite happy to risk his own.

The brigadier's chief-of-staff was his brigade major Geoffrey Hitchcock of the Rifle Brigade. His intelligence, charm and sense of humour, combined with efficiency, made him an ideal senior officer and delightful companion. He had the rare gift of the light touch, which assured him respect without the need to raise his voice and he remained a lifelong friend. Moving to the same post in 21 Brigade 11 (East Africa) Division in South-East Asia Command (SEAC) a few months later, he paid me the compliment of

31

sending for me to join his brigade staff, saying he 'would rather die with his friends'.

One of my new duties was to control a mixed collection of Ethiopian and Somali spies. They gave us information about the activities of *shifta* bandits, Somali and Muslim fanatics, Italians and the Ethiopian Army, whose 14th Brigade stationed south of us at Fich was commanded by a remarkable British gunner officer Colonel Dennis Athill. Another almost legendary figure was Colonel Pat Munday. He commanded the Somalia Gendarmerie at Mogadishu. This force bore the brunt of the task of policing the hostile tribes and pacifying the area in general, since the British government followed its historic policy of only using the army 'in aid of the civil power' as a last resort.

Soon, it was time to move on from Africa to Asia to try to catch up with the war. At the end of January 1945, I duly received orders to proceed to the SEAC as a reinforcement for the 11 (EA) Infantry Division then engaged in the monsoon battle, in the Kabaw valley, crowned by the capture of Kalewa.

After a week's breakneck dash south in an Italian diesel lorry, Kenya was literally 'a sight for sore eyes'. The psalmists' description of the Promised Land as great northern desert wastes gave place to lush green pastures and sparkling streams, and the rocky hills were succeeded by the snow-clad glory of Mount Kenya. A glass of cold Tusker ale in the Outspan in Nyeri was nectar of the gods to thirsty soldiers. Night found us asleep in the inevitable transit camp, exhausted, excited, strangely exhilarated.

The clear notes of the bugle heralded a beautiful morning; a gossamer mist lifted lazily to reveal dew-dappled scarlet acacia and bauhinia trees, hibiscus and lantana shrubs, nasturtiums, zinnias and marigold enshrined in neat green lawns bordered by whitewashed stones. Above all, there was the unique crisp fresh air of the Kenya Highlands, which keeps one warm but never hot, cool but never cold.

A distant cousin from Galway, Patsy Barclay, married to one of Kenya's senior settlers, Captain Hugh Barclay, who had a farm at Menengai near Nakuru in the Rift Valley, kindly asked me to spend my second embarkation leave with them. Since few got a second leave, for most were dead soon after the first, I felt I was living on borrowed time, with every minute infinitely precious.

It gave me my first glimpse of a now vanished world of effortless racial superiority and gracious and leisurely living allied to a very real sense of duty and responsibility, immense self-confidence (a vital prerequisite to the entire role) and a pioneer spirit of self-sacrifice and hard work.

Every morning a Kikuyu syce (groom) would bring my pony to the door and I would gallop across the wide open spaces without ever leaving the Barclay estates before returning to eat a delicious Kenya breakfast of papaw with lime, bacon and eggs, toast and marmalade, and local coffee. During the day, neighbours would ride over for a chat to discuss the crops or the garden and at dinner I was introduced to the informal custom of wearing pyjamas and dressing gowns. At night, I read Baroness Karen Blixen's delightful classic *Out of Africa*, and Elspeth Huxley's *Red Strangers*, which in their several ways epitomized the voice of the Kenya settler of their time, paternalistic no doubt, but with a very real love for their adopted land and its people.

This was the Kenya I remember in 1945. Alongside the spacious farms and gardens of the 'White Highlands', were the over-crowded and eroded lands of the 'native reserves'. The women there walked slowly, for they were bowed down like donkeys with 60-pound loads of firewood or bananas. Lovely at 15, they were old and fat with hard work and child bearing at 35. The young, strong and fortunate who got jobs on the white man's farm, were, for the convenience of their masters, permitted to 'squat' on the land by cultivating a small plot and building a modest hut in which their families could live. They were mostly Kikuyu from the land-hungry Kikuyu reserve, which I was once taken to view almost as a tourist attraction like some grotesque game park or zoo. Even for a 20-year-old newcomer, the stark contrast came as a shock. I kept my views to myself.

The basic wage of an unskilled squatter labourer at that time was six shillings a month (30 pence in today's English currency), which was modest, even in pre-inflation colonial times when a man could buy 100 eggs for a shilling and get drunk on sixpence.

Tanzania: Journey to Republic

'All good things come to an end,' as my father was so fond of saying and, after a night or two at the Gilgil training camp, I found myself on the old KUR & H train again on the way back to Mombasa *en route* for the Far East. On arrival there, we spent a week in a camp at Nyali beach at the height of the hot season, awaiting the troopship to Ceylon. The temperature was 90 degrees Farenheit and the humidity 99 per cent, air-conditioning was unknown and fans were nonexistent. Sleeping naked save for a *kikoi* (coloured Somali cloth) round my loins, I would wake up in pools of sweat in the rosy fingered dawn and dash into the cool breakers.

A fiery phantasmagoria of swimming, sleeping, sunbathing, blue seas, blue skies, green palms, white surf, white sand etched a lazy margin to our beach-bound existence. Within it dwelt the strange fraternity of the transit camp; some coming and some going with little in common save their shared destiny. It was a hothouse for instant friendships and sudden bar quarrels. Brown-skinned Swahili fishermen with dancing eyes and the bright intelligence of Arab and Portuguese ancestors, sped through the waves in fast traditional outrigger canoes (*ngalawa*), hollowed out of the trunks of mangrove trees. A small army of camp followers plied us with coconuts and their delicious juice (*madafu*), with oranges, lemons, limes, tangerines, papaws and groundnuts. In the big mess *banda*, we lived on fresh fish, lobsters and prawns and the ubiquitous Tusker; water was kept cool in these pre-refrigerator days in sheepskin *chagul*s, slung from the branches of shade trees or from the sides of moving lorries. It was an unforgettable tropical dream.

4

Victory in the Far East, 1945–46

One evening early in March we moved secretly in three-ton lorries to Kilindini docks and boarded the regular trooper SS *Dilwara*, setting sail later that night for Colombo, Ceylon. Though the sea was not very rough, few of our *askari* had ever been to sea and many were violently seasick, a condition aggravated by the intense heat in the bowels of the ship and the anxiety of leaving Africa for the first time for unknown shores.

A Belgian Congo unit from the *Force publique* was on board going to reinforce a field ambulance unit attached to our 11th division in Burma. Attired in grey uniforms and kepis, they maintained rigid discipline; a young captain (a doctor) told me that he was shocked to see British officers 'fraternizing' with their black troops, adding that 'the British Empire would come to a sticky end if such behaviour were allowed to continue.' I recalled his words when the *Force publique* mutinied in 1960, murdering a number of officers and their families. The 'fraternization' consisted of officers comforting seasick soldiers and following the time-honoured tradition of the British army in seeing that their men were properly fed before settling down to eat their own meals.

Alone and unescorted, we sailed east relying on speed to beat any Japanese submarine that might still lurk in these waters, where a year earlier a similar troopship carrying female nurses had been torpedoed with heavy loss of life and great popular indignation.

On 17 March 1945 — St Patrick's Day — we arrived safely in Colombo and 'entrained', to use the military expression, for the station at Vavuniya in the uplands, without more ado *en route*, for the East Africa base reinforcements camp at Mankallam in the northern jungles. We were quite overwhelmed by the lush green vegetation, giant jungles, brilliant colours of flowers, birds, butterflies, dark waterlogged atmosphere and humid heat, paddy fields, rubber estates, tea gardens, tarmac roads. The neat legacy of Dutch burghers and Victorian administrators and planters was superimposed on the proud Buddhist kingdoms of antiquity, whose ruined palaces, monasteries and water tanks provided eloquent evidence of a civilization unknown to East Africa. Pools of lotus and water lily added a touch of romance to our progress and the very air was scented with the fragrance of frangipani — the temple flower of many a wayside shrine.

Late at night, we arrived at Vavuniya in the heart of the jungle, which more nearly resembled the Burmese jungle than any other, and wearily clambered into the waiting convoy of lorries for the last leg of our journey to Mankallam, about 20 miles away.

At midnight, we silently traversed the narrow moonlit road through the tall trees of the jungle to the hum of countless insects awake for the cool of the night. In the moonlit radiance one could dimly discern for the first time the tenuous lianas redolent of the celluloid antics of Johnny Weismuller and Sabu — the elephant boy.

Suddenly, time stood still, and I was conscious only of floating through the forest under the stars, blissfully happy, fearless, at one with myself and the trees and the men around me, intoxicated by strange scents and sounds caught up in a mystic euphoria of exhaustion, exhilaration and wonder. The vehicle ground to a halt, there was a raucous shout and the spell was broken. The base reinforcements had arrived.

After spending two-and-a-half months as a battle-school instructor in Ceylon, with a tough Afrikaner called Major van Horsten in command, I met educated Africans from Makerere College, Kampala for the first time. Together, we marched 20 miles a day. We swam in 2000-year-old irrigation tanks and shot a water buffalo by mistake, burying it in a hurry near its abandoned plough. Can shame sink deeper?

Corporal Kimutai, the young Nandi from Kenya, is full of

shining faith, discussing New Testament passages and the next world. Why should they die so far from home for such an unknown cause? A young man wept when his hair was cut off on the sergeant major's orders, not only because his looks were affected but because his tribal custom had been broken — so many tribes, so many customs. Only the English ruler is trusted to take 20 shillings home to the family in Nyeri.

There were weekends in Anuradhapura, Trincomalee and Colombo — reclining Buddhas, dagobas by the dozen and priest-ridden cities of the past. We had lunch at the Galle Face, and drinks at the Grand Oriental Hotel and police mess in Colombo. We went swimming in Mount Lavinia, visited the zoo and the church at St Paul's, Kinsey Road, went dancing at the Silver Slipper and Mountbatten passed by in a jeep on the Kandy Road. There were the Peradinya gardens and the Temple of the Tooth — 'five shillings for the high priest,' said the verger. 'Like hell,' I replied. 'Does the dean of St Paul's get a tip?' We had Sunday pic-nics in Mullaittivu, ate prawn curries with 30 side dishes, went to resthouses with peppermint creams and enjoyed trips in catamarans.

On 1 June 1945, we set off for the front in Burma via the advanced reinforcements camp in Comilla, Assam, where we arrived a fortnight later. After crossing the narrow seas dividing India and Ceylon by ferryboat from Talaimannar to Dhanaskodi, we made a leisurely journey by troop train up the east coast of India to Calcutta through Madras, Trichinopoly, Pondicherry and Cuttack.

The train stopped for hours several times a day to allow the troops to eat on the platforms of the various stations. The heat was appalling and, stripped to the waist and dripping with sweat, we sat limp in the carriages clutching blocks of ice to our bodies in an attempt to alleviate the furnace-like atmosphere. Maunds (100 kilos) of ice in old sacks could be obtained occasionally from friendly stationmasters along the line.

The ghastly poverty of India made an indelible impression on us all. Thousands of human scarecrows stormed the stations fighting each other for the scraps left over from the soldiers' banquet and for the one-anna prize of carrying the smallest piece of luggage. Children maimed and blinded from infancy to increase their begging power soon ceased to startle or stir the conscience. The *askaris*, amazed by the spectacle of the broken-down brothers of the prosperous Asian merchants in East Africa, announced that they would never again allow themselves to be exploited by such miserable creatures.

We reached Calcutta. We changed trains to travel through the dreary rice fields of East Bengal to board the river steamer on the mighty Brahmaputra River — a pleasantly cool interlude — then took yet another and very narrow-gauge railway until 'the morning after the night before' we reached the railhead at Comilla.

As we arrived at our camp near the airstrip, Dakotas flew in the wounded from the front all day long; the rain poured down. The battle raged at Mytkyina — our division had just moved back to India to rest and refit at Ranchi in Bihar Province west of Calcutta.

Casualties from malaria had been nearly as heavy as from the fighting itself, so we were issued with ointment and the new Mepacrine tablets. They made one look yellow after a few weeks and were expected to render one impotent after a few months. Indeed, the 14th Army only stamped out malaria by the draconian step of making it a crime and any soldier contracting it was placed on a charge and duly sentenced as severely as if he had been 'absent without leave' or had stolen from a comrade.

It rained continuously for a month, but company and platoon training continued uninterrupted. We were hardly ever dry and a terrific storm one night blew away half our tents, leaving Yona Sudi, my Nyao orderly from Masasi in southern Tanganyika, high and not dry amid the debris.

We were now superbly fit, running two miles every morning before breakfast and marching 15 miles a day through water-logged rice fields past picturesque pagodas, up and down the steep razor-backed hills in our jungle green battledress and slouch hats. We were fighting fit and fit to fight, as the battle-school slogan of the day had it. Morale was very high as news of new victories came in and the forgotten 14th Army came into its own with the ending of the war in Europe on 8 May 1945.

The moment of truth was surely nigh, but it was not to be. Within a month of joining HQ 21 Brigade in 11 (East Africa) infantry division at Ranchi, the atomic bombs were dropped on Hiroshima and Nagasaki and the war was virtually over. The division had been due to return to Burma at the end of August to relieve the 2nd British division on the Mawchi Road — the scene of bitter fighting. I had just received orders to fly to Rangoon with the advance party in a few days time when the bombs dropped.

On our last leg of a divisional exercise at a little village called Hesadi rumours began to spread that a secret and incredible bomb had been dropped on Japan 'killing millions of people'. Signal officers had picked up broadcasts from Calcutta radio; we waited for hours in an agony of apprehension until an official statement from division headquarters confirmed that the atomic bomb had indeed been dropped and Japan had asked to surrender. A strange mood of short-term disappointment mingled with a deeper long-term relief now set in to produce an amazing anticlimax as the almost unbelievable news of the Japanese surrender on the orders of the god emperor was received. The 15 August 1945 was proclaimed VJ Day; the Second World War was over.

Britain had millions of men under arms and vast victorious fleets of warships and aircraft. It ruled a quarter of the globe in the greatest empire in history where 'the sun never set'. It was ironic that the waves of victory marked the high tide of its fortunes, that it would drain to the dregs the cup of bitterness usually reserved for the vanquished.

As for the army, it found the end of the war if anything a greater strain than the beginning. Millions of men separated from their families for years wanted to go home in a hurry and it was nearly impossible to run down such a highly geared-up machine at once. First in, first out, was the order of the day. An elaborate 'points' scheme taking into account marital status and length of service overseas was promulgated. It was called python, with delightful variations for special cases such as LIAP (leave in addition to python) and LILOP (leave in lieu of python) — to which we added LOLLIPOP with sensual connotations, long fled from memory. In lighter vein, VJ Day was celebrated in our brigade headquarters by a monumental beat-up.

In the big mess tent, drinking started before lunch at noon and continued with occasional breaks for eating until dawn the next day, when the brigadier, a delightful Cameron Highlander called John Macnab, decided to inspect the brigade on horseback. He told me to wake up the syces and get them to saddle our ponies. Dawn broke at 5.00 a.m. or thereabouts and the brigadier mounted his pony only to fall off on the other side. Juma and I gently eased him back into the saddle and we set off at a sharp canter for the headquarters of 2nd (Nyasaland Battalion) KAR a mile or so away.

When we arrived, the guard commander gave the classic order of 'Guard turn out.' And, when he saw the brigade commander, he ordered 'Guard present arms.' As the brigadier threw up his right hand to return the salute, he very gently fell off his mount for the second time. The *askaris* remained at the salute, motionless as statues. With some difficulty, I contrived to dismount and replaced him on his perch.

The advance continued. The brigadier, quite undeterred, announced that he would now inspect the 3rd Battalion NRR under Colonel H. Bayldon a mile away in the other direction. So, off we set at a brisk canter, with the brigadier bewailing the fact that the 2nd KAR had been found sound asleep. When we reached the Northern Rhodesian Battalion, we found them drawn up for parade soon after 7.00 a.m. with Colonel Hugh Bayldon at their head. We rode into the parade ground and faced the serried ranks of 800 officers and men. The colonel brought the battalion to 'attention' and then to the 'present'. But, before the brigadier could reply in the customary manner to these military courtesies, the night's drinking took its toll and he had perforce to dismount and with the slight cover available give a public performance of an essentially private act. My admiration for the King's African Rifles was unbounded. The Northern Rhodesian Regiment did not bat an eyelid as its Bwana Mkubwa relieved himself with a certain abandon and with the same perfect sang-froid as he had met the Japanese fire a few months earlier.

Remounted, the Rhodesians inspected, we set off in the early morning sunshine to inspect the 4th (Uganda) Battalion of the KAR under their one-armed hero Colonel Duncan Geddes. He was a fellow Cameron Highlander, but alas, before we had reached their lines the brigadier's horse had slipped in a rabbit hole, throwing him to the ground and injuring his left arm. We were then within walking distance of our headquarters, which we reached at about 8.00 a.m. The brigadier retired to bed to lick his wounds after telling me to ring up the divisional commander, General Dimoline, and tell him that 'he would be unable to read the lesson in the victory thanksgiving service in Ranchi cathedral that morning.' I went to my tent, fell asleep, and woke 12 hours later with my boots on. The war was really over.

It took some time to get over the shock of guaranteed future existence. The brigadier offered to recommend me for a regular commission in the army. However, when impressive forms were distributed concerning choice of peacetime employment, I returned to my first love, deepened by my experiences in Somaliland, service in the KAR and knowledge of Swahili, and put down colonial service as first choice, foreign service as second choice and army as third choice. A visiting provincial commissioner from Kenya, the redoubtable Sidney Herbert Fazan, encouraged me in my choice. My own Tanganyikan *askari*s, whose advice I sought, were most enthusiastic and did me the honour of inviting me to serve in their own country, an invitation I accepted. It was a decision I never regretted, despite later pleas from friends and relations in Kenya to change my crazy decision and opt for settler country and a better climate. It was over a year before my fate was finally known. Meanwhile, our 'rhino' division began slowly but surely to move home at the end of the year, starting with our 21 Brigade, whose new arrivals like myself were transferred elsewhere, in my case back to the Tanganyikans as a platoon commander in 4/6th Battalion KAR.

In the four months before their return, every effort was made to amuse the restless troops by 'planned recreation'. Military duties were reduced to some extent, though the security situation in Bihar Province kept the division in a state of readiness. Thus, in early September, I was sent in the brigadier's new jeep to Calcutta to buy cups for a gymkhana. One of these, the Epsom Cup, I later had the pleasure of winning myself in the steeplechase, though a far greater feat was keeping my seat in the *askari* stakes for riders of mules bareback.

I was also sent on an unsuccessful mission to the local Rajah of Panchkote near Perulia to buy ponies for the general and brigadier. The Yuvaraj Maharaj of Panchkote was one of hundreds of minor princelings, who boasted I think of a one-gun salute. He greeted me at the gate of his demesne from where a servant had summoned him, a faintly forlorn, fat figure with a flabby pale brown face, chewing betel nut, with bloody red lips, his youth overtaken by overeating and under exercise. He was wearing a shabby white dhoti over knee breeches and was polite though not friendly. Within seconds, I realized that his stable was unlikely to come up to the expectations of the top brass, although he reluctantly allowed me to inspect his rather ramshackle zoo, while doing his best to keep me out of his 'palace', which perversely I was determined to enter. By shameless flattery of the lacklustre peacocks and a pat or two for His Highness's pair of pye-dogs, I at length succeeded in gaining entry.

The entire place had been furnished regardless of cost by a Paris firm in the most lavish and florid manner so that (for example) a chandelier of green emeralds surmounted the billiard table, while an electric tiger pranced around the dining room. The fabulous effect was somewhat lessened, however, when a visit to the lavatory revealed the words 'vacant' on the door.

That extraordinary anticlimactic afternoon was full of surprises, none more so than when, having told HH that I was off to Kashmir on leave the next day, he kindly wrote me an introduction to 'Mr X' himself, with whom he said he had been at school.

Arrived in that earthly paradise a few days later, I lost no time in presenting myself at the great white palace on a hill overlooking the Dal Lake, only to find the maharaja away. However, the introduction led to an invitation to 'tea with the *Tehsildar* [mayor] of Srinagar' — hard-boiled eggs and limited conversation seated on a fine Persian rug. As a palace gate crasher, I was no duffer.

The next fortnight was a dream of brilliant images. These were images of mountains, champagne air and deodar trees, images of *saddhus* and ashes and the Takt-el-Suleiman. There were the motionless houseboats and lazily gliding *shikara* (gondola) to the Shalimar Bagh and the Nishat Bagh (garden of gladness) of lotuses, blue water lilies, roses, jasmine, silken saris and golden women. I remember Sadak Ali at the fifth bridge, walnuts, papier mâché, Nedou's Hotel, the proud Residency and Skinners (a famous shop for tents and camping equipment) on the Bund.

A week's trek in the mountains alone with the faithful Aziz, 15-year-old Fidus Achates and a few Kashmiri porters took me through magnificent scenery to the sacred lake of Gangabal. This was at the foot of Mount Haramoukh and within sight of ten peaks over 15,000 feet high, including the awesome K2. Meditating on life was resumed at sylvan pools, rivulets and waterfalls sprawled on rocks close to heaven, reading *Wesleys' Journal* and the soldiers' khaki and gold Bible, free as the mountain winds.

After stopping at Ganderbal for a hilarious game of hockey with the villagers — a joy beyond language — I returned by long-range *shikara* across the Wular lake past rustling reeds to the countless canals and old wooden bridges of the water city.

Paradise was lost but soon regained by a Kiplingesque pilgrimage to Peshawar; an armed convoy took us through the Khyber Pass to lunch with an Indian Army friend near the Afghan border at Landi Kotal. I caught a glimpse of Dr Brydon's road from Jellalabad, the proud badge of the Somerset Light Infantry. The plaques and badges of British and Indian regiments incised in the rocks, memorials to fallen heroes and thoughts of Alexander's epic march long, long ago moved me deeply.

Then it was back to the Braganza Hotel at Rawalpindi and the swarthy Punjabi Muslims at the station — Greek fairness and Greek features still in their faces. What a station! It was thrilling to wait for the Delhi express in this modern caravanserai of turbans of every shape and colour, saris and jewels, sackcloth and ashes, cooking pots, prayer mats, pilgrims and holy men.

The express trains in India always seemed to leave at unearthly hours of the night and, after watching half India, nay half Asia, go by, I duly boarded the great train — pride of the Raj, together with the Grand Trunk Road and the barrages and irrigation systems of the Punjab. A friendly guard warned me to watch my

43

suitcase, 'Plenty loose — Wallah on train Sahib,' he said — an immortal injunction, which seems to have universal relevance.

Then I was back in the India of the mutiny; the Union flag still flew over the residency at Lucknow amid the ghosts of Havelock's saints; the reveille still sounded in Bareilly — though no longer in Birr. In Delhi, I paid homage to the heroes of the Kashmir Gate; in Cawnpore I recalled the ghastly massacre. My father's old friend Colonel Richard Parsons had fought throughout the mutiny and had had his life saved by an elephant. It was only 90 years earlier, and seemed very close and fresh in the memories of white rulers and Indian subjects; every Indian Army brigade still contained one British battalion. The seventeenth-century Mogul Empire — of which I had had such a delightful glimpse in Kashmir — also lived on in the Red Fort and Peacock throne at Delhi and in the famous Taj Mahal and fort on the Jumna river at Agra, which contains the almost more exquisite Pearl Mosque.

Back from leave at Asansol station, the waiting jeep took me past the collieries at Dhanbad and the great Tata steelworks at Jamshedpur, before delivering me to my tent at Dipatoli camp a few miles from Ranchi. There my old friend Geoffrey Hitchcock (who had recommended Kashmir for leave) gave me a warm welcome. Soon we were riding again every evening together with Brigadier John Macnab and Colonel Duncan Geddes of 4 (Uganda) KAR and Major R. E. (Dick) Stone, the DAQMG, already in the colonial service before the war and later to become Resident of Buganda.

Time flashed past as the departure date approached. There was impressive drinking by all of Muree Beer, Lion Beer, Carews Indian Gin and Calverts Canadian Whiskey. There was the Ranchi Club, the BNR (Bengal and Nagpur Railway) Hotel, Audrey House, dinner and dancing, parties in the big mess tent and, of course, Colonel Richard Miers of the SWB (South Wales Borderers). He commanded the 2nd (NY) Battalion KAR and was tall, dark, handsome, saturnine, sophisticated, stooping and brilliant. One listened mesmerized to his conversation, which was highly intellectual and spiced with a mordant wit. He was not popular with everyone, but I worshipped him from afar. I read an article in a magazine recently describing him as 'one of the finest English-men of his generation', and was not surprised by the tribute.

Soon, 21 Brigade went home and, for a blissfully carefree month I led the simpler life of a platoon commander in 4/6 KAR. This entailed marching ten miles a day through dry Bihar *nullah*s and dusty fields and villages gazing at placid water buffalo, emaciated cattle, donkeys and mangy curs. We played endless games of tenni-quoits in the evening in case we were not sufficiently exhausted.

I shared a tent with a fellow Irishman and brother officer in the Inniskillings, Desmond Chaloner, whom I was later to meet both in Dublin and in Dar es Salaam. Another new friend was my orderly, Madulu Bundala from the Nzega district, who taught me some words of his tribal language, Ki-Nyamwezi, including that loveliest of all greetings, *mwangaruka* (good morning to a man). Indeed, I became so fond of the five or six Wa-Nyamwezi in my platoon that, on being asked on arrival in Tanganyika as a cadet in 1948 where I wished to serve, I replied 'Unyamwezi' without hesitation and was promptly posted there. Later, I met Madulu again at a cattle market and took him on as a servant. But, that is another story.

Early in January 1946, I was interviewed by the divisional commander General W. A. Dimoline ('Dimmy') for the job of his ADC and told to prepare for duty at 'A' mess, Peppe Villas, Dorunda, as soon as possible.

A regimental soldier imagines an ADC to be some kind of glori-fied flunkey who spends his time opening car doors, saluting and generally bowing and scraping: this is a caricature. In fact, the job is tough and demanding for 24 hours a day. A general's aide or personal assistant on the field of battle, or in my case on manoeu-vres inspecting units or in the office at division headquarters, is comptroller of his 'A' mess and has to order the food and drink. I had to choose the menus, keep the accounts (a constant headache), supervise the servants, and take charge of the vehicles and drivers, the flowerbeds and the gardeners.

General Dimoline was 50 at the time, tall with a somewhat portly figure, sparse dark greying hair and moustache, and a red cheerful face. He had a reputation for being a martinet and was certainly a great stickler for the military virtues of discipline, efficiency, smartness and the usual mania about punctuality. Like nearly all officers who had survived the African army, he also possessed a lively imagination and a keen sense of humour. His bark was usually worse than his bite, though he exploded on occasion. He was invariably kind and considerate to his personal staff who all enjoyed working for him. His happiest time of the day was when he inspected his roses before breakfast with a glass of orange juice in one hand and a stick in the other, escorted by a small retinue of officers, gardeners and a servant who refilled the glass when it was empty.

Life with the General was a change indeed for a junior sub-altern, now promoted to captain at 22. For battalion after battalion, I accompanied him on farewell parades in the big Humber saloon with the hand gear, sitting beside a Kikuyu driver called Gikonyo. With a scarlet pennant proudly flying, two white military police motorcyclists in front, two black ones behind, the precision planning on time and distance would always ensure that we arrived exactly five minutes before the time of the parade. Once, the general nearly went frantic because the front left-hand white motorbike spluttered and failed to start. We therefore chucked it out and brought a black motorbike up from the rear, proceeding in a level formation of white and black in front and black behind, which looked fine — like an inverted arrowhead.

Vivid impressions remain. There was a weekend pheasant shoot at a Jesuit mission with the General's delightful Belgian friend Father Jacques (Jacky), the ADC in charge of beaters, after which there was dinner in the refectory of pheasant, philosophy and homemade wine. I remember driving the General to parties in the evening after having reconnoitred the routes in the afternoon, and planning a dinner for the Commander-in-Chief, India, General Sir Claude Auchinleck — nervously carving the duck, getting a rocket for forgetting the orange salad and being consoled by friendly laughter. I recall being amused at the apparent importance old men attached to little things, but remember Dimmy's constant refrain — 'If a thing's worth doing at all, it's worth doing well.'

The senior officers in the mess and the junior staff of mess waiters, orderlies and batmen were wonderfully kind and helpful. Brigadier Radford, the CRA, forgave me for bumping into the back of his jeep. Colonel Norris Irven, the GSO 1 and a gunner, a particularly charming, quiet and gentle man, took me riding in the evenings. Colonel Michael Biggs, the CRE and an army tennis champion, seemed the model of effortless ease and elegance. Colonel Pat Saunders, the DAQMG, was gruff and friendly. Colonel Jimmy Sones, the CSO, who was slightly nearer my own age, took me from time to time in his jeep for dawn swims in a local 'tank' — the site of the divisional aquatic sports, in which we both later participated.

The most important person in my life perhaps was Mulenga Pio, who had virtually run the General's domestic affairs since prewar days, when he commanded 1st NRR at Lusaka. A Bemba by tribe from the then Northern Rhodesia, his slight build concealed great strength, while his cheerful face displayed intelligence and sympathy. He spoke good English — a rare attribute in those days — and worshipped the ground on which his master walked. Amazingly adaptable, he soon spoke a little Urdu and seemed as much at home in Ranchi as in Lusaka. He virtually ran the housekeeping and was completely honest. Another stalwart was my own orderly Donald Diwas, a Mngoni from the Songea district of south Tanganyika. With a brown, round chubby face, a stocky body and legs that were disproportionately thin from early malnutrition, he would chat about his father's tobacco farm and long for home.

The pace quickened as the date for the final withdrawal of the remainder of the division drew nearer. Famine and civil war threatened India. Hundreds were being killed in riots in Calcutta, and thousands were dying of hunger and disease in the streets and even on the platforms of Howrah and Sealdah stations. Following the example of Sir Thomas Rutherford, the governor of Bihar, three-course meals were decreed in all messes and entertaining was limited. 'Quit India' appeared everywhere and a crowd once surrounded my jeep in Ranchi yelling, *Gandhi ki jai* (Long live Ghandi). Yet, the deputy commissioner of Ranchi, one of the last white ICS (Indian Civil Service) officers, told me at lunch that it had all happened before. He said that famine and riot had always been the order of the day and that without the British the whole subcontinent would fall apart, so bitter was the hatred between Hindu and Muslim.

Certainly, one sensed the imminence of vast upheaval — the late afternoon of empire. We were privileged to get a glimpse of the greatest single imperial achievement in all history just a year or so before it came suddenly to an end. The outward and visible signs alone were splendid. Quite apart from the impressive public works already mentioned and the amazingly efficient medical, educational, postal, agricultural and forestry service, there was an outstandingly able and impartial judicial system. Its monumental Indian Civil Procedure Code became a latter-day Code Napoléon for the entire empire, well supported by a fine police force and prison service. Strolling around Calcutta, one entered Clive Square or Dalhousie Street and imagined oneself back in Georgian London. Chowringhee, with its Bengal and United Service clubs, Grand Hotel and Firpo's restaurant, was a sort of cross between Piccadilly and St James, with the maidan thrown in as a sort of oriental Hyde Park.

It was less easy to discern the inward and spiritual grace. However, it was there too in the feats of scholarship and research carried out by generations of Britons into Indian languages and culture, archaeology and religions, flora and fauna, enough to fill whole libraries.

They surveyed the whole country, mapped the Himalayas and then climbed them. Above all, with a breathtaking audacity, they forged from the most disparate elements of the human race a legendary imperial army. It was unique in its composition, in its super efficiency and strength, and in its almost perverse loyalty to an alien raj. The whole incredible machine was coordinated by but a few hundred officers of the élite Indian Civil Service. This itself was not only one of the most efficient and incorruptible instruments of rule known to man, but also the exemplar upon which at least fifty lesser overseas administrations were modelled.

With the advantage of hindsight, it seems crystal clear that once this incredible imperial bastion had fallen after nearly 300 years of such close links with the metropolitan power, the entire colonial structure so haphazardly built up, so loosely scattered around the globe, must surely, gently, disintegrate. New Delhi itself — the seat of power triumphantly enshrined in stone by Lutyens — remains a monument to rival the glories of Greece and Rome.

Enough said of India; our black 'rhino' division gave a most moving 'torchlight tattoo' at an improvised stadium to bid farewell to the people of Bihar and, in particular Ranchi, who had been such kind hosts for a year. It closed fittingly with the massed choirs of the *askari* singing their marching song — an African equivalent of Auld Lang Syne.

Kwa herini ndugu zangu	Goodbye my friends
Kesho na yoyoma	Tomorrow we're off home
Kwa mama na baba	To mother and father.

As I sat beside the General in the torchlight listening to this wistful melody, sung so beautifully and expressing a comradeship soon to end, I felt a great sadness and a lump in my throat. This was shared, I noticed, by the tough old soldier himself. I sensed that somehow things would never be quite the same again. I had an uneasy feeling of fin de siècle, not yet expressed in thought, a premonition perhaps that within the next 30 years almost the entire empire, even the very regiments themselves, would have ceased to exist.

5

Oxford Springboard, 1946–48

One beautiful morning in May, the luxury cruise liner *Monarch of Bermuda* sailed into Mombasa harbour where General Dimoline and his men received a victor's welcome. A large crowd of cheering people, led by the Governor of Kenya, had assembled on the quayside with ships dressed overall, sirens hooting and bands playing. The 11th division had come home — together with the 22nd and 28th independent brigades and the 81st and 82nd West Africa divisions. They had shared in a remarkable African contribution to victory in the Far East. The ethics of using colonial troops in campaigns so far from their own homes seemed dubious to me at the time, for the Japanese threat to say Nigeria must have been minimal. On reflection, however, one must recall some of Hitler's statements on the essential inferiority of the blacks and the virtual certainty of their future enslavement in the event of an Axis victory. Japanese treatment of conquered colonial peoples in Malaya and elsewhere in the Southeast Asia co-prosperity sphere did not encourage one to expect anything better from them.

The British authorities were also scrupulously careful to refrain from using colonial troops to assist other colonial powers to suppress local insurrections. The possible use of our 11th division — mooted at the time — to assist General Douglas Gracey to help the Dutch restore order in Java at the end of the war, is a case in point.

The British have always paid subject peoples the genuine compliment of broadly treating them as they treat themselves by imposing on them similar institutions to those in the United

Kingdom. To a nation that went to such lengths to produce colonial Pygmalions by the dozen, it seemed only logical to bestow the ultimate honour of permission to bear arms and share the common sacrifice. After all, the British had given them the benefit of an international language and literature and the very games they had invented and played, like cricket, soccer and rugby, and had taught them to climb their own mountains and swim their own seas. Subsequent history will, I believe, vindicate this decision.

General Dimoline had been named as future commander-in-chief for East Africa, so my tenure of office as his ADC came to an end in Nairobi. Before we parted, he kindly gave me an excellent recommendation for the colonial service. In the best army tradition, he read it aloud to me, adding, 'That'll get you in my boy, the Colonial Office won't insult me.' He also gave me a beautiful prewar tussore-silk suit that no longer fitted him as a parting present, which I treasured for many years in Tanganyika, where for some time it was my only suit.

A few days later, I was ordered to Cairo for my preliminary colonial service interview. General Dimoline gave me a lift in the special RAF plane taking him and Colonel Irven there on their way home. I was apprehensive on my first flight, the more so when we boarded the tiny three-seater single-engine plane. It flew slowly, lowly and bumpily north, landing every two or three hours to refuel and taking two days to reach our destination. After coming down at godforsaken airstrips in the sand at Malakal and Juba, we reached Khartoum in the late afternoon. General Dimoline was driven away to stay with the KAID, as Commander-in-Chief General Sir W. Platt was picturesquely styled in Arabic, in the imperial anomaly of the Anglo-Egyptian condominium of the Sudan — Bel-es Sudan, the land of the blacks governed by blues, as the wags said.

I spent a night in the Grand Hotel in Khartoum in the stifling June heat. This was where I drank iced coffee for the first time and from where I sent a letter home covered with the lovely 'camel stamps' I had admired all my life. I walked along the banks of the Nile in the cool of the evening and saw the statue of my hero Gordon. He was seated on his camel not far from the steps of the Residency where he had died.

Tanzania: Journey to Republic

We went to Cairo next morning, flying low over the Nile, over the Valley of the Kings at Luxor to Wadi Halfa and on to the airport at Heliopolis — city of the sun — in the afternoon. Staying at the most luxurious transit camp yet at Abbassia, I duly reported a couple of days later for my interview. This was with Mr Tom Vickers at his office at 9 Sharia el Birghas in the centre of the city. In my best tropical service dress uniform, with buttons, shoes and Sam Browne belt shining, a most attractive blonde called Mrs Margaret Nicholson met me. I passed the time of day for ten minutes or so with her before being ushered into Tom Vickers's room for the fateful half-hour. I was nervous, as usual on these occasions, but felt I was doing quite well until asked, 'Are your motives then purely altruistic?' I had to confess that I had never heard of that word. Years later, when I chanced to meet Mrs Nicholson again at the Shelbourne Hotel in Dublin, she told me that our little chat had formed an important part of the interview. I like to think that is why I was told, a day or two later, that I had passed and, 'subject to medical fitness, would proceed to England at earliest opportunity by MEDLOC [via the Mediterranean Sea] for a final interview in Whitehall'. My elation knew no bounds, as I proceeded fit as a fiddle next day to the formality of my medical. Stripped down as usual, the old Polish army doctor listened anxiously with his stethoscope. He then said in a sepulchral voice: 'I am sorry to tell you that you have a clangour on the heart and may drop dead at any minute, so I cannot pass you fit for the colonial service.'

To say that my heart sank is putting it mildly, yet I felt no great fear of death, only an overwhelming disappointment that my colonial service career appeared to have ended before it had begun. I handed Tom Vickers the doctor's report the next day with a plea that a second opinion be sought. I told him that I was a cross-country runner and could not believe that there was anything seriously wrong with my heart. Having assumed that was the end of the matter and that I would return to the KAR in Nairobi, I was pleasantly surprised when he yielded to my arguments. He arranged for an appointment a week or so later with the senior heart specialist for the Middle East — a British RAMC colonel.

Thus, suspended between life and death, between a long sought after career and uncertain employment, I passed a period of silent misery. I had decided not to confide in anyone, or to upset my family by writing. Instead, I sought solace in the Abbassia garrison swimming pool and in the carefree company of tsarist *beau sabreur* Colonel Paul Rodzianko, the noted horseman and a brother officer in the mess. On the appointed day, the kindly colonel examined me and at once put me out of my misery. He explained that I had 'a murmur on the heart, quite common at your age, you'll probably live to be 100'. Not for the first or last time I wept silently with joy and went on my way walking on air.

Soon I was back in England after a rough trip across the Mediterranean and a leisurely week's progress across France. This had been on a broken-down railway system from Toulon to Calais, with delightful long stops for peaches, strawberries and wine in sunlit villages in Touraine. Then came the white cliffs, form filling at Dover Castle, green fields, green trees, flowers, blessed cool of a northern clime and a night at a converted country house in the Midlands. I arrived home late the next day at my grandfather's old rectory at Newcastle Lyons, three miles from Celbridge, where my parents had moved for reasons of economy. I then came back to London for the interview at Dover House, Whitehall. This was before an impressive panel of top colonial and civil service brass, including the great Sir Ralph Furse. He had virtually created the unified colonial administrative service in his capacity as director of recruitment at the Colonial Office and still jealously presided over its postwar recruitment programme.

The day before I left for the interview, we had gone over to tea with the Kirkpatricks at Donacomper. There, I chanced to meet Sir Ivone Kirkpatrick of the Foreign Office, made famous overnight by his interrogation of Rudolf Hess. He was soon to become high commissioner in Germany and was later head of the Foreign Office. He was a small, quiet, unassuming man and I asked him for some tips for the interview. He replied without hesitation that 'one should bear in mind that the same three qualities were essential for both the foreign and colonial services.' These were (1) intellectual curiosity, (2) catholic tastes and (3) humanism. 'Since,' he elaborated, 'one must constantly question what was going on, one must be as happy at an ice hockey match in Moscow as at the Bolshoi Ballet and one must obviously be fond of one's fellow men.' He added that love of travel and languages went without saying. Were he to start his career in 1946, he would choose the colonial service rather than the diplomatic. It gave much greater responsibility at an early age, at a time when modern communications had robbed embassies abroad of their former initiative.

I was heartened by his excellent advice and did my best to work it into my answers whenever possible. It was presumably with good results, for I have certainly never heard a better summing up of an aspirant's qualities; it was exhausting. Searching questions were almost shamelessly fired at me from all sides. 'Why do you want to go to Tanganyika?' 'What are your hobbies?' 'What will you do alone in the bush?' 'I won't be alone,' I retorted, 'I will be surrounded by Africans — I'll make friends with them.' 'How will you build a house?' 'Send for a builder and tell him to build it.' Finally, 'You were at an Irish school called Portora. Where is it? Tell me the names of two well-known men who were educated there.' 'Henry Francis Lyte, the author of Abide with Me,' I replied, 'and Oscar Wilde, from the sublime to the ridiculous.' They all laughed and I felt more relaxed.

After more waiting, I arrived a few weeks later at Amiens Street station in Dublin. I had come for the weekend from the Inniskilling regimental depot at Omagh, to where I had escorted a party of men from the Furness Abbey camp in Barrow-in-Furness. My mother handed me the dread envelope with a Colonial Office imprint: 'Mr Secretary Creech-Jones has asked me to inform you that your appointment as an administrative officer (cadet) to Tanganyika Territory has been approved.' My heart stopped beating. I was in, after all those months of waiting. Cairo clangours and all! I was in, and rarin' to go.

The magic letter had gone on to say that I would be required to attend a 15-month course of training at the universities of Oxford and London. This was the Devonshire course named after the then Duke of Devonshire who was chairman of the committee that established it. On satisfactory completion of this course and yet another medical examination, I would become eligible for final appointment — hence our designation as colonial service proba- tioners on an allowance of £23 a month. More accurately, we were pre-probationers. On arrival in our respective territories, we did the first two years as cadets on probation before being confirmed in due course after passing examinations in language and law.

The course at Oxford lasted from October 1946 until June 1947, the one at London from June to December 1947. The letter also mentioned an immediate 'Class B' release on grounds of urgent national importance. I quickly went back to Furness Abbey and then off to York on 20 September to collect my new grey demob herringbone suit. I bade farewell to the army after just four years of service, which as in so many cases had completely transformed my life. If I had not been selected for the colonial service I would doubtless have served for at least another year, for my release demob group was only 1948.

The Oxford course was essentially a staff course designed to give cadets basic background knowledge of the wide variety of subjects needed for their profession. Oxford was generous with its dons and a brilliant galaxy of talent assembled to instruct us when we reported to delightful one-armed Colonel Drummond on 13 October. Most of them were well-known authors who delighted in recommending their own books, which we then bought at Blackwell's.

Thus, Sir Reginald Coupland lectured on colonial history, Margery Perham on colonial administration, Professor Hancock on colonial economics, and Professors Meyer Fortes and Evans- Pritchard on social anthropology. Landon of Trinity lectured on criminal law, Waldron on the law of evidence, and Fifoot, one of the wittiest speakers I have ever heard, on the interpretation of statutes. Morrison gave dry as dust lectures on soil mechanics, Meek lectured on land tenure and old Longland, a retired provincial commissioner (PC) from Tanganyika, lectured on surveying. Scott Russell, lately released from a Japanese POW camp and a mountaineer of note, lectured us on soil science and later became a lifelong friend. Almost all were national if not

55

international authorities on their respective subjects — we were fortunate indeed.

While it might be thought that the more academic aspects of the Devonshire course bore little relevance to the daily tasks of a district officer in a totally different environment, I felt that it was a useful background. It set the highest standards of excellence, which, suitably adapted to local conditions, provided an ideal framework for almost every activity. It also gave one self-confidence, background knowledge of the local historical, political and economic situation and a feeling of belonging to the world-wide colonial service.

Oxford, which I had first seen snow clad over four years before, filled me with a strange restless melancholy. I felt sadness bred of envy that I had missed the golden carefree days of youth and had, perforce, to rest content with a pale imitation of the real thing. It was difficult to concentrate on academic studies after several years' absence at the war. The nature of our staff course, with its wide-ranging syllabus, left little time for the precious leisure that is so essential a part of a university education.

With a self-conscious introspection, I roamed the streets gazing in awe at the dreaming spires of the old city, trying to drink in hasty gulps the hallowed distillation of so many centuries of history and learning. Sir Ralph Furse came and told us that we were a privileged élite and some of only 800 cadets selected from 40,000 applicants for the colonial administrative service in the first postwar intake. We were among the fortunate few chosen to attend the courses at Oxford and Cambridge, later to merge in London University.

Privileged or no, we certainly had a global outlook, since as a course we were destined soon to serve in territories as varied as Nigeria, Hong Kong, Kenya, Malaya, Fiji, Basutoland, Sierra Leone, and the Gilbert and Ellice Islands. Outwardly, the empire still preserved the awesome appearance of a recessional composed at its zenith. Most of us would live to see its nadir, with flags, maps and names transformed, symbolic of the vast vacuums of power and ideals left mostly in Africa and Asia with the departure of Pax Britannica.

Sir Ralph Furse felt that the Victorian empire had been modelled too closely on the Roman pattern. He compared the great barrages of the Punjab and the grand trunk roads and railways of India with the aqueducts, viaducts and metalled roads of Rome. He compared the Indian Army with the legions, and the collectors in Bengal with the centurions in Spain. He urged us to foster and follow the Greek ideal of spiritual and cultural partnership with subject peoples, on the lines of Alexander's rapprochement with the Persians. He stressed that material power, albeit mellowed by incorruptible administration and financial rectitude, was not enough.

Nearer home, the fascination of the colonial service was the wonderful opportunity it gave one to serve such diverse peoples in such an incredible variety of scattered places. It allowed one to seek sunshine and adventure and the romance of distant lands. One could look forward to an honourable career of modest comfort and reasonable security, and to devote one's life to a noble cause. To this end, our mentors sought to instil in us the Elizabethan ethos of a love of learning combined with a life of action. Steeped in the great traditions of Oxford and Cambridge, we were to be launched in the islands of the Pacific, in the teeming cities of Asia and in the deserts and bush of Africa.

The old white commonwealth of Canada, Australia, New Zealand, and South Africa, created by the Statute of Westminster in 1931, had now been expanded to include the first coloured dominions of India, Pakistan and Ceylon. It was clear that there could be no turning back from the daunting and unprecedented tasks ahead. We were no longer mere rulers but nation builders, planning to build slowly but surely on the solid foundations of solvent treasuries, viable economies, impartial judiciaries and trained local staff. We were to adapt as required the best that Britain could offer in the light of prevailing circumstances.

Our greatest asset was an immense self-confidence bred of centuries of successful imperial administration and recent victory in the Second World War. Our liabilities were our declining power, our increasing subservience to the USA and the irresponsible power of the United Nations. This was not to speak of the shrinking world referred to earlier, which effectively precluded any hope we might have had of running things in our own way and in our own time. It certainly did not occur to us that nearly all our own precious careers were destined to be cut short in midstream. We would spend a good deal of our time literally 'sawing ourselves off' by training our local successors.

Indeed, well before we reached the usual retirement age of 55, we were to see the entire colonial empire of over 50 dependencies virtually disappear. The Colonial Office and colonial service came to an end as governors, government houses, district commissioners, Union Jacks, forts, parades, bands, buglers, clubs and lawns faded into the undergrowth of recent history. Ours was indeed a unique vocation of faith shaken, of hopes unrealized, of charity soured.

I had the good luck to be up at Wadham College with its perfect quad and lovely garden, presided over by its famous warden Maurice Bowra, then at the height of his fame. Three tall magnificently built Fijian princes were the only other members of our course in that college. They were Ratu Edward Cacobau, whose grandfather had ceded Fiji to Queen Victoria, sending her his war club in token thereof, Ratu Penaia Ganilau and Ratu Kamisese Mara, later to become prime minister. Edward had been awarded the Military Cross while serving as a major in the New Zealand Army fighting the Japanese in the Pacific. He was quietly amused when the South African authorities would not let him land when his ship docked at Cape Town.

We were conveniently placed for Rhodes House, the centre of our academic studies where the greater proportion of our lectures took place. Its green copper dome, surmounted by a sculpture of the mythical Rhodesian Zimbabwe bird, gives a distinctive touch to this modern building of Cotswold stone. It had been built by the trustees of the imperialist visionary Cecil John Rhodes to house the finest library of commonwealth studies in the world. It also provides a suitable headquarters for the far-sighted foundation of scholarships that bear his name. These are awarded annually not only to outstanding commonwealth students, but also to Americans and Germans, to the lasting advantage of Oxford's sports teams.

Oxford Springboard, 1946–48

The severity of the notorious winter of 1946/7 was matched only by the austerity of the Labour government, which its cheerless Chancellor of the Exchequer Sir Stafford Cripps, pronounced in jest in Oxford to rhyme with 'peeps', personified. From January to March, the city lay under a dazzling cloak of snow; the river Thames was frozen, coal nearly ran out and power cuts were frequent. Food and clothing were still rationed, so we shivered and dreamed of the future sunshine.

Miraculously, the merciless winter gave way to the ecstasy of an early spring. Shy sun rays timidly pierced dappled clouds to reveal green shoots and buds, crocuses of purple and gold, tender yellow daffodils, blossoms in hedgerows and the half-forgotten music of singing birds. A fleeting glimpse of an Oxford summer followed with punting on the Cherwell and cricket in the parks. There were bicycle rides to Blenheim and Nuneham Courtenay, dawn May Day madrigals from Magdalen tower, reading on a rug under the great college copper beech, amorous advances, college dances and too many exams.

At the end of June, we reluctantly departed to the great lonely city of London. We were to continue our course at the School of Oriental and African Studies and the London School of Economics (LSE), where our Cambridge colleagues were to join us. London University, with its dozens of colleges scattered over an enormous area and tens of thousands of students, seemed less of a university and more of a vast cramming establishment. To add insult to injury, we even had a roll call at the beginning of every lecture — very different from Oxford's gracious invitation to learning.

A friendly Tanganyikan from Tanga, the late George Magembe, taught Swahili very well. He insisted on the highest standards of pronunciation. He managed to put across the elusive Bantu *ng'* prefix as in *ng'ombe* (a cow) by getting the entire class to chant singing *ng'ombe* — a sound that I only mastered many years later.

Sir Archibald Carr-Saunders, celebrated demographer and principal of LSE, welcomed us with a sherry party to introduce us to our lecturers. In this famous and progressive school of politics, future colonial administrators were for the first time to be given a basic training in local government and the social services. Field visits by bus to London County Council building projects, housing estates, schools, clinics, homes for the aged and handicapped, and even sewage farms, supplemented the theoretical lectures. London brought us down to earth in every sense of the word.

The course was followed in September by an imaginative and useful three-week attachment to the three tiers of local government in our own home areas (Oxford in my case as I lived in south Ireland). I spent a week each with the Bullingdon Rural District Council, the Oxford City Council and the Oxfordshire County Council.

There were to be more social anthropology lectures from Audrey Richards and political geography ones from Lucy Mair. There were visits to magistrates' courts, police stations and prisons. Thus, we had a unique opportunity to scrutinize the entire fabric of the body politic of the metropolitan power. Whatever one may feel about the rights and wrongs of recent British colonial policy, there can be no doubt that the postwar colonial administrative officers were superbly equipped and trained for their well-nigh impossible tasks. This was thanks to a handful of enlightened men and women whose thinking was far in advance of their time. Perhaps it was too late.

Some people have criticized the British for rapidly transplanting their own cherished political institutions — built up slowly but surely over 1000 years — to alien soils. Here, they have but followed the example of colonial powers throughout history from the Romans to the Arabs and the French, Belgians, Dutch and Portuguese to a greater or lesser extent in our own time. They have all at least paid the peoples they presumed to rule the compliment of passing on to them the best of their respective civilizations. How different peoples expressed their national genius in their colonies would provide a fascinating field of study. Indeed, determined to see for myself how other colonial powers trained their officers, I spent a week of the Easter vacation visiting the École de France d'outre mer in Paris. I also spent ten days during the summer vacation in the Low Countries visiting the Belgian and Dutch colonial colleges at Antwerp and Leiden respectively. The French training was run on very formal and academic lines, the

Belgian quasi-military, while the Dutch, whose course was attached to Leiden University, had a system more akin to our own.

Back in Oxford again for the local government attachment, I went to a private dance at the little Berkshire village of South Moreton near Didcot. There, I fell in love at first sight with a pretty young woman called Susan — quiet and shy with a lovely voice. We were married at the South Moreton church on 27 December, just in time for her to sail with me to Tanganyika a few weeks later.

Her father, Major-General Gerald Arthur Rickards, a scholar of Eton, was a gallant gunner officer who had been awarded the DSO and MC in the First World War. He and his wife Stella gave Susan and me a welcome leave base in their beautiful Gloucestershire home at Avening, where they had moved soon after our wedding, and were later devoted grandparents to our children, who were virtually brought up by them after they went to nearby boarding schools. Appropriately enough, my cousin Ralph Sadleir, chaplain of Eton, married us.

6

Sailing to Africa, 1948

Leaving London on a grey, cold day on 23 January 1948, we eventually arrived in Dar es Salaam on 26 February. This was after our old Union Castle liner, the *Llangibby Castle*, had broken down for a few days in Marseilles and been delayed for a few nights at Mombasa. Susan and I spent a couple of days at the Port Reitz Hotel in Mombasa, which cost us 15 shillings a day inclusive. Excited by my return to Africa, I showed her over the great Portuguese Fort Jesus and the picturesque streets of the old town.

Slowly we continued our voyage south, calling briefly at Tanga and Zanzibar until early one morning we dropped anchor in the middle of Dar es Salaam harbour. There were no deep-water piers at that time, so our baggage was loaded onto a lighter while we went ashore by launch to the customs jetty. From there, we went to the home of Mr Cheyne, the Secretary for African Affairs, who had asked us to stay for the few days of our induction in the capital. It was the height of the hot season with the temperature in the eighties and the humidity nearly 100 per cent. I remember taking a bath before dinner and putting on a white shirt, which I had to take off a few minutes later because it was soaked with sweat. I replaced it with another when I had managed to cool down a bit, before putting on the jacket local etiquette demanded at the time.

Air-conditioning was still unknown and refrigerators were scarce. Large electric ceiling fans, like old-fashioned aeroplane propellers, did their best to provide some draughts of cooler air. At night the temperature dropped, but by very little in the hot weather from November to March, and one often awoke in a pool of sweat. Mosquito nets were still mandatory and endemic malaria still claimed many victims.

Yet, there were compensations. To what Sultan Seyyid Barghash of Zanzibar had called a 'haven of peace' in 1856 when, attracted by the beauty of the 30-square-mile landlocked natural harbour he established a retreat there, the Germans had added a garden city laid out in rectangles beside the little village of Mzizima. Tall and stately indigenous palm trees were reinforced by scarlet acacia (or flamboyant) trees, which later gave the main street its name. There were exotic avenues of purple jacaranda and Indian almond, of green Cassia simaea and sweet smelling frangipani, of Nandi flame and dust-pink bauhinia. Here and there, ancient baobab trees surveyed the passing scene with timeless gaze, while the lovely black-green mango trees gave fruit and shade to the passing crowd. 'The Potamus will never see the mango on the mango tree,' sang T. S. Eliot with an excess of poetic licence. Mangrove swamps ringed the city and groves of gossamer casuarinas wept in the breeze along the sands. Solid stone bungalows were built to accommodate soldiers and civil servants. They had verandas, balconies and high ceilings and were painted white. A fine governor's palace in the Arab style of architecture was built facing the Indian Ocean just north of the harbour entrance. Destroyed by Royal Navy gunfire in 1914, the building was later rebuilt after the First World War as the British governor's residence. After independence in 1961, it became the state house and official residence of the president of the republic.

Everywhere, the bougainvillaea reigned supreme. In all its vivid colours, it climbed and clambered along whitewashed walls and old trees, succumbing gladly to the gardeners' and topiarists' cuts in multicoloured hedges, festive arches and strange beasts. Less spectacular shrubs vied for position, scarlet poinsettias and hibiscus, classical red and white oleanders, yellow alamanda, coral creeper, pungent smelling lantana and sweet scented myrtle and jasmine. The heady fragrance of the gardens — deadened by the sullen heat of the day — blended with the slight dank sea breeze to bring an intoxicatingly lovely aroma.

This was the garden city of the white guardians. A mini Whitehall built around the shores of the harbour along the Azania front consisted of fine old half-timbered German buildings with red corrugated-iron roofs. These housed the secretariat, treasury, high court, police headquarters and other government departments. Further south, lining the harbour as far as the customs jetty, were the Dar es Salaam Club, Lutheran church, New Africa Hotel, Standard Bank of South Africa, White Fathers' mission and St Joseph's Roman Catholic cathedral. (Built by the Germans in 1895, St Joseph's was one of the oldest buildings in the city.) The railway station lay behind them. This had been built in 1903 as the terminus for the 770-mile-long central line to Kigoma on Lake Tanganyika. The main shopping centre in Acacia Avenue, the Indian bazaar and the great dusty open space of Mnazi Mmoja (one coconut tree) separated the town from the overcrowded ramshackle huts of the African area beyond.

A few nineteenth-century Arab buildings, one of which housed the prisons' department headquarters, survived here and there. There were few tarmac streets and the only pavement appeared to be in Acacia Avenue. Motorcars were the prerogative of Europeans, though doubtless a few of the richer Indian merchants possessed them. A few Africans owned bicycles, a few could afford a ride on an overcrowded bus, but the great majority walked.

Tourists or casual visitors were virtually unknown. There were therefore very few hotels, for everyone stayed with friends or colleagues, or in government resthouses or camps. A rickshaw rank outside the New Africa Hotel catered for the needs of the many travellers in ships ashore for the day. I both pitied and admired these men who had the strength and courage to haul their human cargo at a trot through the torrid streets — stripped to the waist, displaying splendid biceps, and torsos shining with sweat.

There was one other hotel besides the New Africa at which Europeans could stay — the Splendid — owned by a Greek in Acacia Avenue. The only cinema, the Empire, owned by a Goan, had been going since 1925. There were a few European banks, businesses, garages and wholesale shops with old colonial names like Smith Mackenzie, Dalgety's, Gailey & Roberts, Howse & McGeorge, Wigglesworth and J. S. Davies, in addition to the great oil companies and shipping lines. Hundreds of Indian *duka*s, nearly all of them small retail shops, specialized in groceries, clothing, carpets, curios and jewellery. The great African market at Kariakoo, where the British carrier corps of African porters had camped in the First World War, provided a profusion of meat, poultry, fruit and vegetables.

The more prosperous African men wore the plain white cotton robes or *kanzu* and either a white embroidered skullcap called a *kofia* or a red fez — they were nearly all barefoot. The women who could afford to wore red, green, blue, or yellow and black cotton pieces called *khanga*s draped round their bodies, while the rest wore cheap black *khanikis*.

The African population lived in square, eight-roomed, single-storeyed houses made of mud and wattle and roofed with coconut palm fronds or four-gallon petrol tins, bright when new but quick to rust. An average family was fortunate to rent a single room for itself for five shillings a month. Some of the richer Arab and Swahili landlords, however, often owned several houses, which brought in a considerable income. A corridor with four rooms on each side would lead from the entrance to a small backyard. Communal kitchens and lavatories of the simplest kind would be at the back under the shade of a banana or papaw tree. There was no piped water and no electricity, only the ubiquitous four-gallon petrol tins (*debe*) and hurricane lamps or candles. One would hear the monotonous thud of pestle and mortar as maize was being pounded into flour for the next meal — a monotony frequently relieved by the merry peal of female laughter and the crying of undernourished babies. In the evening, as darkness veiled the squalor, whining mosquitoes would mercilessly attack the defenceless denizens, who were too poor and ignorant to buy mosquito nets or prophylactic pills.

Men and women ate separately. The men often took their dinner together outside the front door sitting on the street. It was the only real meal of the day — a great tray filled with rice or maize porridge, seasoned with gravy and beans or dried shark, with some oranges, mangoes or bananas as dessert. It was eaten with the hands in biblical style, carefully kneaded and mixed with the vegetables, munched with the appreciation of those to whom hunger is no stranger.

Breakfast was a cup of tea and a bowl of maize gruel. Lunch was often a cup of tea, a cake and a doze under an Indian almond tree. It was small wonder that half the children died before the age of one and a quarter of them before the age of fifteen. Average life expectancy was only 35 and average income about £20 a head per annum. Few could afford meat, usually only eaten once or twice a year at weddings or religious festivals. Chicken was recommended for special occasions — *kuku ni chakula cha siku kuu* (chicken is the food for a feast).

Alcoholic drinks, forbidden by the Koran, and European drinks virtually denied Africans by the colonial government, were in any case beyond the purse of the vast majority. Local brews were made variously from millet, rice, banana, cashew, coconuts and honey — by old ladies on the premises in 44-gallon drums. They were cheap and not very intoxicating, unless consumed in great quantities, which they often were. Two refreshing soft drinks, which were very popular in Dar es Salaam, were coconut juice (*togwa*) and ginger (*tangawizi*) — 20 glasses cost one shilling. It was a cheap round!

There was little privacy, so the trivial round was conducted with a dignified ritual, without which such a harsh existence would have proved unendurable. Discipline, politeness and old world courtesy, combined in one key Swahili word *adabu*, play an all-important part in African tribal life. The exquisite courtesy of an African village embraces elaborate Arabic greetings and inquiries after health and fortune, bowing with hand on heart. More earthy Bantu attributes of cheerfulness, spontaneous hospitality and tact, expressed in warm two-handed handshakes, afford a unique welcome to visitors, especially foreigners. A visitor is never forgotten. A return to a familiar place after five, ten or even twenty years brings an unforgettable welcome as he or she is readmitted to the warm charm of a family circle.

The upcountry passenger train left Dar es Salaam station for the interior three days a week, on Tuesdays, Thursdays and Saturdays; one spoke of catching the Thursday train, not the 4.15. The journey was considered quite an adventure and the stations became so many venues for social gatherings *en route*. When the train arrived at bigger centres like Morogoro, Dodoma and Tabora, it would stop for half-an-hour or so and impromptu parties would take place in the comfortable dining car, where no licensing laws seemed to operate. The entire population for miles around came to every tiny station to sell fruit and eggs to third-class passengers and meet their friends. Children and even some grown-ups would run out of their homes to cheer the train on its way. They would watch the great *gari-la-moshi* (car of smoke) slowly steaming along, sometimes almost at walking pace as it climbed a steep gradient.

Before boarding the train we spent the statutory week in the capital being briefed by senior officers, being posted to our various stations upcountry, drawing advances of pay, clearing our kit through the customs, licensing our guns and so on. We were also introduced to many of our brother officers by means of dinner parties and lunch parties and the famous tropical cocktail parties held as the sun goes down (at 7.00 p.m.) known as sundowners.

My wife joined other wives in shopping for our new home in Seifi's Household Stores, in Kassums, and Haji and Patels. With our wedding present money, we bought a Persian rug for £18 in Mooloo's and a tropical wireless set for £48 in Souza Junior Dias Ltd, an unlikely sounding Goan establishment.

We called formally on the governor, the chief secretary and the chief justice by signing special visitors books left in the porches of their residences. This all-powerful triumvirate formed the inner circle of the colonial Establishment of the day, and failure to call on them was unthinkable since it could mean exclusion from the coveted invitation lists to the various receptions and parties, which made up local white society. Such calls had to be repeated on all visits to the capital and, on proceeding on home leave, the mysterious letters PPC (*pour prendre congé*) accompanied them.

Most exciting of all was our interview with the administrative secretary, Sir John Lamb, a modest, capable and charming man, who posted us to our individual preferences — an immense morale booster. I asked to go to one of the districts inhabited by the

Wanyamwezi (people of the moon) in Western Province, since I had so much enjoyed serving with them in the King's African Rifles. To my surprise and without any hesitation, Sir John posted me to the Nzega district 65 miles northwest of Tabora *en route* to Mwanza. It was known for its dusty plains, great herds of cattle and shortage of water. On the way, we were first to spend a week at Tabora, the headquarters of Western Province, for further local briefing by the provincial commissioner and his staff.

Another senior official, Bobbie Maguire, impressed us by stressing the importance of making our homes as comfortable as possible. He advised us to bring out from home any little treasures we might have, since Tanganyika was our home now 'for the duration'. I took his advice and never regretted it. It was vital to one's morale during the vicissitudes of the long hot years in splendid isolation to have a real haven, where one could forget the pressing cares of the day and relax in familiar surroundings created by a picture from home, an old cushion or a favourite book.

On arrival at Tabora station 30 hours after leaving the coast, the district commissioner C. F. C. V. (Bill) Cadiz and his wife Phyllis met us. They kindly had us to stay for a few days in accordance with the provincial administration's admirable custom of never consigning a brother officer to a local hotel or government resthouse. Bill Cadiz, tall and athletic looking, was an experienced DC. He had distinguished himself for his exceptional fluency in the Swahili language in a service that prided itself on maintaining the highest standards of Swahili of any government in East Africa. Also, his father had been DC Tabora before him, soon after the First World War. He attributed his somewhat singular surname to the fact that he was descended from an Armada sailor washed ashore near Galway in one of the storms that marred its unfortunate journey in 1588.

The next morning, PC Western Province Mr R. W. Varian gave me the laconic advice 'to keep my mouth shut and my bowels open'. A famous big game hunter, who had once shot a lion in the lavatory in the Tabora girls' school, he inquired if I had seen any wild animals yet. When I replied that all I had seen was a snake coming out from under the secretariat building in Dar es Salaam, he said, 'A snake coming out of the Secretariat — it must have been Maguire!' Ralph Varian was on his last tour of service. An Irishman of Huguenot stock from Dublin, a graduate of Trinity College Dublin and a hockey international, he was a bush district officer of the old school. He had never served in the secretariat and felt the same piteous contempt for its officials as a frontline brigadier might feel for a staff officer in the War Office — hence doubtless his remark about Bobbie Maguire.

Tabora is a pleasant town about 4000 feet up the great central plateau, so is fairly cool at night. It is 500 miles from the coast and 250 miles from Lake Tanganyika on the old Arab caravan route from Bagamoyo to Ujiji. David Livingstone spent some time at Unyanyembe ('place of the mango trees') in a flat-roofed hut (*tembe*) just outside the town on his last journey. The Germans had built a great stone fort there — as they did in their stations throughout the country. In fact, the Swahili word for fort '*boma*' became synonymous with the district office and has remained so to this day.

For a few months during a critical phase of the East African campaign in 1916, which the German commander General von Lettow-Vorbeck immortalized, the Germans moved their capital to Tabora. It was here, in the railway workshops, that the famous numismatic curiosity, the 'Tabora sovereign', was minted. After the war, the British built a railway to Mwanza on Lake Victoria. This joined the central line and thus made it a suitable site on which to found the élite Tabora boys' school. Rainfall was sparse and the climate was dusty and dry, which produced the acacia bush thorn-scrub vegetation so typical of much of Tanganyika. Water and food shortages were chronic, though a big dam-building programme was well underway when we arrived. Cool green avenues of Cassia simaea trees led from the *boma* to the town. They went past the earth 'browns' of the golf course, the hard tennis courts and the cricket ground of the club. They went past the tiny replica of an English village church to the straggling ramshackle shops and houses of the bazaar.

On the right of the road near the railway station was the fine hotel. This, together with the New Africa Hotel in Dar es Salaam and the district commissioner's house overlooking the lake at Kigoma, had been built for the planned state visit of the German crown prince, 'Little Willie', in 1914. However, the visit had been cancelled because of the outbreak of war. All three buildings were known as the Kaiserhof. Many years later, one of the Kaiser's grandsons, Prince Burkhardt of Prussia, visited Dar es Salaam. He told me that he had seen the imperial eagle of the German empire still standing on the roof of the New Africa Hotel. Tanganyika was divided into eight provinces, each of which had about seven districts, making 56 districts in all. Their administrative staffs ranged from five district officers in the more important districts to one in small outstations. Only 20 or so district officers then staffed the secretariat in the capital, making a total administrative staff of 300 officers, including about 40 who were always on leave. To save travelling costs, one went home on leave every two-and-a-half years for five months.

Western Province was the second largest province in Tanganyika. It contained the three Nyamwezi districts of Tabora, Nzega and Kahama, to the northwest on either side of the Mwanza railway line. It also included the mixed Nyamwezi/Manyema tribal area of Mpanda, to the southwest of which was the recently discovered Uruwira lead mine. The mountainous Ufipa district was in its southwest corner, stretching along the lake to the Northern Rhodesian border near Abercorn. The Kigoma district included the large historical Swahili town of Ujiji where Stanley found Livingstone in 1871. It also included the wild Buha highlands to the north, which stretched west to the borders of the Belgian protectorate of Rwanda–Urundi. Buha was divided into the two lovely districts of Kasulu and Kibondo. There were eight districts altogether in the province, which had a population of about a million people. The provincial commissioner, his eight district commissioners and about a dozen district officers ruled it indirectly through traditional chiefs. The district officers were known as Bwana *Shauri* (Mr Problems). This was because they spent most of their time listening to the fascinating variety of human affairs, complaints, dramas, quarrels and land disputes that were prevalent in rural society. They heard some in court and

70

some out of it, some in the office and some on safari, in local parlance. This charming sobriquet coined by the subject peoples themselves goes far to explain the relaxed nature of British rule and the wonderfully friendly relations on the whole between rulers and ruled.

Indeed, it is unfair even to try to translate such a unique legacy of Swahili linguistic genius as the word *shauri*, so appropriately chosen by the inhabitants of Tanganyika to describe a district officer's multifarious duties. These are more varied in scope even than those of his illustrious predecessor, the collector of the Indian civil service. The collector's honourable vocation, created by the ephemeral circumstances of the past century, was unprecedented in its well nigh limitless responsibilities and opportunities. It was unmatched by all previous imperial officials from Persian satraps to Roman centurions, from Chinese mandarins to Turkish governors, right down to the more military French, Dutch, Belgian, German and Portuguese administrators of the early twentieth century.

Thus, *shauri* could appear in such varied contexts as *shauri ya mungu* (act of God), *shauri yako* (your own fault), *shauri yangu* (my own business), and so on *ad infinitum*.

Meanwhile, the youngest and most junior *bwana shauri* in the territory sat and perused the annual reports of the eight districts in the PC's office; they seemed incredibly dull. 'The rainfall in Kahama was more than usual and the maize crop halved'; 'cases of theft were on the increase in Kigoma Township'; 'The hospital roof leaked in Nzega'; and 'more trees were being planted in Kasulu to stop soil erosion'. Here was parish-pump politics with a vengeance — I supposed I had really chosen the right job. However, the Union flag flew proudly over the office, on the front of the PC's chauffeur-driven Chevrolet and over the great grey stone fortress where smart police sentries in blue jerseys, puttees and tarbushes, armed with the old Lee-Enfield 303 rifles, saluted smartly as we passed. The power seemed to be there; I was not too sure about the glory.

Susan and I sat beside the driver in the front of Hasham Remtulla's old five-ton lorry, all our worldly goods loaded in the back, as we set off down the dusty red murram road that led to

Nzega. The journey took about two-and-a-half hours on a fairly good road. We drove through the Miombo thorn bush past scattered villages 'of mud and wattle made', over numerous wooden bridges, sometimes set at rakish angles to the road, often approached unawares after exciting bends. There were PWD camps every ten miles, gangs of labourers filling the potholes with earth and gravel, digging the deep broad drains on either side of the road, waving cheerfully as we sped by.

7

Upcountry Cadet, 1948–49

I t was early March and the land was parched, eagerly awaiting the onset of the long rains. Scorched earth and tree stumps marked the forest clearings of shifting cultivators in their quest for virgin soil. Clumps of cassava, sweet potatoes and groundnuts climbed casually up the gentle hills and carpets of green rice and sugar cane lay along the valley bottoms shaded by tall fever trees.

The hump and horn of scrawny cattle meandered down bush tracks led by little boy herdsmen to the music of iron bells. Long wooden cylinders of 'hives for the honey bee' were suspended from the branches of acacia trees to give at least some milk and honey to this arid land. Suddenly, the bush gave way to neat avenues of dark green Cassia simaea trees interspersed with white and yellow frangipani. They led to a low whitewashed building with a red corrugated iron roof in front of which the Union flag flew proudly in the warm afternoon breeze from a tall white flag-pole set in a lawn surrounded by whitewashed stones. This was the district office headquarters of Nzega district, known in Swahili as the *boma*. From there, avenues lined with scarlet acacia and jacaranda trees, oleander and bougainvillaea radiated to the hospital, police lines, prison, stores, village and market. They also led to the government officials' half-dozen small red and white bungalows, surrounded by neat gardens of marigolds, petunias and euphorbia hedges, with a much prized red murram tennis court in the background.

It was tea time; a cheerful New Zealand DO, Sam Humphries, and his lovely wife Jean carried us off to their home, supervised our unpacking, produced servants out of a hat and, all in all, gave us a wonderful welcome. Later, the DC Peter Bleackley and his wife Rachel had the entire station — a dozen European officers and their wives — to a sundowner to meet us on their veranda.

We had strayed into another world. It was an isolated yet fiercely dedicated world. Its rulers were aloof yet possessively proud of their district and their people. Men and women were on duty seven days a week and 24 hours a day. This was the colonial service in the field, actually in an 'outpost of empire', charged with implementing the latest ideals and policies of Oxford academics and Westminster politicians.

As we relaxed in the cool of the evening, dull provincial office reports came alive as waves of conversation in an unfamiliar jargon swept over us. 'Were the women really beginning to come and have their babies at Paddy Mitchell's new clinic?' 'Did they consult witch doctors as well as an insurance policy?' 'Would the large dams built by the Water Development Department at Nzega and Ulaya fill up to their full capacity in the coming rains?' 'Were the spillways all right or would they burst or overflow and flood the surrounding villages?' 'How many acres of rice and other crops could be irrigated behind them?' 'How many more dams could we afford to build?' 'Could we put fish in them, swim in them, sail on them?'

At the cattle market the next week, the new cattle rate was one shilling per beast, 50 cents for calves, which was difficult to assess because, as they said, no one likes to tell you how many they have got. Unyamwezi creameries run by Jim Mitchison and a joint effort with the Tabora and Kahama creameries sells hundreds of tons of ghee, mainly to Indians for cooking fat. We must persuade farmers to sell their surplus milk. We must persuade farmers to dig compost pits and use cattle dung on their crops. We must persuade them to collect maize stalks on wooden stands, to keep reserves of seed, to plant cassava as a famine reserve, to dig latrines. We must persuade the people to go to hospital, to send their children to school, to pay their 12 shillings a year taxes, to refrain from getting drunk. We must persuade them, persuade them, persuade them. It was small wonder that, lunching with us at Handeni a few years later, the governor Sir Edward Twining turned to Susan and said, 'I won't apologize for talking shop; in our job shop is life.'

It was exciting to be alive, exciting to go to bed for the very first time in our own home. The next day was somewhat of an anti-climax. The DC gave me a small party of six 'station hands' with instructions to refloat and clean up a canoe that had run aground on the shore of the Nzega dam. This was in preparation for a picnic tea his wife and her Canadian guest Franie planned to hold that afternoon. It really brought me down to earth; there was to be no visit to a chief or parley with a witch, no hunt for a murderer or reading of the Riot Act. My grand ideas dispelled in an instant, though I quite enjoyed the task allotted to my party. It gave me a chance to get to know some of the station hands whose multifarious duties ranged from cutting grass, tending the gardens, growing vegetables and maintaining the buildings, to marking out the tennis court and putting up the net. As in the King's African Rifles, there was no strict dividing line between hours of work and hours of leisure, which in the nature of things tended to co-mingle.

I shared the DO's office with Sam Humphries who initiated me into the art of hearing tax defaulters' cases in our capacity of third-class magistrates. They almost all naturally pleaded guilty in default of their tax receipts for the year or years in question. They were then sentenced to a month's extramural labour for each year tax was due. This was a mild form of imprisonment to enable them to pay off their dues to the state by giving a period of free labour. During this period, they stayed at home with friends or relatives, or (if they came from afar) in a camp. Cynics said that the intensity of the DO's tax drive was in inverse proportion to his wife's plans for a rockery or duck pond.

My first job on arrival in the office at 7.30 a.m. was the rather tedious one of counting the cash in the strongroom not to speak of the ivory tusks and rhino horns deposited there for safe custody. The East Africa copper coinage of the day had holes in the middle of the coins, which could be tied together for safety on bits of string; they were very, very dirty. I held one key of the strongroom door, the Indian cashier the other, to reduce the risk of internal theft. When the sealed canvas bags, each containing 2000 shillings, filled the room to overflowing, they were transferred in some secrecy by lorry under police escort to provincial headquarters. Once the policemen stole the lot, but that is another story.

We had scarcely finished unpacking our boxes at Nzega when, in typical service fashion, we were ordered to the neighbouring district of Kahama. This was to replace the well-known RAF fighter ace Wing Commander G. R. A. M. 'Robin' Johnston DSO DFC who had shot down 29 German planes. He had suddenly been transferred to Mpwapwa district in Central Province to form a new district at the groundnut scheme headquarters at Kongwa. It was felt that his distinguished war record and tough personality would help him deal with the exceptional problems created by the influx of so many British ex-servicemen and their camp followers.

For us, therefore, Nzega was something of a false start, for we were only there for three weeks before moving to Kahama — a sister district that had formerly been administered from Nzega. Before leaving, however, I was summoned to the hospital to take down a 'dying declaration'. An angry husband, who he named in a matter of fact tone of voice before dying calmly a few minutes later, had stabbed some poor fellow in the stomach. I had to read the relevant section of the penal code to him before taking down his last statement.

We and our repacked possessions were duly driven a few hours further on down the dusty road to Kahama in the ubiquitous three-ton district lorry. There, a white district office with a charming thatched roof was surrounded by a colourful garden, which featured an ancient vine mounted on a wooden trellis. This gave a pleasantly informal aspect to the inevitable white stones, white flagpole and red, white and blue flag. Avenues of evergreen Cassia simaea led from one small bungalow to another — all built for a few hundred pounds by the PWD and containing exactly the same furniture down to the last chair. There was no sign of the grand piano in the district commissioner's house as portrayed in *Man of Two Worlds*, the film about Tanganyika I had seen a year or so earlier.

The DC, Donald Flatt, with a first in Greats from Merton College, Oxford was then in his mid-thirties with about ten years of service behind him. He had lost his wife a few years earlier in tragic circumstances and had remarried an American missionary nurse called Ruth Safemaster, who had already spent many dedicated years working under an eye specialist at the Lutheran mission at Kiomboi in the Singida district of the Central Province.

Tall, dark and handsome with a slightly saturnine, serious look, his fellow administrators thought he took life a shade seriously, though they respected his deeply held religious beliefs. Some said a little unkindly that, 'When he was a DC he looked like a missionary and then after he became a missionary he looked like a DC.'

A man of exceptional integrity, he was an incredibly conscientious administrator, even going to the lengths of keeping a big book with every government and treasury circular and circular letter duly inscribed in it — a book he very kindly presented to me on his departure to the mission at Moshi. On Sunday mornings, his wife personally conducted a church service in Swahili for the 30 or so prisoners in the Kahama gaol — a captive congregation in every sense of the word.

So keen was he on the district that he often sent me on safari over the weekends so that I would be back in the office on Monday mornings to help with the mail. Ten days a month on safari was the rule in his district, so that really 'close' administration could be maintained. Woe betide the chief whose tax collection was behind schedule, or school attendance 'disappointing'. Inspection books were kept at every hospital, dispensary and school in the district to keep a constant check on progress.

Our staff also boasted an agricultural assistant, Bill Yeo from Devon. He was a practical farmer, the salt of the earth; a sleeping sickness officer Ron West, who was immensely keen on his job; a resettlement officer Charles Parry, who had known Cecil Rhodes; and a PWD officer Charlie Cleton who had a lovely Seychelloise wife called Terry. The remaining thirty-odd government departments came under the administration, whose 'Poohbah' officers found themselves responsible for a bewildering variety of diverse duties they could never have discharged without the help of a devoted cadre of Asian and African NCOs.

Roman-style government was the order of the day, with priority given to maintenance of law and order and tax collection. Without taxes, the creation of wealth needed to finance vital water, health and education services could not even be contemplated.

The DC was a first-class magistrate with powers to imprison for up to two years and to impose a 2000-shilling fine (plus 24 strokes of the cane for certain offences such as rape and cattle theft). I, as a third-class magistrate, only had powers to imprison for up to three months and to impose a 500-shilling fine. We both made preliminary enquiries into more serious cases — mainly murder and manslaughter, which were referred for trial by the High Court on circuit at Tabora — to establish whether or not there was a prima facie case for the accused to answer. Great importance was attached to judicial work. We tried to mete out justice, as fairly and speedily as we could for a variety of excellent reasons, not least of which was the very limited accommodation in the lockup (*mabus*). In this laudable aim we were helped by the fact that, as administrators, police officers, prison officers and coroners, we were able to dispense with the preliminaries to some extent. It was a help to know that the accused was a 'well-known' thief or the murder victim a 'hot-tempered drunkard'. It was a shade more complicated in the court itself when the magistrate found himself the counsel for both the prosecution and the defence.

The role of the magistrate does not appear so strange when one realizes that from time immemorial the chiefs had played much the same part of ruler and judge in their own traditional society. Perhaps surprisingly to Westerners, they countenanced neither prisons nor executions, since all punitive sanctions were imposed in the form of compensation to the injured party.

It was also tempered by the fact that the High Court exercised appellate and revisional powers and kept a very close eye indeed on the administration of justice in the lower courts. A parallel structure of native courts handled nearly all civil cases based on native law and custom and all petty criminal cases. Lugard's disciple Sir Donald Cameron introduced this vital offshoot of indirect rule on the Nigerian model in the 1920s. Here the DC, wearing yet another hat, sat as an appeal court of first instance — the first rung on a ladder that led to the governor himself.

The chief sat as judge in his *baraza*, a low whitewashed mud-brick building with a thatched or corrugated iron roof. It was open at one end and had a low dais with two small rooms leading off it at the other — one an office and one a lockup. There were no windows in the auditorium, which was surrounded by low walls and pillars with accommodation for a hundred or so inside and thousands outside. The chief, normally assisted by two court elders as assessors, sat on a chair behind a wooden table on the dais, while his court clerk (*karani*) made a record of the case, collected fines, court fees and taxes, and issued the vital receipts (*stakabadhi*).

Like medieval kings, few chiefs could write, relying on their court seal (*muhuri*). The lesser elders, witnesses and so forth made their mark in the approved style, so the court register and documents were spattered with thumbprints. Everything happened at the *baraza*, for quite apart from being the courthouse it was the focus for all local and indeed central government activities in the chiefdom. Meetings were held, disputes over land, cattle and women thrashed out, revenue collected, workers paid, mail delivered, drums of petrol and sacks of grain dumped. It was HQ bush.

The chief maintained law and order with the help of three or four unarmed tribal police or messengers, his various subchiefs, village headmen and elders. The DC had half a dozen policemen who could be armed in an emergency with old .303 rifles, which they also carried when escorting prisoners or large sums of money. There was also a small prison, like a Beau Geste fort, with accommodation for about 30 prisoners and another six or so prison warders to look after them. The 'eyes and ears' of the administration, however, were undoubtedly the élite band of *boma* messengers (*ma-tarishi*). These were local tribesmen, in this case Wanyamwezi or Wasumbwa, many of whom had served the government for twenty or thirty years. The head messenger Nassoro, who combined the qualities of a sergeant major with those of a diplomat, attended the DC, while Ngwaya and later cheerful little Mayengo, son of Chief Lwassa of Runzewe, looked after me.

They sat on a bench outside the office doors on the veranda, wearing plain khaki shorts and tunic, scarlet fez and barefoot, carrying a small thin cane, which was more a badge of office than a weapon. They knew everything, everyone and every place. They were guides, philosophers and friends to the foreign rulers and acted as popular interpreters in every sense of the word between rulers and ruled.

They worked cheerfully for seven days a week and 24 hours a day for the princely sum of £2 a month. They were indefatigable, indomitable and incredibly loyal. They organized foot safaris, pitched camp, killed snakes, collected chickens and eggs, apprehended lunatics, arrested thieves and even on occasion quieted noisy demonstrators. They tendered advice when asked to do so that was nearly always wise and fair. They must have a prominent place among the unsung heroes of Africa, for they gave so much and expected so little. They were true exemplars of Milton's words; 'They also serve who only stand and wait,' which my preparatory school headmaster Captain Clifford Lloyd had taken as the text for his sermon on my last Sunday at school.

Law and order having been thus established and maintained in such apparently effortless and economic fashion, the twin pillar in the imperial system, the collection of revenue, could safely be set up. The payment of tribute in some form or another has ever been a vital ingredient of government by consent, however authoritarian or democratic, royal or republican it may be. Since it creates a symbolic bond between the collectors and their fiefs, your overlord will protect you from rivals if only to ensure that you continue to pay your dues to him.

It gives the payer a stake in the state, however humble, an interest proportionate to his means in the prosperity of the nation. In a hitherto wholly subsistence economy, it gave the African peasant a small incentive towards the essential modern creation of a cash economy with all the paraphernalia of agricultural and cattle markets and the complementary provision of attractive consumer goods, which only money could buy. Thus, they made the transition from skins to shirts and *khanga*s, and later to suits and hats. They went from bare feet to shoes (if not as comfortable, at least protection against bilharzia), from walking to bicycling, from hoes to ploughs. They progressed from witch doctors to modern medicine and education — in short, a fascinating survey in microcosm of the whole development of society and government from Babylon to modern times.

Most important of all from the point of view of the Establishment, it provides a ready-made register of all the inhabitants, an essential prerequisite to any efficient administration. Woe betide the DC, chief or subchief who had not collected at least 90 per cent of his tax by the end of January. Tax collection was the inevitable yardstick of all administrative efficiency and zeal in such a system, even of love and respect because an unpopular chief's taxpayers slowly melted away. Since the chiefs' salaries and to some extent the DC's promotion prospects rested respectively on the number of taxpayers and the percentage of tax collected, the incentives speak for themselves.

If the *boma* messengers were the day-to-day routine link between DC and villagers, the chiefs were the formal and symbolic political and constitutional link between government and people — a role that was always delicate, at times tense, even dangerous. The tortuous traditional complexities of tribal rule, hedged in as they were by ritual and magic and often bedevilled by family, friends and *fitina* (intrigue), were difficult enough to contend with in themselves. This is not to mention the extra burden of acting as buffer between ultra-conservative and naturally suspicious tribesmen and ultra-officious (to African eyes) and impatient foreigners, full of crazy ideas and outlandish plans.

The Kahama chiefs were local aristocrats whose families had ruled their people for centuries, though even by modest Tanganyikan standards they were minor rulers with but little to distinguish them from the majority of their subjects. Their salaries ranged from £50 a month for Chief Kishimba of Kahama chiefdom, in some ways a paramount chief, to only £2 a month for poor old Chief Hole-Hole of Ulewe II, whose kind offer to present Susan a superb leopard skin I unfortunately had to decline.

Chief Kishimba was undoubtedly *primus inter pares* and his court was situated on the delightful rocky hill of Zongomera, a few miles from Kahama, in a series of scattered compounds under the mango trees surrounded by thorn *zariba*. The houses were beautiful examples of traditional Nyamwezi craftsmanship, with excellent thatch and fine timber from the local forests, plastered in mud and sometimes daubed in lime.

The chief was very distinguished looking — tallish and slender with an inquisitive and scholarly look on his brown face. His fine hands with thin sensitive fingers looked as if they and their antecedents hadn't done 'a hand's turn' for 1000 years. He usually wore khaki trousers, a white open-necked shirt with long sleeves and a pair of white tennis shoes. He always carried the symbolic ebony and wildebeest-tail fly switch, the mark of a ruler.

As his subjects entered his presence, the men bowed and gave charming ceremonial low handclaps, to which, in Soviet style, the chief gave a gentle clap in exchange. When two chiefs met, subtle nuances entered into the clapping style in the manner of two Japanese bowing each other out. One could at least generally find out, however, which of the two thought himself the more important. Even the white officers were accorded this courtesy, which I always appreciated, even though, somewhat churlishly I fear, we only responded with a slight inclination of the head.

Another chief, Andrea Mhanda of Ngogwa chiefdom, always greeted his guests with a salute by his state drummers. This would be exquisitely performed on venerable drums of all shapes and sizes, some of them hundreds of years old, by a team of all age groups. He seemed rather old and gloomy, walked with a stoop and resisted all change in a determined manner.

Chief Lumerezi had ruled his hilly fortress of Mbogwe for 40 years and, like his neighbour Chief Kisozo of Ushirombo, always wore a large cowrie shell on his head as a badge of office. He had at least a dozen wives, was small and brown but stockily built and immensely strong, with a twinkle in his eye and a great sense of humour. Once, at the end of the dry season, I watched him turn out his entire chiefdom with the drums to fight a spectacular bushfire for most of the night. The excited shouts of the men, the ululation of the women, the barking of the dogs could be heard against the strange sizzling of flame and thorn, the sighing of the wind and the more hopeful noise of the branches beating out the encroaching fires. The entire sky was lit up for miles as the flames hissed and crackled out of the stifling clouds of acrid smoke.

The chief stood calmly, giving orders to his subchiefs, elders and messengers, exhorting here, rebuking there, occasionally joining the beaters himself, until in the early hours the battle was won, leaving great blackened hillsides and smoking ash in its wake.

What characters these chiefs were. For good or ill, they were on duty, like district officers, 24 hours a day for seven days a week, their lives inextricably interwoven with those of their people. Although the titles were hereditary, eldest sons did not automatically succeed to the chiefdom if too infirm or stupid, and the elders usually succeeded in selecting the best available candidate. With so many women and children around, there was no shortage of applicants. Another advantage of the system was that half the people in the chiefdom were usually related in some way to the ruler so had a vested interest in maintaining the status quo.

Not only did the chief have to unite and lead his people and represent their best interests to the colonial power, but he also had to reconcile the living with the dead. Failure in this respect could incur the wrath of the ancestral spirits (*mizimu*) and awful retribution in the shape of drought, famine, disease and death. In such agricultural and pastoral communities, rain was the key to life itself and failure to ensure an adequate supply for his people could traditionally lead to a chief's removal or even death. Thus, every family hamlet had its miniature hut for the spirits, which was kept supplied with symbolic offerings of beer and grain. Special sacrificial festivals (*tambiko*) were held on appropriate days to placate the spirits of given individuals, usually fathers and grandfathers because, sensibly, the most recently departed got top priority. The chief was responsible for satisfactory relations with the ancestral spirits as a whole and, on big feast days, chickens, goats and even cattle were sacrificed by the fearful living to the silent dead.

The missionaries formed a 'third estate' in our remote world. In the Western Province, the famous White Fathers' Roman Catholic order that Cardinal Lavigerie founded in the previous century reigned supreme. Its mission stations were oases of civilization in that wild land, with whitewashed stone or mud-brick churches, schools, dispensaries, well-kept farms and gardens, orange groves and avenues of trees and flowering shrubs.

Dressed in white cassocks — a habit modelled on the djellaba and burnous of the North African desert — the White Fathers would speed around dusty bush tracks on their motorbikes visiting bush schools and sick parishioners. While their dedication and discipline were admirable, the dedication of the wonderful White Sisters was heroic. While the priests and brothers returned home (usually France, Holland or Switzerland) once in every ten years, the nuns left their homes forever, staying in Africa until they died. One wonderful old lady at the Ushirombo mission had served there for 50 years, waiting for the day when she would join her friends in the little cemetery in the mango trees.

Father Beh from Alsace was father superior at Ushirombo and felt equally proud of his choir and football team. He liked having guests, for he then had permission to serve his homemade orange wine at dinner. It was a great joy to spend a weekend there in a mud-brick resthouse with iron bars on the small windows to keep out leopards, whose sawing noise could often be heard at night. On the Saturday afternoon, Father Beh, cassock and all, and I played football with the schoolboys; on Sunday morning my wife and I attended High Mass and listened to the beautiful voices of the children's choir, which Father Beh had built up over the years.

We sometimes shared the resthouse with Charles Parry, the sleeping sickness resettlement officer who had met Cecil Rhodes. He was a marvellous old man who at one time had been a chorister in St Paul's Cathedral. He had never married and had spent a lifetime wandering around Africa, often living in a tent on safari for months on end. On the rare occasions he surfaced at district headquarters, he would celebrate round the clock so superbly that we said he had sundowners and sunrisers.

Further west at the Runzewe mission, where we had the honour of sleeping in the bishop's room, old Father Martin, an 80-year-old Breton with a flowing white beard, presided. He still toured the dusty roads and tracks on his motorcycle inspecting mission schools and dispensaries in remote outstations, visiting the sick and comforting the dying. Indeed, there never seemed to be a place so remote that others remoter didn't spring from it deeper yet into the wilderness.

Nearer the Kahama *boma* lay the Mbulu mission, where two Dutch priests, Father James the hunter and Father John the scholar, bibliophile and philatelist coexisted amicably. They had just completed a large dam, which provided a good water supply for the villagers and excellent duck shooting for Father James and his guests. At Lowa, not far away, the saintly and haggard-looking Mr Brandstrom of the Swedish Free Mission lived in a small, spotlessly clean house with his thin, fair wife and pale children surrounded by his faithful evangelical flock. Once a tall and handsome man, austerity and frequent attacks of malaria had reduced him to a stooping yellow shadow of his former self, until only the piercing blue eyes shining from his parchment face revealed the inner fires which still burned so brightly.

I felt deep admiration for this man and his family, who suffered so much illness and isolation for their faith. I remember taking coffee and Swedish cakes with them one morning, with a bright red and white tablecloth on the table and cushion covers to match and seeing them all set off later in a very old rickety brown car.

In common with the rest of the country, large areas of Kahama were infested with tsetse fly, which causes sleeping sickness in humans and trypanosomaisis in cattle and horses. This meant that riding was only possible in a few mountain areas. The small chiefdom of Mpunze with only a few hundred inhabitants was literally dying out from the depredations of the scissors-winged tsetse fly. Such is the power of tradition, however, that the people not unnaturally refused to consider government advice to move to 'fresh fields and pastures new' free of the dreaded fly only fifteen or so miles away from district headquarters.

Young, fat Chief Emmanuel was quite ineffective, so the DC gave Ron West and me the job of persuading the populace to leave their homes. This we did through massive government support in the form of tax exemption for a number of years, digging wells, and building a *baraza*, school, dispensary and chief's house. Advance parties were brought over by lorry on day trips to spy out the land flowing with milk and honey. Little by little, our propaganda began to work, first with the young people who were always eager for excitement, then with the women who were quick to sense the advantages of a more convenient water supply, and finally with the conservative elderly gentlemen themselves. We camped at New Mpunze for a week during the actual move in the dry season, while relays of lorries lifted the inhabitants and their belongings village by village to a new and more promising life. Suitable arrangements were made for safeguarding the ancestral tombs and visiting them in the future. Years later, I was thrilled to meet someone from the new settlement who told me that it was flourishing. Peace had had another of her victories.

There were also defeats. One of these was the appalling rinderpest epidemic that decimated the Nyamwezi cattle in 1949. Ken Aspinall, the veterinary officer for Nzega, who later became director of veterinary services for Nyasaland, and his gallant band of field officers and veterinary assistants worked round the clock. They vaccinated thousands of cattle herded into the long narrow stockades known as cattle crushes, normally used for regular dipping to get rid of ticks responsible for ECF (East Coast Fever). All went well for a bit, then disaster struck. The new wonder vaccine flown down from the famed veterinary laboratories at Kabete in Kenya, instead of immunizing the cattle killed them off in hundreds. Angry farmers refused to have their cattle vaccinated and, in one or two cases, mobs attacked the unfortunate vets who had to be rescued by the police. Worst of all, the prestige of the veterinary department suffered a severe blow from which it took several years to recover.

The little town of Kahama was my responsibility and every Saturday morning I inspected it for two or three hours accompanied by the township supervisor, Mr Khan. His great achievement had been to build a new marketplace for £150, complete with red corrugated-iron roof. We planted hundreds of *mharita* (soap trees) on the edge of the dam as an antidote to the bilharzia snails, which could bring in their wake the much feared delayed action disease, which often erupted 20 or even 30 years later.

We ended our round with a visit to the prison where I received a particularly warm welcome, maybe because there were few rival attractions. It must have seemed amusing to see the solicitous white district officer coming to ask if there were 'any complaints'.

Indian, Arab and Somali traders and a handful of Canadian gold miners at the Issaka railhead made up our small immigrant community. Harban Singh, our *boma* cashier, was an excellent tennis player. This gained him social acceptance by the Europeans and his hospitality was notorious. He was so liberal with the whisky that one often had to pour it away into his garden when no one was looking.

The Arabs, mostly illegal immigrants from Muscat and Oman, carried out petty trading of the meanest kind in the most remote trading centres. The Somalis as usual were proud and arrogant cattle traders and refused to be classified as 'Africans' in the 1948 census. One of them, irate at charges of impotence being levelled against him by his lovely young wife, instantly unveiled the allegedly faulty weapon. He would doubtless have proceeded to an impressive display of firepower had he not been seized by the police and subsequently fined ten shillings for contempt of court.

Johnny Baker, Mel Thompson, and Bob Ewing ran the Canuck gold mine where I first saw a shining gold brick. At weekends, they invited us to shoot wild duck, Egyptian geese, partridge and guinea fowl on the shore of the new dam at Issaka.

Between Issaka and Kahama lay Isegehe, where a pilot development scheme had been launched. Its laudable aim was to create a model village where everyone tie-ridged their fields, dug latrines and compost pits, saved their maize stalks for manure, sent their children to school and their wives to the new maternity clinic. Chief Kishimba's prime minister Wakili Mlolwa, a tall, handsome and dynamic young man who had been educated at the Tabora school to Standard 8, supervised the operation. The title *Wakili* (an Arabic word) was variously used to mean a regent or deputy, or less frequently an agent or even an advocate. In this instance, it had become fashionable for the government to appoint bright young men to take over the more progressive development side of an uneducated chief's duties, with the powers of a deputy.

Mlolwa and his generation really believed in development and struggled to free their people from the age-old chains of a feudal tribal society that had changed little in 1000 years. They saw us as their allies in this task and befriended us accordingly. Consciously or unconsciously, they were laying the foundations of their country's independence — they looked for wider horizons. In nearly all cases, they were the first men in their families since the beginning of time to be educated. They laboured under immense handicaps. They came from homes where books, letters, pictures, radios, maps, carpets, chairs, tables and even beds had never been known. English was a third language following the vernacular and Swahili. They learned geography, but many had never seen the sea. Their ancestors had never built a bridge or made a wheel. The wonder is not how small their brains are, but how great has been their intellectual achievement and imaginative insight during recent decades.

8

To the Shores of Lake Tanganyika, 1949–50

After a year in the Nyamwezi districts of Nzega and Kahama, we were moved early in 1949 more than 200 miles further west to the mountainous Buha district on the shores of Lake Tanganyika. Here, a few thousand Watusi aristocrats, pale and proud cattle owners, in a situation comparable with that of the Hutu and Tutsi tribes in the neighbouring Belgian protectorate of Rwanda–Urundi, ruled 300,000 dark-skinned tribesmen.

The paramount chief was a beautiful woman of 19 or so called Mwami Teresa Ntare. She had been educated up to Standard 8 at the Tabora girls' school. She was married to an agricultural instructor called George, who always carried their baby boy Constantine while his wife held a *baraza*. Her family had ruled the Waha for centuries in a somewhat unusual matrilineal dynasty from their beautiful mountain stronghold Heru Juu, five miles from Kasulu, and 2500 feet up a winding escarpment due west of the *boma*. On ceremonial occasions, her loyal, almost entirely male subjects would prostrate themselves before her with a great cry of *buha bugare* (O great drum of Buha).

I found her very beguiling. On several occasions I went to her *baraza* intending to give her a stern reprimand about poor attendance at the local primary school or forest fires, only to be gently ushered into her private office for a charming tête-à-tête. Her dulcet tone and friendly, if not quite amorous, glances of injured innocence proved too much for a susceptible 25-year-old and the planned rocket fizzled out into a mild plea for improvement.

She also possessed a very old, almost antique motorcar. When it was roadworthy, she was occasionally driven to church on Sunday to the White Fathers' mission at Kabanga, five miles east of Kasulu in the plains where the old Dutch Bishop Van Sambeek held sway. She was the only African in the district at the time to own a car; indeed, I doubt if there were more than two or three in the entire Western Province.

The vast majority of her people wore cattle skins fashioned into simple garments, while the young unmarried women went gracefully bare-breasted, water pot on head, to the manner born, always greeting us on the roadside with the wonderfully joyous ululation whose marvellous spontaneity is so characteristic of an African welcome.

Indeed, as the men filed into the office in the morning to register the usual variety of complaints, my young messenger Ilika used to spray them with DDT pesticide to remove the large number of flies that swarmed all over their skins. At first I was shocked by this procedure, which did not seem to reflect the human rights guaranteed by the United Nations Charter, but once I saw that the recipients seemed to take the spraying completely for granted, I too became reconciled to it.

Corporal punishment was a different matter. Two years of imprisonment with hard labour (IHL) and 24 strokes of the cane was the maximum punishment laid down by the penal code for cattle theft. This was the most prevalent crime in the district at that time and was often accompanied by brutal assault and, occasionally, even murder or manslaughter when the owners put up a stout resistance. Coincidentally, it was the maximum punishment that could be imposed by a district commissioner with the powers of a first-class magistrate, subject always of course to confirmation by the High Court in distant Dar es Salaam — 800 miles away. Once confirmed, the sentence was carried out locally and an ornate ritual followed. A sack filled with maize was placed on the floor of the DC's office in the presence of the DC himself, the medical assistant from the small *boma* hospital and the head messenger Shija, who acted as 'executioner'. The unfortunate prisoner was then led in by a warder, stripped of his shorts and a piece of white cloth soaked in paraffin oil placed over his bare bottom, presumably to afford some slight protection. The warder produced a medical certificate stating that the prisoner was fit enough to endure the sentence. Shija then beat the man slowly and deliberately, calling out the numbers after each stroke until the sentence was completed. The victims normally behaved with great courage and rarely whimpered, but should there be bleeding, excessive bruising or distress, the DC could (and sometimes did) halt the punishment immediately.

Although not one of my favourite duties, I was unwittingly introduced to it on the very first day of our arrival at Kasulu. As the old Kahama three-ton district lorry carrying Susan, me and all we possessed came to a halt outside the DC's office, we heard to our surprise the unmistakable sounds of the swishing of a cane from within. Jock Scott, the district officer I was replacing, told us to wait until the beating was over when the DC, the legendary John Young, would see us.

John was a remarkable character who concealed beneath a gruff manner a real affection for his unruly charges. A 37-year-old Scot from Helensburgh in the Clyde estuary near Glasgow, he was lucky to have inherited a small fortune in the shape of a rubber plantation in Ceylon and two fishing trawlers on the Clyde.

The official mail from Tabora and Dar es Salaam came in a special lorry from Kigoma every Tuesday morning. It left again with the outgoing mail on Tuesday afternoon, only giving us an hour or two to reply by return to urgent letters. There was no telephone, but a rather archaic form of telegram occasionally arrived via the stationmaster at the Kigoma railhead, having been passed down the line from station to station by an antique signalling machine called a pantophone. The messages were often corrupted and took days to arrive. We were certainly not under any great pressure. Quite the reverse; we only worked in the office from 7.00 a.m. to 2.00 p.m., walking the hundred yards or so home for breakfast at 9.00 am. We then had a siesta after lunch before emerging after tea at 5.00 p.m. for a game of tennis or golf before sundown and the ritual drink on turret or veranda that accompanied the glorious Kasulu sunsets and the eerie honking of the African hornbill.

John Young was a living legend. He was the very embodiment of a bush DC, a latter-day Sanders of the River. He had no career ambitions whatsoever and a great contempt for the penpushers of the Dar es Salaam secretariat. He saw them as a Government House coterie of ambitious officers, often pushed by even more determined wives who used their beauty and charm to good effect to get their husbands transferred on promotion to yet another secretariat in Lagos, Accra, Kuala Lumpur, Suva or Kingston, Jamaica. All he asked for was to be left alone in the bush to enjoy himself and at the same time to seek justice for his people in his own way. The colonial service probably needed a sprinkling of John Youngs. His independence of spirit was exemplified by his somewhat cavalier attitude to responsibility. This became apparent when he insisted on taking Susan and me with him on one of his very rare visits to the little fishing village of Kagunga on the shores of Lake Tanganyika, which could only be visited comfortably by motor launch from Kigoma. It was a subchiefdom of the great mountain chiefdom of Nkalinzi, ruled by the somewhat austere figure of Mwami Batega. Its fearsome fastnesses dropped more than 6000 feet down to the lake in a series of spectacular ridges, crags and cliffs, rarely if ever scaled by teenage goatherds.

John had decided to spend a week there camping on the beach, meeting the fishermen and their families informally, swimming and reading. The climax of the visit would be a formal *baraza* on the last day, when complaints would be heard and government policy explained.

To get there we borrowed the DC Kigoma's old motor launch *Imara* (Swahili for strong). We all drove down to Kigoma in the tram (John's Bedford station wagon) and spent the night before the journey with the delightful middle-aged DC, Geoffrey Popplewell and his wife Isabel in their palatial residence, the Kaiserhof, with its superb view over Lake Tanganyika.

Geoffrey Popplewell, though another bush DC of the old school, was as conservative and traditional as John was eccentric and rebellious. He had the greatest respect for authority and established custom and was conscientious almost to a fault. He was horrified by John's decision to leave the Kasulu *boma* virtually unmanned for a week, and told him so. John replied with his inimitable chuckle and touch of Scots accent, 'They'll get on far better without us.' Next day we set off for Kagunga in the *Imara* for the four-hour journey north along the beautiful lakeshore. After an hour or so we passed the world famous chimpanzee game park at Gombe, called in Swahili *Shamba la Bibi* (literally meaning the Lady's Estate) after the Empress of Germany. The celebrated naturalist Jane Goodall has since devoted her life to the study and care of her beloved chimps there.

Like all the denizens of the lakeshore, the village headman Jumbe Rashidi wore the coastal Swahili dress of white *kanzu* and red fez or white embroidered skullcap (*kofia*). He kept us well supplied with chickens and eggs at the going rate of 100 eggs for a shilling and 50 cents for a chicken.

Preparing for my higher standard Swahili examination, I read *King Solomon's Mines* by Rider Haggard in its Swahili translation (*Mashimo Ya Mfalme Sulemani*) and the *1001 Nights* (*Alfu Lela Wa Lela*) from cover to cover, looking up any new words in the dictionary as I went along. For several months before the exam, I had got up at 6.00 a.m. every day before going to the office and solemnly learned every word in the entire Swahili dictionary — of which there were 30,000 in all.

The German rulers before the First World War had beautifully laid out the station at Kasulu, and the good work was continued by their British successors who shared a love of forestry and gardening. On a ridge between two valleys about a mile long and perhaps 200 yards wide, avenues of Eucalyptus citriodora, with their exquisite lemon scented fragrance lined the roads, interspersed with dark green cedars and cypresses and the feathery grevillea robusta trees.

Four government bungalows lined the upper road leading to the DC's fort, while opposite them were situated the hospital, school (standards one to six), tennis court and mini-golf course on the gently undulating slope leading down to the district office, police station and courthouse.

At Heru Juu, apart from Mwami Ntare's tribal headquarters, there was a very old Church Missionary Society (CMS) mission house and church partially concealed by a forest called Giwahuru. Two Australian clergymen called Chittleborough and McGorlick, who came under the diocese of Central Tanganyika at Dodoma, ran this. The CMS represented the extreme evangelical wing of the Anglican communion and its Australian element was most austere.

In contrast, the highest Anglo-Catholic diocese of the Anglican communion is that of Zanzibar, from where it moved in the early years of the century to headquarters at Magila in the Tanga district of eastern Tanganyika. The German government took the sensible decision to divide the whole country into spheres of influence between the various denominations. For example, the Church of Sweden was allocated Bukoba district, the Swedish Free Mission Kahama, the Moravians Tabora, the American Inland Mission Lake Province, and the Roman Catholic Benedictines Songea district in the Southern Province, where they built great cathedrals at Peramiho and Ndanda. Mount Kilimanjaro was divided between the Holy Ghost Fathers and the Lutherans and the Protestants and Anglo-Catholics were left well apart. The vast White Fathers' mission was allowed nearly everywhere.

Under British rule, these distinctions became somewhat blurred and bitter quarrels sometimes ensued over rival spheres of influence. Unlike Unyamwezi, the White Fathers' mission made few converts in the Buha highlands — one priest told me he made three converts in 27 years. His forlorn mission included a medical and educational centre that was fairly well patronized by the local animists. Things were quite different in the plains where the White Fathers flourished at Kabanga and Makere.

Susan and I were sent off on wonderful safaris in the highlands for a week at a time. We were driven to our destination in the district's three-ton lorry, which returned to collect us at the agreed rendezvous later on. There was not really a great deal of work to do in the formal sense, apart from checking current cases in the local court and visiting the rare primary schools and dispensaries. The people were backward and largely uninterested in education or progress of any kind. It was a fairly primitive society, little changed over hundreds of years where the men herded cattle, sheep and goats and the women planted small plots of maize, millet and sorghum in the windswept soil. The missions usually planted coffee and citrus trees. Clumps of bananas and papaws were common, while most huts had little vegetable plots of pumpkins (*mboga*), also the generic name for all vegetables, beans and spinach. Great grassy plains on the highland plateau swept by strong winds made agriculture and afforestation alike rare and difficult. There was little or no indigenous rainforest left, save occasional sacred groves where spiritual leaders had been buried long ago.

The very names spell magic — Manyovu and Nkalinzi, Buhinga and Buyenze, Biharo and Bunyoro Bunganda. Mtwale (subchief) Victoria of Buhinga was a tired, prematurely aged woman of 30 or so in a faded blue cotton dress. Wakili Chuleha of Manyovu was tough and able, ambitious in khaki slacks and shirt. Manyovu was where we would spend a week at a time 6000 feet up in a splendid brick resthouse in the mountains with a glorious tall waterfall within walking distance. Here we were 40 miles from Kasulu; the further one went the wilder and more lawless were the people.

Twenty miles further on, on a rough scenic road with tantalizing glimpses of the great lake below, came Nkalinzi, seat of the 'King of the Black Mountains' himself, the formidable (and venerable) Mwami Batega.

Susan was now — New Year 1950 — expecting our first baby and the usual discussion ensued as to whether she would go to the nearest government hospital at Tabora, 500 miles away, or even further to the better equipped and staffed Kampala hospital in Uganda. Fortunately, we were spared the agonizing decision by the timely arrival of a young American doctor Bill Taylor and his wife Liz, both in their late twenties and full of enthusiasm to establish a modern, well-equipped Seventh Day Adventist hospital at our beloved Manyovu of all places. It was to be called the Heri (peace/ joy) Mission Hospital.

Meanwhile, building started on the hospital, their new house having been built before their arrival, we became fast friends and they kindly invited Susan to stay with them in early February for the birth of the baby which Bill would deliver, assisted by Liz who was a trained nurse. He was a graduate of the University of

California and he took care of Susan from the time of arrival. The baby duly arrived according to plan on 3 February, a lovely little girl christened Caroline Lucy in due course in our sitting room at Kasulu by Padre McGorlick of the CMS mission.

John Young kindly lent me his car and driver Hassan to take me up to Manyovu to see the baby after the exciting news of her arrival had reached the *boma* on a Saturday afternoon.

Soon afterwards, the governor His Excellency Sir Edward Twining came on an official visit accompanied by his wife Lady (May) Twining. She herself was an excellent doctor whom he had married many years before when they were both serving in Uganda — he as a district officer and she as a government doctor. On his arrival in Dar es Salaam the year before, Twining had summoned all eight PCs and other senior officials to a meeting at Government House and addressed them thus:

> Gentlemen, you may like to know how I became a governor. When a district officer in Uganda, I failed my Swahili exam and was sent to Mauritius as labour commissioner. After that I never looked back, proceeding to be governor of North Borneo via St Lucia in the West Indies before coming here. So had I not failed that exam I would still be counting pickaxes at some *boma* in Uganda.

Twining, whose large and jovial exterior concealed a sensitive and bright intelligence, was perhaps the most dynamic and powerful man to govern Tanganyika since Lord Lugard's great disciple Sir Donald Cameron had introduced the Nigerian doctrine of indirect rule through the tribal chiefs in the 1920s. A scion of Twining's tea, he had started life as a regular soldier in The Worcestershire Regiment and had served in the 'troubles' in Ireland after the First World War. A colourful figure, he believed in putting Tanganyika on the map and freeing it from its subservience to Kenya by encouraging foreign investment and development by personality and good public relations. He often described Dar es Salaam derisively as 'a city of branch managers' — the head offices almost invariably being in Nairobi, the Kenyan capital.

When he left eight years later, he had largely succeeded in this aim and retired full of honours as Baron Twining of Tanganyika and Godalming in the county of Surrey, the only Tanganyikan governor to be ennobled; He liked dressing up in his full dress blue and gold uniform with cocked hat plumes and sword. Rightly, I think, he attached great importance to ceremonial parades, bands, naval visits, Armistice Day services, state openings of the Legislative Council and ceremonial *baraza*s, which represented the symbolic trappings of power and authority to a people whose own dignity and background greatly appreciated such outward and visible signs.

Whenever possible, he brought the police band — which he loved on occasion to conduct himself — with him on safari, well aware of the popular love of music and display. On the occasion of his first visit, a vast crowd of tribesmen poured in from all over the district to the beautiful setting of the Kasulu golf course and gave him a great welcome, and the DC John Young a fine farewell. Afterwards, Lady Twining called on us to inspect Lucy and to give Susan welcome advice on looking after her.

John went off on leave to Scotland and, to my delight, I was given charge of the district for six months or so until my own leave was due in September 1950. I was then duly gazetted district commissioner at the age of 25.

Francis Townsend, younger brother of Group-Captain Peter Townsend, the celebrated Battle of Britain pilot, equerry to the King and unsuccessful suitor for the hand of Princess Margaret, arrived soon afterwards as my district officer. Fortunately, he was the proud possessor of a new Land Rover and was most generous in driving us around, even on one occasion taking us into Urundi for a delightful weekend at the Hotel Paguidas in Usumbura. We were impressed by the wonderful forests planted by the Belgians on the hillsides and the long straight roads lined by avenues of eucalyptus. These were maintained by chain gangs of manacled prisoners supervised by *askari* of the famous Congo Army, the *Force publique* detachments of which were stationed at every Belgian *boma* in addition to the usual police post.

I was very conscious of the privileged position I had as the

British representative on an international border, entitled indeed to fly the Union Jack on my vehicle when paying an official visit.

With shades perhaps of my earlier ambition to join the diplomatic service, I always jumped at any opportunity to practise my French on my Belgian neighbours, few of whom spoke any English. On one occasion, I went by myself on an official visit to Monsieur François — the Belgian Resident, equivalent to our provincial commissioner, at his headquarters at Kitega, visiting the lovely station at Bururi *en route*. Monsieur and Madame François kindly put me up for the night and gave me a superb Belgian dinner. I can still remember the wonderful scent of the cedars and cypresses after the rain.

As always, I was struck by the very paternalistic, authoritarian style of Belgian rule — destined to reap such a tragic whirlwind ten years later with the mutiny of the *Force publique* soon after the independence of the Congo in 1960.

I greatly enjoyed running the district on my own with little or no interference from Tabora and none from Dar es Salaam. I concentrated on improving the roads, especially the five-mile escarpment from Kasulu to Heru Juu. I was very proud of a new mountain road called the Buyenze Loop, cut for three miles or so through the mountains, to link Buyenze with the main district road running from Kasulu, Heru Juu to Manyovu. We took advantage of a tribal custom whereby all able-bodied men from 16 to 60 give up to a month a year's free labour for public works. We had hundreds of men a day working with pickaxes, shovels and *karais*, digging laboriously to drive the road through the dry red laterite soil.

I spent many happy hours with them planning the work with road foreman Asumani, stressing the importance of deep storm drains on both sides and a perfect camber — a sloping crest of the road for the rainwater to drain off during the usual thunderstorms. Whenever possible, I joined in for an hour or two, stripped to the waist and singing the choruses of the great African working songs. The men had a real incentive in that the completed road link would be a short cut to the markets where they sold their maize, beans and other crops, and also of course would shorten the distance to schools, hospitals and so on. There were celebrations when the road was finally completed shortly before I left on leave in September 1950, and it was still going strong when I returned to Kasulu on safari from Dar es Salaam 20 years later.

So, after a memorable first tour of nearly three years, we flew home by Sunderland flying boat from Lake Naivasha in western Kenya, famous for its millions of pink flamingos. We went by easy stages, landing on the Nile at Khartoum in the late afternoon, in the floodlit harbour at Alexandria at midnight, and in the lovely harbour at Augusta in Sicily at dawn the next morning. There we stopped for a few hours to refuel, have breakfast and a shave.

The flying boat was spacious and comfortable, and there was even a cocktail bar on the upper deck. We took off at about 10.00 a.m. and landed on Southampton water at about 3.00 p.m. to be met by Susan's parents and my mother. They gave us a wonderful welcome and were thrilled at the first sight of their granddaughter Caroline Lucy. As we drove to London in the airways bus, we passed the centurion tanks of the 8th Royal Irish Hussars, my brother Digby's regiment, on their way to embark at Southampton *en route* to the Korean War. I managed to see him for a couple of days in London before he too had to follow his tanks on board.

9

Academic Interlude, 1950–51

The Devonshire second course at Oxford and Cambridge respectively was designed to enable young DOs who had usually completed both the first course and their probationary tours as DOs (cadets) to specialize for a further two academic terms (Michaelmas and Hilary) on a subject relevant to their work, in the light of the experience they had already acquired. I chose to study public finance under the famous Professor Hicks, whose wife Ursula was also one of my tutors. We had to submit a 100-page thesis on a special subject at the end of the course and I selected 'indirect taxation in Tanganyika' — a fascinating and somewhat obscure subject with a limited bibliography.

The course was preceded by a colonial service summer school held at Cambridge in late September under the chairmanship of Sir John Shaw, the tall, distinguished looking governor of Trinidad. I shared rooms in Queens College with A. C. W. (Tony) Lee, a brother officer from Tanganyika who had sailed out to Dar es Salaam with us on the *Llangibby Castle* and who had since been stationed in the Lake Province. Participants came from all over the world including a most amusing Portuguese district officer from Macao and a number of French and Belgian officers from West Africa and the Congo. It was a very civilized event with only a few sessions each day, allowing plenty of time to meet one's colleagues in the friendly atmosphere of Cambridge colleges and pubs.

Much as I loved the wild primeval unspoilt glory of Africa, it was always a balm to the spirit to return from time to time to the gentler and more familiar charms of one's native land. A return was symbolised, whenever possible, by a visit to the national shrine of Westminster Abbey, which I had first visited with my mother at the age of nine. The coronation chair had thrilled me even then, the shield carried by Henry V at the battle of Agincourt in 1415 and the tomb of Queen Elizabeth I.

David Livingstone's grave in the nave had introduced an African dimension to the cathedral, which always represented for me the very heart of Britain and the old British Empire, if not the very centre of the world itself. I never left it without feeling reinvigorated and inspired anew to pursue 'my first avowed intent'.

It is fitting indeed that, as I write, I have just seen the plans for a great commemorative service to be held in the abbey on Tuesday 25 May 1999 to mark the ending of Her Majesty's Overseas Civil Service to which Her Majesty the Queen has been invited. A plaque in memory of members of the colonial service was unveiled some years ago in the cloisters. The British Empire itself virtually came to an end at midnight on 30 June 1997 when Hong Kong was returned to China after 150 years of British rule.

I went back to Oxford in October 1950 for the start of the second Devonshire course. It was based in the Colonial Service Club in South Parks Road, round the corner from Wadham College, where many of us stayed, and Rhodes House, where we all studied. Jerry Cornes, the famous Olympic runner who had served as a district officer in Nigeria and Palestine, had succeeded Colonel Drummond as course supervisor.

The future prime minister of Ghana Dr Busia, then a young district officer, was with us as were the heirs to the sultans of Kedah and Perak from Malaya and two charming Zanzibaris, Hilal Barwani and Sefu Jahadmy, the former accompanied by a beautiful, petite, veiled wife.

Several years later, they killed a sheep in my honour at Chake Chake on the clove-scented island of Pemba when I was on an official visit there in the public relations department; Barwani was district officer and Jahadmy the education officer.

I found the course intensely interesting as I struggled to grasp the intricacies of economics and public finance, taxation (direct and indirect), international trade, balance of payments, invisible exports, and so on, which were subjects I had never fully understood and always found difficult. Indeed, it was for this reason

101

that I had decided to tackle what was for me the most difficult, rather than the easiest subject.

I had always been intrigued by balance of payments and spent hours trying to understand how it was calculated. The effort must have stood me in good stead, for years later, in the run up to independence in 1960/1, I lectured in Swahili on simple economics to adult education classes in the Arnautoglu Hall community centre in Mnazi Mmoja, Dar es Salaam. I defined money as 'sweat plus skill allied to the natural resources of the earth' in an effort to dispel the fashionable fallacy that vast sums of money would be printed when Tanganyika achieved its independence. To this end, we printed posters showing the number of bags of coffee or cotton required to fund a year at university and the numbers of bags of produce needed for export to Britain to enable us to import a Land Rover or an operating theatre.

On indirect taxation in Tanganyika, I read every one of the dozen or so books that had any bearing on the subject and greatly enjoyed writing a thesis. This I lodged safely in the library of Rhodes House, where I trust it still lies, fondly believing it to be a unique work.

We had a few weeks left before returning to Africa and joined old friends from the Western Province, Robin and Jock Risley on a motor tour of the Low Countries and Paris, with visits to cathedrals, churches and art galleries being the main targets. We felt starved of 'culture' in the African bush and thought that, like camels, we could drink it up in Europe and store it in our humps for the cultural deserts ahead.

We drove through Delft, Haarlem, Amsterdam and the Hague, marvelling at the treasures of the Rijks Museum and Mauritshuis, of Rembrandt, Vermeer, Frans Hals and Van Gogh. We drove through Belgium over the historic Arnhem and Nijmegen bridges to the great cathedral of Malines, the *Vieux Place* and *Enfant pis* in Brussels, to the haunting bells of Lierre, the gargoyle encrusted cathedral of Laon and finally to incomparable Paris itself. There, on our last night before going to Chartres, I received a telegram from Dar es Salaam ordering me to return at once to Tanganyika and proceed to Handeni in Tanga Province as DC.

10

Monarch of all I Survey, 1951–52

We arrived in Handeni early in May 1951 at the end of the rainy season. The district lorry had been sent to the Tanga airport to collect us in torrential rain and we had to set off immediately on the 106-mile journey before the new dam at Muheza flooded the main road — 30 miles west of Tanga. We were, I believe, the last vehicle to get through before the flood.

Though we left Tanga soon after lunch, because of the appalling conditions we did not reach Handeni until nearly dusk. Exhausted as we were, we received a warm welcome from my predecessor Robin Thorne and his beautiful golden-haired wife Joan — nicknamed Helen of Troy because of her perfect classical features.

They lived at the top of a hill in an old German fort separated from the *boma*'s various administrative offices by a garden court-yard. A gleaming brass maxim gun on a tripod on their lofty whitewashed veranda was trained to 'fire' down the long avenue of frangipani that led to the front door. A relic from a brief skirmish in 1915 in the First World War described in Francis Brett Young's *Marching on Tanga*, the victims lie buried in a small immaculately kept war cemetery with Christ's thorn hedges nearby.

The Thorne's great excitement was the baby elephant tethered to a tree in the garden, which had been brought in a few days earlier after poachers had killed its mother. Lucy, tired as she was, was thrilled by it and had a close look before going to bed. It stayed with us for a few months, growing fast, before being rescued by the game department. It was a great tourist attraction.

Handeni, one of Tanganyika's 56 districts, is situated in Tanga

103

Province (one of eight provinces) in the northeast of the country. Nothing could have provided a greater contrast with Kasulu in the far west. Its 75,000 people were scattered in tiny villages and hamlets over 5000 square miles of dull, dry bush country at an average altitude of 2000 feet. The people were mainly Zigua in the east and Nguu in the hilly west.

They were the same ethnic people as the Bondei around Muheza and as the Sambaa in Lushoto and Korogwe district to the northeast and north respectively of Handeni. Legend has it that the Bondei lived in the valleys and the Sambaa spread to the mountains to the west. Perhaps feeling squeezed out, the Zigula seized the land to the south and the Nguu (or Ngulu) moved into the western hills on the borders of Masailand.

In marked contradistinction to the Nyamwezi and Waha peoples of the west, they were shy, reserved in the presence of strangers, and almost sullen. Once one got to know them, however, they revealed hidden depths of character, with considerable intellect, sense of humour and fierce loyalty. These qualities have enabled many of them to play a distinguished part in the new Tanzania, out of all proportion to their numbers.

Their proximity to the Arab-Muslim civilization of the coast and to the three historic ports of Bagamoyo, Sadani and Pangani exposed them to the incursions of Arab slave traders. At the same time, the transfer of the UMCA bishop of Zanzibar to Magila at the beginning of the century led to a great drive for Christian converts in Tanga Province. Many mission schools, hospitals and dispensaries were established and churches built throughout the area.

Five miles from the *boma* on the Korogwe road lay the long established UMCA mission at Kideleko. This was a veritable oasis of civilization with a vast thatched roof church, a splendid hospital, and boys' and girls' secondary schools. The priest in charge, Father Neil Russell, a 48-year-old Scot from Edinburgh, was an ascetic and scholarly man of prayer, greatly admired and loved by the Zigua, Christian and Muslim alike, who became a legend in his lifetime.

The Thornes had asked him to tea to meet us the day after our arrival and the sight of this bearded, gaunt, almost Christ-like figure in a khaki cassock and sandals immediately inspired us. He was like a Franciscan monk in a Renaissance painting. His clear, direct gaze and quiet authoritative voice were awesome and unsympathetic people could find him alarming. He said that he hoped we would come to church on Sundays; when I replied that, work permitting, I hoped to do so, he asked what work could possibly be more important than worshipping God and setting an example to the congregation.

We tried to follow his advice and attended his wonderful services as often as possible in the great church. It would be packed full with hundreds of people every Sunday, men on the right and women on the left, summoned to prayer by the beat of a great drum. Many of the women had their babies slung on their backs in the folds of their colourful *khangas* (coloured cotton dresses). Despite the occasional hullabaloo, the babies were remarkably well behaved while they endured two hours or so of the excellent Swahili version of the beautiful Anglo-Catholic liturgy of the 1549 prayer book. The singing was unaccompanied and joyful, the chants reverently intoned and the whole atmosphere profoundly spiritual and moving. There was an important secular by-product too in that I got to know many of my fellow worshippers over a cup of tea after the service in Neil Russell's rondavel. This was an advantage because I came across many of them in the course of my official duties.

District officers came and went, but missionaries often stayed for a lifetime. By and large, only the most exceptional administrative officer would have as great a knowledge of the local people's languages and customs than they would. Neil Russell became a great friend of mine and, every Monday evening for more than two-and-a-half years, Susan and I would drive to Kideleko after tea. Then, while she taught needlework to hospital patients, I would sit on Neil's veranda looking out over the bush to the distant Nguu hills. We discussed just about everything in heaven and on earth.

We also talked about local affairs and I found his experience and wisdom invaluable in tackling the daily tasks confronting me. When mutually convenient, we sometimes did joint safaris. It was a wonderful experience to take part in the Holy Communion services he held in tiny bush churches for a dozen or so worshippers in remote corners of the district, recalling the earliest days of the church nearly 2000 years earlier.

Father Neil, like St Francis of Assisi who tamed a wolf at Gubbio, could speak quietly to a lion blocking his way on the Mazingara road before continuing his journey on his bicycle. He could gently persuade a madman, who terrorized people in Chanika town, to drop his knife. And, he could make an enormous black snake, which was thought to harbour an evil spirit and was frightening children at Kwamkono, vanish into thin air by making the sign of the cross over it. He had great respect for Muslims and, in his early days as a curate at Magila, was said to have called his flock to prayer at dawn like a muezzin from his minaret. He ate very little, living mainly on cassava, corn cobs and peanuts and gave most of his £30 a year allowance back to the church.

With him at Kideleko mission were three indomitable ladies, Dr Sitwell who ran the hospital, Miss Reynolds, head of the St Paul's boys' secondary school and Miss Eira Lloyd from Wales, headmistress of the girls' school. They ate their simple meals together at the table in the *mezani*, where Father Neil only joined them for lunch after High Mass on Sundays. They lived austere lives in primitive, uncomfortable conditions, their entire lives dedicated exclusively to the poor Zigua whom they selflessly nursed, taught and served. Out-of-date copies of the *Church Times* and a small library of religious books provided their sole entertainment; occasionally we persuaded them to cycle over to us for tea and tennis.

The local people preferred the mission hospital because they had to pay a few pence for the drugs and thought they must be more effective than the free ones. Also, there was no doubt that the love and care of the mission staff for their patients and pupils transcended the more mundane services of government employees. To a greater or lesser degree, this was true throughout the country.

There was a smaller mission station at Kwamkono, 25 miles north of Handeni, a few miles to the east of the Korogwe road. The mother superior of this convent of the Community of the Sacred Passion (CSP) was a dynamic 80-year-old nun called Sister

Pauline. She was a Cockney from London's East End and was assisted by a most saintly aristocrat called Sister Magdalen. Together with a handful of young African nuns, whose vocation was a total denial of the traditional role of women in their tribal societies, they ran an excellent little hospital and primary school. Susan and I loved staying with them on safari and attending the beautifully sung office of compline in the evening in their tiny wooden chapel. It was a rocky area and even more remote and peaceful than Kideleko itself. Near the mission was the great stone precipice of Mungu Yeye (God himself), where hundreds of years earlier, sacrificial victims had been thrown over the cliff to propitiate angry gods and ancestors when the rains failed.

At the *boma* in Handeni, a small district team of government officials met every Monday morning in my office to coordinate plans for the week ahead. Two of these were Yorkshiremen — DO Denis Blain who had been one of General Orde Wingate's Chindits in the Burma campaign against the Japanese and the agricultural officer John Ainley. A district assistant called Eddie Davey who had survived being torpedoed as a Merchant Navy seaman in the Atlantic Ocean in the Second World War and a water development engineer called MacPherson were also in the team.

They all lived in government bungalows within a few hundred yards of the *boma*; we were about ten Europeans in all, including wives and children. For recreation we had a hard tennis court in front of the DC's house and a unique squash court in a corner of the courtyard immediately below the flagpole turret, which also served as a grandstand and intimate sundowner venue. It had a lovely view of the sun setting over the Nguu hills in the west. A famous former DC before the war, John Ransom, was said to have sent a telegram to the High Court in Dar es Salaam saying, 'Please send £50 urgently required for court,' on receipt of which a few weeks later he had built the squash court. We also had modest gardens featuring the usual zinnia, marigold and petunia, and some really magnificent purple bougainvillaea planted by the Germans.

A new feature was a splendid dam holding millions of gallons of water, which the Water Development Department had just completed to provide a permanent water supply for the small township of Chanika — a few hundred yards away across the valley.

I shall never forget the fresh hopeful smell of parched earth at the end of the torrid dry season, after the blessed drops of the first rain had consecrated the soil and laid the acrid dust. Soon, the first bright green shoots of young grass would lay a verdant carpet across the featureless miombo forests of the bush, fertilized by the ash residue of the pungent-scented forest fires at the end of the previous dry season.

To have any effective control over a large and scattered population with only two British administrative officers and a dozen policemen, it was necessary to use some sort of indirect rule. This had been informally instituted during the German colonial period (1890–1918) when chiefs had been appointed. Prior to that, however, though Zigua clan leaders had exercised political power in times of emergency, there had been no centralized political authority. In 1926, Sir Donald Cameron introduced Lord Lugard's Nigerian policy of indirect rule throughout the land and formally recognized nine chiefs in Handeni district. By the early 1950s, chieftaincy was well established. As the Tanganyika annual report stated, 'chiefs are traditional rulers of their people, forming the basis for local government, round whom the system of councils has been built up.'

Inspired by the first secret ballot election ever held in colonial Africa in the Gold Coast (now Ghana) in 1951, I introduced the first secret ballot election in Tanganyika in 1952. On this occasion, largely illiterate voters elected nine members, one for each chiefdom, to the *ufungilo* (local council) at Handeni, which comprised 27 members — nine chiefs, nine elected members and nine more nominated by the DC. I tried to nominate experts in important fields like agriculture, health and education. One of these was Ali Kambi, the chief agricultural instructor, who was a man of enormous influence in the district.

The secret ballot itself involved voters placing their thumbprint against the name on the taxpayers' roll and then placing a small piece of paper into one of three coloured boxes. 'To make assurance doubly sure', there was one colour for each individual who stood behind his own box to show himself to the assembled electorate of only a few hundred voters, before voting commenced.

Previously, candidates had been elected by a show of hands in open *baraza*. This, however, often degenerated into a slanging match in which domineering speakers, sometimes witches, almost terrorized the people into voting for their man.

The ultraconservative Zigua were suspicious of the new system until they discovered it really did produce the candidate they wanted. The election of a new chief in Mgera chiefdom a few months earlier had provided a suitable opportunity to carry out the first experimental election. Although my new car, a blue Austin A70 pick-up, was stoned in an early display of hostility, once the people realized that their favourite man had indeed been elected in the red box, they adopted the new method with great enthusiasm. The handsome young Mussa Massomo, who had just completed Standard 12 at the Tabora boys' school (originally for sons of chiefs) was by an enormous majority elected as Zumbe chief of Mgera.

Back at the *boma*, an old grey-headed messenger called Sufiani sat on a bench on the veranda outside my office door slowly embroidering a black and white Muslim *kofia* (skullcap), which he sold for ten shillings each. Like the late Salim Mhapi, he too was to be awarded his sovereign's certificate and badge for long and faithful service to the British Crown, which I had the honour of presenting to him in his remote village before leaving Handeni towards the end of 1953. Inside the office, banging away on old typewriters and antiquated copying machines, laboured the chief clerk Athmani Kitojo, an Mbondei from Muheza and his cheerful young assistant Charles Kibaja, also an Mbondei in his bright yellow shirt.

With them was a rather wild young Zigua clerk, John Frank, who had been educated locally at St Pauls at Kideleko and whose former wife Teresa was Lucy's *ayah* (nanny). Soon after I came, John Frank got involved in some complicated litigation over his divorce, which culminated in his writing a long letter of complaint to His Excellency the Governor, with copies to his Grace the Archbishop of Canterbury and the Secretary General of the United Nations in New York.

The cashier was a small brown cheerful man from Tanga called Nuru, an Msegeju by tribe like his friend and compatriot Mamboleo Makoko, the hospital assistant, whom I was to meet again in London many years later.

My friends Athmani and Charles were tireless workers. They were loyal, dedicated to their work and acted as faithful advisers, reflecting to some extent the voices of the young African intelligentsia. How they mastered my handwriting was nothing short of miraculous; I even managed to train Athmani to take dictation straight on the typewriter. His pride and joy was his new motorcycle and I was deeply saddened to hear a few years later that he had been killed instantly on it in a bad road accident in Tanga.

Not far from the *boma*, near the council chamber stood a baobab tree from which the Germans had hanged the last Mzigua who had killed his twins in 1909 — a grim reminder of the draconian justice for which the Germans were famed. 'You could leave a shilling in the road for a week and no one would dare to steal it,' I was told, when reminded that British rule commanded less respect than German rule. Twins had been considered a bad omen for centuries and local custom had demanded their instant dispatch.

The chairman of the council was our friend and ally Zumbe Hemedi Sonyo, the chief of Magamba, nine miles down the Bagamoyo road southeast of Handeni. Tall and slim, about 35 years old with a twinkle in his eye, he was far and away the most progressive of the very conservative old Muslim chiefs. Although he had only received an elementary education, he had an innate intelligence and great powers of leadership.

He cycled to Handeni several days a week and I often drove out to see him for a cup of tea and a general chat. He had two charming wives, the younger of whom was the road foreman Mselemu's beautiful daughter. (Her brother Abdulla worked for us many years later in Dar es Salaam.) He also had a splendid family retainer called Sa'Mokiwa (son of Mokiwa), whose family had served the chief's family for generations and had originally been household slaves. Now he doubled as bodyguard, personal attendant and general factotum, deeming it an honour to fill this unpaid role.

110

After the wives had been presented, Zumbe Hemedi always called out '*Sa'Mokiwa! Lete chai na mayai*' (Sa'Mokiwa! Bring tea and hard-boiled eggs). The big brown teapot and a tin of condensed milk would soon arrive accompanied by at least six hard-boiled eggs and salt in a saucer. The routine never varied.

What Zumbe Hemedi lacked in formal education, he more than made up in wisdom and certainly believed in leading from the front. His favourite saying was *uisfuate maneno ya watu, au utaharibika* (do not do what the people tell you or you will be finished). He usually wore a traditional white kanzu and embroidered *kisibau* (waistcoat) with a scarlet fez, but on state occasions he wore European style white shirt, slacks, jacket and fez. Older chiefs wore rather rustic looking turbans. Their Muslim subjects generally also wore variations on the same dress, while the Christians wore shirts and trousers, or shorts for the younger men.

On Empire Day, 24 May, Queen Victoria's birthday, I wore my white full-dress uniform with ceremonial sword and took the salute at a parade of all 50 or so schools in the district and their delightful fife and drum bands. This review was followed by a buffet lunch in our house for government officers and their wives, missionaries and other expatriates from remote areas. One such expatriate was Mr Czurn, a tall Czech who ran the great Mninga forest concession at Kang'ata on the Morogoro road on behalf of the timber merchants William Mallinson & Sons.

The lunch party was followed by a tea party for the chiefs and some of the top *boma* African staff. I can see them all now, toying politely with unfamiliar European food, beautifully dressed, courteous and dignified. Apart from the chiefs of Magamba and Mgera already mentioned, those present included:

(1) Zumbe Mohammed Mlinde of Mswaki, 25 miles west of Handeni on the Mgera Road, who was elderly and austere;
(2) rather old and crafty-looking Zumbe Saidi Mdoe of the Chanika chiefdom right on my doorstep;
(3) Zumbe Ali Mazora of Mazingara, 30 miles southeast of the *boma* beyond Magamba, youngish, obese, weak and scruffy;
(4) Zumbe Swalehe Saidi of Mgambo chiefdom, 40 miles east of

headquarters, a naughty-looking old man with a mischievous grin and reputation for *fitina* and sorcery;

(5) reckless, feckless wild looking and young Chief Andrea Mhanda of the remote little chiefdom of Kwamsisi on the Pangani border;

(6) the young chief Omari Ngora of equally remote Kwekivu in the southwest corner of the district, only accessible by a road like a dry river bed;

(7) Zumbe Omari Ndaro of the lovely little mountain chiefdom of Kimbe (white bird) between Kwekivu and the main Morogoro road, who was an equally venerable neighbour; Zumbe Omari, small, wizened and wise with a twinkle in his eye and a joke on his lips, beloved by his people; and

(8) last but not least Jumbe Lekipondo, headman of a few thousand Masai and Kwavi nomads who grazed their cattle on the Kiberashi plains near the Masai district border beyond Mgera to the west. He was a slim, cheerful middle-aged man dressed on special occasions in a faded old dinner jacket. When one of the cakes was passed around and the Zigua chiefs politely cut themselves slices, Jumbe Lekipondo seized the whole cake and put it in his pocket, to the shock and outrage of his more sedate peers.

We only had a few Masai on our western plains, but they were intrepid walkers and great travellers, and I had often met them before in Kenya and elsewhere. With the Zulus, they were perhaps Africa's most glamorous tribe, famed throughout the world for their courage, honesty and beauty. Since God had given them all the cattle in the world, recapturing their own property was a sacred duty. When they sometimes appeared in my court charged with cattle theft, they always pleaded guilty with disdain and, when a man was killed in a skirmish, went to their deaths with sublime courage. They would not lift a finger to do any menial work like cultivating crops or working on the roads or dams. They were aristocratic cattle owners, nomads who apparently owed their superb figures and supreme physical fitness to endless exercise and a diet of blood and milk.

They had virtually coexisted with lion, rhino, buffalo, elephant and other dangerous animals in the Ngorongoro crater near Arusha and elsewhere from time immemorial and feared neither man nor beast. They were bronze paladins of the African bush, spiritual heirs to the immortal Spartans of ancient Greece, with all their panache and charisma; they spent hours 'doing' their hair and adorning themselves like guardsmen preparing for a big parade.

I once gave a young Masai *moran* (warrior) a lift. With his long spear sticking out of the window, the conversation for some reason turned to weeping. When I said, 'Masai warriors never weep,' he replied 'Of course we do. A man who doesn't cry has no soul.'

I had a Masai cattle bell mounted on my desk, with the sweetest tones I have ever heard to remind me of the lovely orchestra of the herd as they advanced across the steppe. Behind my head hung a portrait of the sovereign, King George VI until his death in 1952 and thereafter Queen Elizabeth II. Upcountry, I wore the administration's standard uniform, white short-sleeved shirt with khaki shorts and stockings and brown shoes; in Dar es Salaam and other coastal areas, white shorts and stockings were worn, so we were all white like the Royal Navy. This dress could of course be suitably modified on safari, when trousers were usually worn because of the prevalence of tsetse flies and mosquitoes, or off duty when we often sported coloured shirts. Shorts were seldom if ever worn in the office after independence, probably in deference to Muslim sensibilities, but one could wear shirts of any type or colour.

We also had a field service uniform, khaki slacks and jacket with a wonderful Sanders of the River-type pith helmet, sweeping down at the rear to protect one's neck from sunstroke, with the brass territorial badge of a giraffe. Although I believe it was worn a lot in the old days on safari, it was seldom worn in my day and then only on some semi-state occasion, such as an informal visit by a governor. The white full-dress uniform to which I have already referred was worn more often, on all special occasions, both in Dar es Salaam and upcountry. An embarrassing incident occurred during my first year as DC. This happened when, in my judicial capacity as a first-class magistrate, I sentenced Zumbe Saidi Mdoe to one-year's imprisonment for stealing 200 shillings from his local native treasury, only to have a High Court judge sitting in

Handeni quash the sentence on appeal later because of a legal technicality. Friends of the chief collected the £40 or so needed to hire Mr Donaldson, Tanga's only European advocate, to defend him. In the resulting euphoria, a mob in Chanika badly beat up the young educated Mhaya sub-inspector Nestor Msikula, who had prosecuted him, while another gang wreaked vengeance on my car by pushing it out of the garage beside the *boma* into the nearby bush during the night. I felt mortified and my relations with my local chief remained strained for the rest of my stay. There was certainly an argument for separating the judiciary from the administration.

Back in the office, I was busy with pet schemes. I was appalled by the primitive medical services, consisting of a modest government hospital at district headquarters, a small dispensary run by an African 'dresser' at each chief's HQ, plus of course the excellent mission hospital run by Dr Sitwell at Kideleko and Sister Pauline's little hospital at Kwamkono.

I routinely came across very sick or injured people on the road and naturally tried to help in any way possible, generally by bringing them to Kideleko. On one occasion, a woman, fortunately attended by her mother, gave birth in the back of my pick-up. On another, I dashed down the Morogoro road to pick up a middle-aged European couple whose car had crashed into a tree near Kang'ata, leaving them both seriously injured. I fear many people must have died in their homes or on the road through lack of transport. The little dispensaries could only cope with malaria and dysentery, and kept a small supply of key basic drugs. We discussed the problem in the *ufungilo* and decided to get a native treasury ambulance, the first in the country, in an attempt to ameliorate the situation. We had the ambulance specially modified and equipped at a garage in Tanga. I was thrilled when it arrived a few months later, complete with red cross and Handeni council markings. It stayed at district headquarters, but was soon in great demand and roaring around the district almost non-stop; few projects proved more rewarding.

In the agricultural sector, farmers suffered greatly from the depredations of wild pigs (*nguruwe*) and baboons (*nyani*). We were lucky to have a brilliant and dedicated young naturalist, Hugh Lamprey, posted to us as a field officer in the game department, responsible for coordinating crop protection measures. He stayed several years and did a marvellous job. Later, he achieved international fame and spent the best years of his life as an expert on elephant and other big game in the Serengeti National Park. He was an excellent photographer and took beautiful black and white photographs of golden weavers in the fort's courtyard.

Asians comprised a small but important group that had been settled in Handeni since German times. About 30 families, Hindu and Ismaili, lived in Chanika, another ten in smaller marketplaces. All were traders, the wealthier ones dealing in produce, mainly maize and cotton, the others selling a variety of petty goods. There were also a few Sikhs, cheerful, bearded, independent men who worked timber concessions and insisted on giving us enormous glasses of whisky at any time of the day or night.

This small community played a vital role in the life of the people out of all proportion to their numbers; they were incredibly hard working, honest and thrifty. They provided almost the only source of private transport and venture capital, the only petrol pumps and spare parts stores, and the only primitive garages. They were great fixers, always anxious to help the government; if they could not provide something themselves, they always knew someone in Tanga, Korogwe, Moshi or even Dar es Salaam who could. Better still, their lorries were always going to Tanga or Moshi and could take policemen, messengers or the sick when urgently needed.

There were two key men in Chanika. Esak Esmail, the Muslim leader, was an intelligent, slightly domineering man who seemed to control practically everything from the markets and garages to the mosque. The other was my special friend Kheraj Bhimji, the Hindu who had a delightfully good-natured grin and sense of humour. I spent hours sitting in his untidy *duka* (shop) drinking Coke or Fanta and hearing all the local gossip.

Other traders I recall were fat, cheerful Hasham Remtulla, who specialized in the transport business; Gulam Hussein; and Merali. The big man was Shariff in Korogwe, for whom many of the lesser traders were local agents. He had a first-class garage and repair workshop, grain stores, flour mills, a fleet of lorries and a luxury saloon car.

The DO and I used to alternate, one touring the district, the other remaining in the office, usually for a week at a time. Whether on safari or in the *boma*, one of our major tasks was to see an endless line of people with *mashauri* (personal matters that required attention). These consisted of a wide range of different problems, including appeals from native courts and complaints. At the *boma* we acted as magistrates, coroners, registrars of births, deaths, and marriages, police officers, and prison officers. On one or two occasions I found a dead body in the bush. I would then carry out an inquest on it as the coroner, arrest the murderer as a police officer, lock him up in the local gaol as a prison officer, and try him as a magistrate, all in the space of a few days.

On safari, we inspected roads, schools, dispensaries and native treasury books, met chiefs and councillors, held *baraza*s and checked works in progress. We also represented all the other government departments, many of whose representatives from education, health, police, game, forestry, tsetse control and water development departments made periodic visits and occasionally prolonged stays.

Meanwhile, at the *boma* I could tolerate routine activities, for there was always an opportunity to engage in my pet projects. One of my proudest achievements was to establish the Handeni Museum. I conceived of the idea immediately after my arrival in August 1951. The Handeni District Tribal Council (as it then was) agreed to start a museum with the twofold object of preserving the memories of the past and of encouraging present-day arts and crafts. The first exhibits to appear reflected the stormy history of the Zigua and Nguu tribes: Portuguese and Arab cannons, grim reminders of successive occupations, African swords, shields and clubs used by the chiefs' great grandfathers to fight the Masai, pillage their neighbours or execute their subjects. Most of these weapons were traditional royal symbols lent by the chiefs and, in some cases, they possessed ritual significance.

Some of the chiefs also lent the copper and brass trays, wooden chests and gold bracelets that Arab slave traders had presented to

116

1. ABOVE. Old Fort, Kilwa Island – scene of the earliest Swahili coinage and poetry.

2. BELOW. Aerial view of Zanzibar. Beit-el-Ajaib: Palace of Wonders in foreground.

3. ABOVE. University College, Dar-es-Salaam at Ubungo.

4. LEFT. Zanzibar Cathedral – Built on the site of the old Slave Market.

5. ABOVE. State House (formerly Government House), Dar-es-Salaam.
6. BELOW. Tanzania Pavilion, EXPO' 70, Osaka, Japan. '...one of the 12 best...'

7. ABOVE. His Eminence Cardinal Laurian Rugambwa of Bukoba – First African Prince of the Church.

8. LEFT. Trumpeting elephant in the Serengeti National Park.

their ancestors in return for safe passages (*hongo*), ivory and slaves. It was decided to house the museum in the council chamber of the native administration building which was speedily done up for the purpose. Local carpenters made glass-fronted showcases for the smaller objects and books of the existing library, while the larger exhibits were prominently displayed around the walls. The idea was to avoid the sterile atmosphere of a museum and, it was hoped, inspire contemporary councils with the visible evidence of past glories not merely to seek an alien heritage.

This dual purpose was symbolised in a statue of Seuta, the warrior hero of Zigua and Nguu. The unveiling of this statue by PC Tanga Mr Harry Gill on 5 December 1951 marked the formal opening of the museum. Seuta means 'son of the bow' in Kizigua and the name was bestowed on a legendary figure called Mganga. Mganga was reputed to have led his people in a guerrilla war against the Portuguese, teaching them for the first time the use of the bow and arrow as a weapon of war. The Portuguese would have been based at Fort Jesus in Mombasa and their raids would probably have occurred in the late seventeenth century.

The bow and arrow thus became the emblem of the Zigua and Nguu people and the chairman of the council's office was renamed Seuta. The statue itself was beautifully made in clay by Paulo Nkanyemka, the council secretary, who had studied at Makerere University, Kampala under the celebrated art teacher Mrs Trowell, who inspired generations of East African artists and sculptors. It depicts Seuta aiming his bow and arrow at an unseen foe.

The council also produced an excellent local newspaper in the Zigua language called *Muli dya Zigula Na Ngulu* (Light of Zigua and Nguu). It was edited by a remarkable young patriot and enthusiast called Zakayo Chabai, whose journal gave the museum full support. It was mainly cultural, but in stating its claims to greater Uzigua had a very gentle political content. It sought to revive irredentist Zigua claims, which if successful would have involved ceding the lush Turiani area of northern Morogoro district and the Miono area of northern Bagamoyo district to Handeni district, not to speak of the Mkwaja corridor leading to the sea through the southern Pangani district.

117

It was undoubtedly true that these areas were all part of the historic homeland of the Zigua people before the German government fixed the arbitrary colonial district boundaries at the turn of the century. While I was sympathetic to these ideas and even raised them tentatively with my more senior colleagues, it was hardly surprising that they were unenthusiastic and preferred to maintain the status quo rather than dismember their own districts.

Zakayo Chabai was also a great Ki-Zigua linguist, historian and scholar, and published a booklet on Ki-Zigua proverbs, the most common of which is *gumbo dina malema mgosi* (famine brings misfortunes, Sir). He also did a lot of research into the history of his tribe. He told me that Zigua settlers had trekked more than 1000 miles north to the seaport of Kismayu in southern Somalia and established a colony there which, so far as I know, is still extant, still speaking Ki-Zigua as well as Somali.

After a beer or two, Zakayo would dream of a great U-Seuta empire, combining Ubondei, Usambara and Uzigula Mkulu, that stretched from the Kenya border to the Wami River and from Masailand to the Indian Ocean. The beer, strictly speaking, would have been illegal at that time, for current legislation prohibited 'natives' from purchasing or consuming European liquor — presumably to protect them from the evils of debt and drunkenness. Similarly, the Credit to Natives Restriction Act stopped institutions and individuals from lending more than a modest sum to Africans, also from the paternalistic motive of keeping them and their families out of debt. These laws were well intentioned and I remember an impassioned speech by the greatly respected Church Army Captain Bennett from Bukoba vigorously opposing their repeal in the pre-independence Legislative Council in Dar es Salaam.

Zumbe Mussa Massomo's election to the vacant chiefdom of Mgera, which I have just described, was occasioned by the tragic death of his predecessor Wakili Salim Mhapi in mysterious circumstances. *Wakili* was the Ki-Swahili for 'regent' generally an uncle or guardian to the young schoolboy princeling — in this case Mussa Massomo.

Salim Mhapi was a tough chief of the old school aged about 60. As a young *askari* in General von Lettow-Vorbeck's German East

African army, he had been awarded the Iron Cross for bravery in action against the British. Short, stockily built, with a smiling brown face, he had a great sense of humour and bright intelligence.

He was greatly respected and admired by all and I enjoyed my visits to his beautiful mountain fastness in the heart of the Nguu hills, stretching away towards Kibaya and the great Masai grasslands to the west. When I had been in Handeni nearly a year I got a message to say that Salim Mhapi was very ill and I should go to see him. I drove at once the 40 miles to Mgera where I found the old chief grey with fear, lying in bed, clutching a piece of paper with Arabic writing on it, which he said was a death spell placed on him by a notorious wizard in Pangani. I did my best to comfort him and arranged for Dr Sitwell to visit him the next day. She could find absolutely nothing physically wrong with him, but agreed that he had apparently been bewitched and was terrified.

Sadly, despite all our efforts, he slowly declined and died after ten days or so, but not before I had invested him with the 'king's certificate and badge for chiefs', which he had just been awarded for loyal service to the crown. We gave him a state funeral with the Union Jack draped round his coffin and I made a short graveside oration, wearing my white full-dress uniform and sword. It was a moving occasion attended by thousands of people from all over the district.

On the return journey to Handeni, the native treasury lorry crashed at a bend in the road and overturned, killing two people and injuring a dozen or so. Sadly, the dead included my devoted young messenger Juma Kitamu who was only just 21 and on his honeymoon.

A few hours later, our drawing room at the fort was turned into a casualty clearing station. Susan and Jean Blain did their best to tend the wounded and shocked and Juma, the wonderful old cook we had inherited from the Flatts at Kahama, made endless mugs of hot sweet tea and soup to sustain the survivors.

The two dead bodies lay under the frangipani trees beside the tennis court in front of the house. As the sun set at the close of that dreadful day, I drove Juma home to his village a few miles down the Magamba road. There, as the tragic news slowly sank in, I witnessed the most poignant scenes of grief as the stricken bride and her family began the most heart-rending wailing I had ever heard. Redolent of a dying deer, it was not hard to follow the Pauline injunction 'to weep with those that weep'.

From that day on, I began to feel increasingly conscious of a deep emotional bond with the Zigua people, which transcended my normal desires and ambitions to do my duty to the best of my ability and to make Handeni the best run district in the territory. Subsequent joys and sorrows only served to strengthen that feeling, reinforced always by the constant support and encouragement I received from Father Neil Russell and the Christian community at Kideleko.

Meanwhile, after his funeral, as we began to assess the consequences of Salim Mhapi's death and the reasons for the lorry crash, ugly whispers began to circulate. It was said that not only had the late chief of Mgera been bewitched but that he had in turn, for some unfathomable reason, bewitched the ill-starred lorry, thus extending the scale of the bizarre disaster.

Witchcraft has always influenced African society and it still does. The comparatively recent advent of Islam and Christianity has done little to alter the situation, save in a few exceptional cases, where deep religious faith has conquered its terrors.

The *wa-chawi* (witches) were the evil practitioners of black magic; the notorious Pangani witch was thought to have cast the fatal spell on poor Salim Mhapi. The *wa-ganga* (witchdoctors or healers), however, were kindly GPs who provided the antidote to such evil spells and indeed also treated — generally with plant or herb-based medicines — the comparatively rare cases of 'ordinary' illness not attributable to witchcraft. In addition to the professionals, there were plenty of enthusiastic amateurs who could bewitch or terrify their enemies by sheer malevolence and hatred, often bred by jealousy, which was a besetting sin of the Zigua, according to Father Russell.

The island of Pemba, north of Zanzibar, has long been notorious for the study of 'black arts' and was even said to have a 'university' of witchcraft. Zigua peasants were very superstitious and often spoke of witches who could set houses on fire from hundreds of yards away; of men being turned into lions for years at a time; and of women being impregnated by nocturnal spirits in their husbands' absence, a fairly useful misfortune. The financial element, while important, was not paramount. The most common cases were ordinary illness, which witchcraft was often mistakenly believed to cause. Patients often insured themselves by visiting both the witchdoctor and the European hospital or dispensary.

Guilt was often an important factor and one of my office clerks was convinced he had a snake in his stomach after seducing a friend's fiancée. When shown an X-ray that proved there was nothing there, he recovered at once. Witchdoctors could also sometimes predict the future by killing chickens and 'taking the omens' in Roman style, and produce love potions (*dawa ya mapenzi*). *Dawa ya Mapenzi* was the title of a popular Ki-Swahili film made a few years before independence in which Rashidi Kawawa (the future vice-president) played the leading role.

Witchdoctors often employed dancers and drummers to cure the sick, placate ancestral spirits and bring rain and the three great classical Zigua *ngomas* — Mbuji, Mselego and Selo — were often used to further these ends. They were a splendid sight (and sound) arrayed in animal skins and feathers with bells on their legs and shaking castanets (*manyanga*) as they swayed to the rhythm of their venerable drums.

Soon afterwards another tragedy occurred in a small hamlet on the main road from Mgera to Handeni when almost all its inhabitants died from eating poisonous mushrooms over the space of just a few hours. Certain varieties of the delicious wild mushrooms that sprang up after the rains in the African bush were difficult to distinguish from their deadly toadstool counterparts. Juma always carried out an inspection before buying them from the itinerant sellers who regularly came to the door at this time.

I never ceased to marvel at African courage, endurance, honesty, cleanliness and high spirits in the face of such adverse circumstances and their fatalism in times of drought, famine, disease and death. The nobility of character expressed in the beautiful manners of the villagers was reflected throughout Tanganyika.

11

The Handeni Famine, 1953

Handeni's economy rested entirely on agriculture and the agricultural officer, John Ainley, was the most important technical officer on the station. He was aided and abetted by the tireless veteran Ali Kambi who led a dedicated band of agricultural assistants. Their major task was to encourage the growing of cassava as a famine reserve crop; it is a root crop that can survive for up to three years under the soil, even when the rains fail. In Europe, the hated school pudding tapioca is derived from cassava. Under native authority law every taxpayer in the district had to plant one acre of cassava and they were also encouraged to cultivate their land, especially on hillsides, with contour ridges and 'tie ridges' to prevent soil erosion caused by heavy rainfall. The Zigua farmers on the whole cooperated extremely well with the agricultural experts, whose advice they quickly realized was in their best interests.

John Ainley also promoted cotton and castor-seed cash crops, while a little rice and sugar cane were also grown in swampy areas. Concentration on maize as a staple crop was a major factor in the recurrent food shortages, which plagued the district, as the plant is so susceptible to drought. A year of well-distributed rainfall gave a good crop that was easily harvested, with less work involved than with cotton. When the harvest was good, the farmers often sold much maize to obtain cash, leaving themselves with scanty food resources for the following year following the well-known Swahili proverb *ponda mali kufa kuaja* (crash the cash, death's coming), our equivalent of 'eat, drink and be merry, for tomorrow we die.'

In any event, the soft variety of maize was vulnerable to weevil attack and is not easily or efficiently stored at home, though the vital 'seed corn' was normally kept carefully in a safe place. The main rainfall pattern itself, which sets the seasonal structure, comprises the *masika* (long and relatively heavy rains) from March to June, followed by the cool season, June to October, then the *vuli* (short, light rains) from October to December, and the hot season from December to March. Thus, there were two seasons and no real spring or autumn, though green shoots came up at the end of the *masika* and the countryside became appallingly dry and dusty in September before the *vuli* rains. From time to time either the long or short rains failed. Occasionally, both did, in which case disaster would strike and a food shortage would turn into a famine, with the pathetic withered stalks of maize dying in the fields. The agricultural officer encouraged farmers to sell their surplus maize to government appointed private traders so that it could be stored as a reserve against food shortages. Storage costs were high, however, and farmers bought maize at much higher prices than they had originally received. This was naturally a constant grievance.

The private traders the government appointed were our old friends Shariff in Korogwe, and Esak Esmail and Kheraj Bhimji in Chanika. In normal years, their modest godown (store) sufficed because the surplus maize moved swiftly (one way only) from the local markets based broadly on the chief's headquarters to the bigger traders in Korogwe, Tanga and elsewhere.

The grain storage department, run by Dicky Lloyd and Danny O'Loughlin in Korogwe, provided an invaluable backup in times of food shortage. They had several enormous stores in Korogwe, holding 15,000 tons of maize, whose moisture content was regularly checked by experts to avoid rotting, evaporation loss and infestation by rats, weevils or other pests. At Chanika, we had two small grain stores holding 150 tons each in strategic reserve, with smaller stores at the chiefs' headquarters. The grain storage department bought its share of the surplus maize in times of plenty from the traders through the usual channels, and topped it up by extra purchases from time to time as required. If the local surplus proved inadequate, they brought supplies from Northern Province or Morogoro, or even imported maize from as far afield as the

United States. Foreign maize had an unfamiliar flavour and was unpopular, but since really hungry people eat almost anything, this did not pose a problem. The grain storage department operated throughout the territory and was always extremely efficient and helpful. Indeed, perhaps one of the British colonial authorities' greatest achievements, not only in Tanganyika but also throughout the empire, was the success they had in preventing loss of life and serious malnutrition. This was done by giving the highest priority to a coordinated policy of preventing food shortages in the first place through enlightened agricultural policies. These were strictly enforced in the field and supported by a network of strategically sited grain stores in case food shortages became inevitable, and backed up by teams of dedicated medical and education officers, for children were particularly vulnerable.

This policy, varied to suit local conditions and different circumstances, had been a legacy bequeathed by the government of India, which had had 200 years' experience in fighting the most fearful famines and epidemics in the harshest of climatic conditions. As usual, when our famine struck it was difficult to determine the precise dates of its beginning and end. For a start, there were considerable ecological variations within the district itself; there could be heavy rain in the Tamota forests of the Nguu uplands and 20 miles away or so at Kwekivu it could be as dry as a desert. People were drowned when dry riverbeds suddenly became torrents as a result of the thunderstorms miles upstream.

Communications were poor and transport primitive. The only telephone line linking the *boma* to the main network at Korogwe was carried on poles beside the main road and was knocked down by playful elephants from time to time, leading to several days' delay while repairs were completed.

In early January 1953, our worst fears were confirmed in spectacular fashion. The 1952 *masika* rains had been poor; the *vuli* rains had virtually failed, so we knew that stocks must soon run out. We placed ourselves on red alert and warned the grain storage department at Korogwe and the provincial commissioner at Tanga. John Ainley had also informed his department through his own departmental channels. A desperate message reached me one

124

morning from Zumbe Ali Mazora of Mazingara chiefdom, 30 miles to the southeast, informing me that the remote village of Tambara, 20 miles or so to the west of Mazingara, had completely run out of food and the people were facing starvation. Urgent action was obviously needed. We loaded the native treasury three-ton lorry to its full capacity with 30 sacks of maize and set off immediately for Mazingara on the reasonably good district road, arriving around lunchtime. Neither any other government officer nor I had ever heard of Tambara, let alone been there. There was no road and nothing bigger than a bicycle had ever travelled there. The primitive track or footpath went through typical dry acacia scrub and our poor lorry had literally to batter its way through the bush like a cross between a tank and a bulldozer.

We had picked up Chief Ali at his *baraza* and I had brought the head messenger, Sufiani, along with me, plus the ubiquitous turn boy or driver's mate, whose quaint name derived from his original role in early lorries of turning over the crankshaft to start the engine. We also took a couple of stout lads armed with pangas or machetes to cut down the branches in our path and clear a way for our precious cargo. We calculated that the villagers of Tambara must scarcely have eaten for at least a week, although they had one old well for water. Impatient and impulsive at the best of times, I nearly exploded with frustration as the lorry proceeded agonizingly slowly to fight its way through the bush; it swayed like an overladen merchantman in a stormy sea — sometimes a boy fell off and had to be hauled up again.

Occasionally, we hit a mile of relatively tree-free dusty plain that had been burned out for tillage. Then we charged ahead at full speed through the dusty humid heat of the afternoon. We had a few groundnuts and a Coke on the way; it seemed obscene to eat at such a time. Once or twice we passed a small hamlet where curious people surrounded us, anxious in a uniquely African way to give advice, show us the way and give us directions. They had a vested interest in the success of our expedition — their own supplies were almost exhausted and I remember we dropped one or two boys off on the way, which had the twofold effect of lightening our overloaded vehicle and affording succour.

At long last, after four or five weary sweating hours, we made our almost triumphal entry into the pathetic little stricken village of Tambara, just before sunset when the first faint emerging breezes cooled the overheated engine of the lorry and were a soothing balm to our exhausted spirits. I shall never forget the scene on our arrival — so much sudden joy and relief transcending the long anxious weeks of suffering and fear. The entire population of the village, perhaps 50 people in all, was huddled together on the ground near the headman's hut in different stages of exhaustion, hunger, sickness and despair. As usual, the young men were the strongest and the old people, women and children were the weakest and most vulnerable.

Nevertheless, as our lorry slowly entered the forest clearing and stopped beside them, an extraordinary cry of joy went up, led by the unique ululation of the women as a solitary drum started to beat. A beautiful 18-year-old woman's hair had turned completely white — a sight that has haunted me ever since. The men began to unload the sacks of maize; the women began to prepare a meal; the sun began to set; the people embraced us; the children laughed again; I cried with joy. No one had died. Tambara was saved.

The sights and sounds of that sad yet oddly exhilarating day left an indelible mark on my memory. Although I worked on local famine relief for the next four months and would, many years later, be placed in charge of famine relief coordination for the whole of Tanzania, that was my 'baptism of fire', so to speak. I have never consciously thrown away good food from that day to this.

Indeed, of all the many varied and fascinating duties that fell to the lot of a district officer under British or African rule, none was more rewarding than feeding the hungry. It was apolitical and obviously received all-party support — it was totally simple and straightforward, and the results speedy, spectacular and much appreciated by all.

Except in exceptional cases, such as Tambara, no free food was distributed for fairly obvious reasons. A free-for-all would have ensued with every able-bodied scavenger grabbing all he could get, and perhaps even reselling it. Instead, free supplies were reserved for hospitals, schools and midwifery clinics and for those old enough to be exempt from payment of poll tax.

Able-bodied men worked for their family food ration, which was fixed arbitrarily at one kilo of *dona* (maize flour) a head per day, worth one shilling. We followed the time-honoured system of building and maintaining useful public works, popular since the Roman Empire, which in Handeni district included the construction of 50 small dams totalling a million gallons of water each, sited and designed by the water development department.

The dams provided drinking water for man and beast and irrigation for several acres of rice or sugar cane behind their walls. Each dam had a spillway on one side, down which excessive floodwaters could flow after heavy rain. Some men were employed on road improvement schemes, or to build new roads, sink wells or construct new schools and houses. At the height of the famine in early March, 3000 men a day were employed throughout the district's low-lying Zigua areas. The silver lining to the dark cloud of the famine was the extra development capital injected into the district to fund these essential relief works, which would not otherwise have been built.

The dam-building programme was my delight because, my love of water aside, it was wonderful to see the dry dusty Ziguan plains transformed by a patchwork of small silver pools dotted around the countryside, the offspring of the great Handeni dam itself. Whenever I could, I would join in the digging for a few hours, stripped to the waist in the sun, singing with the swinging of the axe and hoe, proud and happy to be in the front line of action. It was also nice to spend a few hours away from the administrative worries of the crisis — the finances, inspection visits by officers from numerous departments, repairs to broken bridges and lorries, and endless letters, queries and answering awkward questions.

Sometimes disaster struck. Most notably, an old lady leaning down to fill her calabash with water lost her balance, fell into the new dam at Magamba and was drowned in six feet of water, more than fulfilling the Zigua proverb *gumbo dina malema mgosi* (famine brings misfortune) to which I have already alluded.

On a less sombre note, a herd of 40 elephants drank the entire dam dry at Kwedilima, a village in the Mgambo chiefdom — as surprising as it was infuriating. Slowly, the famine became more widespread as requests for help began to trickle and then flood in from far and near. By February, the famine was in full swing and by far the greater part of my time and energies were devoted to it. Indeed, making a virtue of necessity as it were, it was perhaps fortunate that Susan had flown home to prepare to have our second child in October 1952. That left me ideally placed to work around the clock, seven days a week, on organizing, directing and coordinating all aspects of famine relief work.

All local leave was cancelled, weekends off were a thing of the past, and 20 rather than 10 days a month were spent on safari. I never went home unless to meet vital visitors concerned with the famine and to sign monthly pay cheques and accounts. In retrospect, I became almost obsessed with the situation and have never worked so hard in my life. On several occasions, I fell asleep in my chair during lunch, to be gently awakened by the faithful Juma as he carried round the next course.

By now too, Denis Blain had been transferred to Same district as DO to my old friend Mervyn Smithyman, a tea planter from Nyasaland (now Malawi) who had commanded 13 Battalion KAR in the 11 (EA) Division in Burma. A splendid young man called David Brokensha, a bachelor with an invaluable Land Rover succeeded him; intelligent and sensitive, he was destined to become a lifelong friend. Son of a High Court judge in Durban, he was a South African of Cornish descent who had fought in the 2 SA Division in the western desert and had been captured at Tobruk. He later took an anthropology degree at Cambridge, which subsequently became the prelude to a distinguished academic career as an anthropologist in West Africa and California, where he later held the chair in anthropology at the University of California in Santa Barbara.

I could have wished for no more able and congenial companion in the daunting task that faced us. A good friend on a small outstation in Africa is a great blessing, especially when, like David, he has a delightful sense of humour. Unlike the fighting services, with their wardrooms and officers' messes, or even the foreign service with embassy colleagues and the social life of a capital city, a bush district officer remained an essentially lonely figure. He was aloof of necessity and to some extent cut off from both the expatriate and native communities. It is quite a strain to be seen to be totally honest, impartial and incorruptible for 24 hours a day, 365 days a year. Yet, no other standard is conceivable for a man who represents his sovereign and country in a remote place and has the honour to live and work under his nation's proud flag. It was small wonder that this life accentuated people's character traits and eccentricities, so that several lived on long after their departure or even death in the collective folklore of many an African tribe.

I was proud to have belonged to such a 'band of brothers' as the colonial administrative service in general and the Tanganyika administration in particular. The latter numbered in its ranks at that time two holders of the Victoria Cross for gallantry, several Royal Navy veterans and Royal Air Force wartime aces. There was a submarine captain, heroes of the French Resistance, Chindits from Burma, guerrilla leaders from Abyssinia, not to speak of Oxford and Cambridge blues by the dozen. There were former rugby internationals, a handful of élite officers from Australia, New Zealand, South Africa and Canada, and several authors, artists, photographers, mountaineers and ornithologists of some distinction.

They were certainly a good advertisement for Sir Ralph Furse's far-sighted and inspired recruitment policy and vision for a future nonracial Commonwealth of Nations. With their fair share of human frailty, they nearly all possessed an inner dedication to that vision, albeit concealed beneath a cloak of British reserve and modesty. Above all, they were honest and incorruptible, only one or two falling by the wayside, almost always after getting into debt.

Schools were always considered a top priority for free food and care, for growing teenagers and small children who assumed many adult responsibilities far sooner than their Western counterparts were particularly susceptible to malnutrition. In such a harsh environment, every hand counted and little boys tended cattle and goats and scared away birds soon after they could walk. Little girls played a similar role, helping their mothers to sweep the floor with crisp homemade brooms composed of branches, and to collect firewood.

Holidays were rare, tending to be confined to important Muslim festivals such as Idd-ul-Fitr at the end of the austere fast of Ramadan when, with a bit of luck, one might expect a gift of new clothes. So ingenious were the children, however, that they even made their own toys. Zigua bicycles, complete with wooden wheels, frame and handlebars, regularly raced down the steep hill from the *boma* to Chanika; the annual bicycle race on a Saturday afternoon was one of the events of the season. Casualties were numerous, but fortunately minor.

When I visited schools during the famine I used to hold a simple general knowledge quiz in each classroom, giving each winner a prize of one shilling, which was enough to buy a kilo of *dona* flour. Many years afterwards and right up to the end of my time in Africa in 1973, I used to bump into former prizewinners. They would tell me just how much that little coin had meant to them at that terrible time, so much so in fact that they had never forgotten it. They even remembered the questions, which had long since faded from my memory. The school system in Tanganyika at that time consisted of primary and middle schools, which I have mentioned. Pupils attending the rare secondary school, from Standard 9 to Standard 12, ended the course by sitting the Cambridge overseas school certificate — a greatly sought after and much prized qualification. Mission schools aside, there was normally one government secondary school in each of the eight provinces, ours being at Tanga. Later, a few select government and mission secondary schools added Standards 13 and 14 to prepare pupils for university entrance examinations.

The medical officer at Korogwe was a remarkable Polish Jew called Dr Izzy Laufer, who had received his medical degree from the historic Italian University of Padua. He was dark and chubby with a round, cheerful face and large horn-rimmed spectacles; he exuded confidence and bonhomie. Like many of his fellow countrymen who had endured hardship and suffering in the war, he had a sharp and slightly cynical sense of humour and, for a man in his early forties, a great understanding of life. A bon viveur — he nonetheless was always prepared to join me on the most arduous safaris into the worst famine areas to check any signs of approaching malnutrition among the population in general and the old, sick and young in particular. To this end, he inspected all schools and dispensaries in the famine areas and came down at once whenever we needed him. On his advice, whenever I visited Kwamsisi chiefdom on the Pangani district border, I would drive 25 miles down the road to the little fishing village of Mkwaja on the Indian Ocean. There, I would load the back of my pick-up with hundreds of coconuts, which I would later distribute to the deserving recipients Dr Laufer had nominated in the various schools and villages along the route of my return journey. Both the flesh of the coconut and the refreshing liquid inside (*madafu*) were thought to be of great nutritional value.

As Mkwaja was in Pangani district, as a matter of courtesy I always informed my friend Peter Haynes, who had taken over from Tony Golding as the DC, of my impending visits there. I loved the excuse to visit Mkwaja to collect coconuts and always found time to strip off and plunge into the waves for a cooling dip in the sea. Kwamsisi was Uzigua's most isolated and remote chiefdom and its young ruler, wild Zumbe Andrea Mhanda, had no interest in any kind of progress or development. His personal appearance was unprepossessing; unshaven, with a dirty white *kanzu*, he seemed wanton, bedraggled and dishevelled. He did not inspire confidence and, with bloodshot eyes from heavy drinking, often looked debauched. The resthouse too was dirty and badly kept. The forest reverberated to the roar of lions, the menacing sawing of leopards and the horrible eerie cry of hyenas.

There were only a few thousand inhabitants in Kwamsisi's scattered, sparsely populated villages. Being tormented by tsetse fly, they could not keep livestock and their chickens must have been the scrawniest on earth. Cultivation too was minimal, with small patches of maize, millet and sorghum in clearings in the bush — classic examples of 'shifting cultivation', a rough African equivalent of the rotation of crops designed to suit totally different circumstances. Whereas in Britain, for example, land is a precious and valuable commodity held for hundreds of years by individual land tenure, in Africa a vast amount of land (generally with very poor soil) belongs to the community as a whole. It is vested in the local chief, who approves individual applications for rights to cultivate in certain areas, a duty sometimes delegated to subchiefs and village headmen. As the farmers have plenty of poor soil, they tend to burn the bush at the end of the dry season to acquire ash as a simple fertilizer and to destroy the numerous pests and bugs.

Three other unusual episodes enlivened our existence — a Masai cattle raid, the gallantry of Police Sergeant Timotheo and ancestral graves on the edge of a sisal estate. Early in 1953, a band of about 60 Masai *moran* attacked a herd of Zigua cattle on the extreme northwestern border of the district, killing a herdsman and stealing more than 100 head of *zebu* (humped) cattle — reclaiming them from their point of view. I summoned the Masai elders to a formal *baraza* the next day near the site of the attack. But, before meeting them, I took the precaution of asking the police commander in Tanga to send me at once his élite police motorized company of 100 or so men specially trained to deal with riots.

With only a handful of policemen at my disposal locally, it seemed prudent in the circumstances to have a strong force in strategic reserve to back up the negotiations, without being in any way provocative. Discussions with Masai on the ultra-sensitive almost religious subject of cattle were notoriously difficult. The brutal murder in Kenya just after the war of Major Grant, the DC of Narok, still lingered in our minds. He had insisted on confiscating a sacred white bull from a young *moran* cattle thief at a big *baraza*. The insult to his deeply held beliefs was too much for the young man, who had run his spear through the much loved DC, killing him on the spot — a crime for which he was later hanged after making a full confession.

After several hours of difficult negotiation, the elders agreed to my strict terms of returning all the stolen cattle, plus 20 or so extra as compensation to the victim's family.

Soon afterwards, a young man went crazy at Kideleko mission, taking a panga in his right hand and a knife in his left and terrorizing the hospital outpatients and schoolchildren. On hearing the

132

news, my resourceful police sergeant Timotheo mysteriously asked me for the loan of a blanket, which we took with us in my car, plus a couple of police *askari* as we set off for the mission. We then cornered the unfortunate man, whose name I have long since forgotten, against the wall of the hospital, while the gallant Timotheo chatted casually to him and, distracting his attention for a second, hauled the blanket over him while we moved in and disarmed him. We later sent him off safely for hospital treatment in Tanga, while Sergeant Timotheo was awarded a police gallantry certificate for his bravery.

The last episode, and in some ways the most disturbing in its wider implications, concerned a small sacred grove of trees containing ancestral graves near the little village of Kwamgwe on the Korogwe/Handeni district borders, to the northeast of the district headquarters. On the Korogwe side of the border lay the important Kwamgwe Sisal Estate. This belonged to the biggest sisal estate company, Bird & Company. Its chairman, the redoubtable Sir Eldred Hitchcock, was uncrowned king of the Tanga sisal barons, the half-dozen or so millionaires who controlled the Tanganyikan sisal industry, the territory's leading export with a crop of 120,000 tons per annum — the biggest in the world. At that time, which was during the Korean War, Tanganyikan sisal was used to manufacture ropes for the US and British navies and its price boomed to well over £100 a ton. Almost the entire length of the dusty ribbon of the Tanga–Mombo road to Moshi was through a green sea of spiky sisal.

The Kwangwe estate wished to straighten out its own demesne and the provincial commissioner told me that Sir Eldred would be 'most displeased' if the villagers were not 'persuaded' to hand over this enclave as soon as possible. I duly went to Kwamgwe and held a *baraza* on the spot with the village elders, who explained at length the traditional and religious significance of the sacred burial grove. I, for my part, put forward the official government line, which stressed the importance of the sisal industry and so on. The villagers, however, were implacable and, on balance, I was convinced that natural justice was on their side. Moreover, the great British colonial principle was that 'where the rights of immigrants

133

and natives should clash, the latter should prevail.' My own personal philosophy was that the DC should always be 51 per cent for his local people and only 49 per cent for the remote government in Dar es Salaam. However, I realize that this view was regarded as heretical and that it should probably be the other way round.

Be that as it may, I wrote a concise report to the PC closing with the recommendation that Sir Eldred's request should be politely but firmly refused. The local villagers would never willingly give up their sacred grove, even for the modest compensation (a few thousand shillings), a fortune to them, that was on offer. With a fairly menacing telephone call, the high command tried to persuade me to change my mind, but to no avail. I was absolutely adamant and totally convinced of the justice of our cause.

At all events, the sacred grove was still inviolate when I left the district at the end of the year, and I have never subsequently heard what transpired — perhaps it was just as well.

12

The Air Crash, 1953–54

By April 1953 the rains had arrived and the parched earth gave way to the green shoots of recovery, above all hope slowly began to return. The end of the famine was at last in sight as the dams filled up and even sometimes overflowed, and short-term vegetable crops such as beans, pulses and pumpkins could be eaten.

Travel was more difficult when the roads flooded and became waterlogged. The sand rapidly turned to mud and I had one nightmare journey from Kimbe to Handeni with a temperature of 103 degrees from malaria. I seemed to spend most of the day on the road being dug out of the sand in the morning and pushed out of the mud in the afternoon. Branches had to be cut from trees to form a carpet on the mud to stop the wheels spinning fruitlessly round. Finally, we broke free and reached the main Morogoro–Korogwe road near Kang'ata, turned left and sped north for home at 30 miles an hour. Nothing can describe the marvellous feeling of relief and exhilaration on returning safely home after a few days on safari, heightened on this occasion by a desire to collapse into bed and sleep and rest one's weary, aching, sweating body.

One seemed to get a heightened sense of living from the fact that almost every safari was an adventure with engines breaking down, tyres puncturing, bridges occasionally being washed away, or roads being impassable. We would never, for example, say 'We will be back at 2.00 p.m.', but rather 'sometime on Tuesday'.

Like our ancestors travelling the seas in sailing ships or crossing continents on horseback or in coaches, we found journeys challenging, interesting, physically demanding, but never easy. For the Zigua, and indeed all Tanganyikan Africans, safari was a necessary evil. It often involved tramping hundreds of miles with one's worldly goods balanced on a pole over the shoulder — Dick Whittington style — or, if lucky, long bicycle rides or being squeezed into the back of an overcrowded bus with screaming babies and squawking chickens in humid, fetid conditions. It was small wonder that a popular Swahili song started with the words '*Kesho safari, kweli taabu*' (a journey tomorrow, truly trouble).

The white man's latest marvel, the aeroplane, which gave travel in Africa a new dimension, would occasionally crash in some of the most remote and inhospitable country on earth, thus rendering the task of location and rescue that much more difficult. Africans had a charming word for an aircraft, *ndege* (bird) and an even more romantic one for an airman, *mwana hewa* (child of the air).

One Sunday afternoon in April while David Brokensha and I were playing tennis, a small aeroplane circled low over the *boma* and dropped something near the tennis court in a metal container. It contained a short message: 'CAA [Central African Airways] Viking VPYEY flying from Nairobi to Johannesburg via Salisbury [now Harare] is missing, last seen flying south towards your district. Grateful search, locate and report back earliest Aviation Nairobi.'

With adrenaline flowing, we abandoned our tennis match for an emergency meeting in my sitting room. Enquiries in the town of Chanika revealed that an airliner had been seen a few hours earlier flying southeast in the general direction of Dar es Salaam, which had the nearest suitable airport at which to land if it were in any kind of trouble. David and I decided therefore to take the old road to Dar es Salaam via Bagamoyo on the coast — the shortest way as the crow flies. John Ainley and Eddie Davey (who had also been playing tennis) took their vehicles due south and southwest respectively so that, it was hoped, all possible airspace would be covered. Although not raining on our tennis court, there were ominous dark clouds to the south with the odd thunderclap and flash of lightning, which was not unusual at the height of the rainy season. Because of the appalling state of the local district roads, we chose to travel in David's four-wheel-drive Land Rover.

We hastily packed overnight bags, filled the petrol tanks and were off at about 4.00 p.m., an hour or so after receiving the aerial message. Nine miles down the road at Magamba, Zumbe Hemedi Sonyo heard reports of an aircraft flying southeast in the morning apparently quite normally. We drove on through Mazingara stopping to ask at every village on the road and a remarkable unsolicited intelligence service appeared to have 'shadowed' the Viking throughout the entire length of its journey.

With muddy roads and frequent stops, not to speak of occasional thunderstorms and heavy rain, we made slow progress. Dusk was approaching as we turned east onto the Kwamsisi road. For hour after hour, we crawled along in the dark through heavy rain until at long last we reached Kwamsisi. There we heard the sad news that an aircraft had indeed crashed into the hills that morning close to the remote village of Kwedifunda, about twelve miles away near the Pangani district border. Though my memories of that dreadful night are confused, I know that Zumbe Andrea and I reached Kwedifunda around midnight in pitch dark and driving rain. Through thick bush, we travelled in bottom gear along rough tracks to our unlikely destination where no white man, let alone government official, had ever been before. It was even whispered that none of the 30 or so villagers had ever paid tax in their lives. They were virtually outlaws, yet I was to remember their courage, honesty and cheerfulness for the rest of my life.

They produced a young man called Musa who had actually seen the aeroplane crashing into the bush on the side of the hill above the village. That night to us, and later at the court of inquiry in Dar es Salaam sometime afterwards, he vividly described the onomatopoeic boom-boom-boom noise he had heard. Experts at the Royal Aircraft Establishment (RAE) at Farnborough interpreted it as the sound of a wing breaking off the fuselage of an airliner. The villagers reported pieces of the aircraft, luggage and dead bodies scattered for miles around. By then, it was too dark to start a detailed search for bodies and wreckage. We had succeeded in achieving our first objective of locating the plane and establishing its unhappy fate.

Our next task was to inform the local aviation authorities so that the grim procedures that follow such disasters could be set in motion as quickly as possible. There was no radio, telephone or telegraph anywhere near. There was apparently some kind of signal station at the little port of Sadani on the Indian Ocean in the northern Bagamoyo district where it might be possible to 'tap into' the coastal telephone line from Tanga to Dar es Salaam and, we hoped, get a message through to headquarters.

So, promising to return the next day and exhorting the locals to touch nothing, we retraced our steps through the bush. We drove all night along ghastly little roads out of the Handeni district, out of Tanga Province and into the Bagamoyo district in Eastern Province, justifiably breaching all the normal colonial service protocol in view of the desperate urgency of the situation.

We drove all night with David at the wheel of his own Land Rover, while I tried, not always successfully, to read the map and navigate along tracks that passed as 'district roads'. We reached Sadani at first light and I have never been so glad to see the sea and echo the cries of Alexander's weary soldiers in India *thalassa! thalassa!*

As the first rays of a glorious African sunrise turned the calm ripples of the sea to turquoise blue, peach and gold, we drove down the beach to the water's edge and with one accord removed our dusty clothes and plunged into the cool clean embrace of the welcoming surf. Neither of us has ever forgotten this bathe, which at once blessed our sleepless, exhausted bodies, minds and spirits, and washed away the terrors of the night.

Restored, we found something to eat and drank a cup of hot, sweet tea. We then set off for the signal station where, with the reluctant help of a young signalman who said he was breaking all the regulations, we at last succeeded in getting through to the post office headquarters in Dar es Salaam and relaying our message to those concerned. I was possessed with a strange sense that I alone had vital information that others eagerly sought for various and compelling reasons. David and I felt our shared responsibility keenly and it was a great relief to discharge our duty and shed the burden. Our first task had been done.

It was now time to return to the disaster area and face what ghastly scenes might confront us there. As the sun rose and warmed us, we returned along the now familiar and sunny route, arriving at Kwedifunda by midday and setting off immediately with local guides to the scene of the crash. We walked slowly up the valley in the heat of the day under a blazing sun. A sickly odour of death pervaded the atmosphere and vultures hovered overhead. We saw the first body — bloated, blackened and covered in a mass of flies and insects — lying obscenely in a clump of trees. As we approached the main wreck of the aircraft higher up the hill, we passed ever increasing numbers of suitcases, some burst open to reveal pathetic reminders of their dead owners. Clothes, bank notes, tennis rackets, teddy bears and dolls littered the bush, some dangling grotesquely from the branches of trees.

Suddenly, in a clearing we saw the remnants of Viking VPYEY split in half with its left wing missing and the cockpit and main passenger cabin broken into two. The front section contained the bodies of the pilot, co-pilot and two passengers still strapped to their seats, while the rear section was empty. There had been 13 passengers and crew on board and the bodies of the remaining nine, including that of the air hostess — the only woman on board — were scattered along the hillside and the valley for a mile or so, like an unsuccessful parachute drop.

One of the passengers was the US consul in Nairobi who had been delivering a box of secret papers and $100,000 in notes to the US consulate in Salisbury, Rhodesia. It subsequently transpired that the villagers recovered 99.6 per cent of all the cash in dollar bills strewn for miles around the bush. They also recovered the bulk of the secret papers and almost all the possessions and property (still intact) of the dead passengers and crew — hence my earlier tribute to them. The headman told us that devout Muslims of the village regarded stealing from the dead as blasphemy and had therefore scrupulously handed in everything they could find.

The missing wing of the aeroplane was found nearly half a mile away and the tailpiece a mile away in the opposite direction, while dozens of smaller pieces of wreckage, including the nose, were scattered around the bush.

Soon after we had returned to the village in the comparative cool of the evening, the first fruits of our dawn message appeared with the arrival of my friend Peter Haynes (DC Pangani) with a safari tent, food and beer. We turned in early and slept like logs. The next day, to our surprise and delight, the well-known 'white hunter' from Arusha, Bowker Douglas arrived with the luxury caravanserai of large tents, tables, tablecloths, cutlery, servants and delicious food and drink provided for millionaires on a game safari.

The government had hired this camp, not for our convenience but to house the crash investigation experts from the RAE, the US consul general for Nairobi and other top brass in the manner to which they were accustomed. Nonetheless, we were invited to join this luxury mess and, as we tucked into fabulous meals and sipped whisky and soda on beautiful canvas chairs, we underwent a real rags to riches transformation.

Reinforcements poured in all that day, including the RAE investigators from England, civil aviation experts and airline representatives. Most of our district team arrived, including John Ainley, Eddie Davey and someone from the game department, who turned up with a radio set, which put us in touch again with the outside world. On Wednesday morning, the aviation experts started to inspect the wreckage carefully, packing up and examining the black box and other key components for forwarding to their laboratories in England. Another aircraft appeared overhead and took aerial photographs of the scene. Their preliminary finding — to be confirmed later — was that the crash was caused by the frightening condition known as metal fatigue, which had caused the first wing to break off and then the stricken aircraft to break in two. The immediate cause was probably heavy turbulence caused by one of the thunderstorms raging that Sunday morning.

Our job was to collect the 13 bodies, place them on improvised stretchers and carry them the mile or so downhill to a waiting five-ton lorry, which the provincial commissioner of Tanga had sent to convey them the 180 miles or so to the government hospital there. It was easy to remove the four bodies from the forward section of the wrecked Viking, but it was an appalling task to collect the nine remaining ones, which had by now been exposed to the harsh elements for three days. They were in a ghastly condition, resembling a Brueghel depiction of the horrors of hell. They looked more like dead cattle than humans, so swollen they had become, stinking of putrefaction, infested with insects and flies, surrounded by carrion beasts and birds.

The gallant inhabitants of Kwedifunda, a hitherto unknown bush village whose name was now broadcast across eastern Africa, formed the main body of stretcher-bearers, spurred on by me, David and our *boma* and Kwamsisi messengers. We worked all day in great heat and, from time to time, men overcome by the grisly sights, sounds and smells fell out to vomit by the wayside. On one or two occasions, they simply refused to go on and wanted to give up. Somehow we coaxed, threatened and cajoled them back to their disgusting task.

At last the lorry was loaded, the obscene cargo was covered with tarpaulins and the driver set off for Tanga. On arrival, the hospital staff had to wear gas masks to unload the bodies, which, after a hurried inquest, were buried in a mass grave of quicklime.

The next day — Thursday — we returned to Handeni to resume our normal (or rather abnormal) duties in the famine relief operations, which were in full swing.

After a month or so, Musa and I were summoned to Dar es Salaam to attend the official inquiry into the crash. It was held in the High Court overlooking the beautiful harbour lined with scarlet acacia and Indian almond trees. To save time, we were told to fly there from Tanga and, I must confess, I felt apprehensive about taking to the air so soon after the crash. As for poor Musa, who had hardly ever left his village in his life and the only aeroplane he had ever seen had broken up in front of his eyes and come crashing down like a meteor near his home, I was concerned for him. I need not have worried. Smartly dressed in a spotless white *kanzu* and embroidered *kofia*, he was as cool as a cucumber and greatly enjoyed the flight to Dar es Salaam and his stay there. Better still, he gave his evidence calmly, clearly and with the utmost conviction, and the court was most impressed. Indeed, his brilliant mimicking of the sound of the Viking breaking up proved decisive in the court's finding that metal fatigue, the hidden cancer of all aircraft, was responsible for the disaster, and I believe that research into its mysterious causes has continued ever since.

I received an official letter of thanks from the government, signed by the chief secretary — a rare accolade — which my friends said might act as credit to offset any future misdeeds. The provincial commissioner, Mr J. C. Clarke, kindly ordered me to Tanga for a few days' rest after this ordeal and had me to stay in the guest turret of his beautiful house by the sea. My visit was somewhat marred, however, by getting a fish bone stuck in my throat for about twenty minutes at a grand dinner party, causing me acute anxiety and embarrassment. They were about to call a doctor when I swallowed it. I was living life dangerously.

The air crash left scars that took time to heal. It, combined with the prolonged and exhausting strain of the famine and no doubt the six-month absence from my wife and children, left me emotionally and physically drained. My judgement must have been impaired. Soon after Susan's return with the new baby, our son Gerald born on 23 February, I foolishly rejected a thoughtful offer the provincial commissioner made in May 1953, which his staff officer, my old friend Robin Risley, conveyed to me personally. This was to send me home on leave after more than two years' service, in view of the considerable pressure I had endured. At 29, with my life having become closely, almost obsessively, committed to Handeni district and its loveable people to the temporary exclusion of almost all else, I made the fatal mistake of thinking myself indispensable. I also laboured under the delusion that it was my sacred duty to remain at my post until the end of 1953 or early 1954 when the first phase of the district development plan would have been successfully completed. Robin Risley pleaded with me to take early leave, but to no avail. I paid the price of my folly with a breakdown in health a few months later, which in retrospect may have been a blessing in disguise.

Before then, however, we celebrated the coronation of beautiful young Queen Elizabeth II on 2 June 1953, only a few hours after the first conquest of Mount Everest by Sir Edmund Hillary and Sherpa Tenzing. It seemed like the dawn of a new Elizabethan era and inspired us all in our bush fortress with high hopes for the future, dreams of transmuting our colonial empire into a great multiracial commonwealth of self-governing nations across the world, united under a rejuvenated and brighter crown.

A few months later, Douglas Swannie, who ran the social development department's film unit in Dar es Salaam, toured all nine chiefdoms with his mobile film unit, showing vast, appreciative audiences a superb colour film of the coronation.

I did not know it at the time, but Handeni would be my last bush station. In addition to my main tasks of representing the sovereign, maintaining law, dispensing justice, collecting revenue and ruling the district through the chiefs, I was responsible for various other duties there. I was the administrator-general dealing with bankruptcies, the registrar of births, deaths and marriages, the coroner, the police (prisons) probation officer and a representative for the agriculture, education, forestry, game, grain storage, labour, medical, veterinary and water development departments. I was the postmaster, executive officer for Chanika township, chairman of the district team and a representative of the departments of civil aviation, customs, hides and skins, public relations, public works, social development and tsetse fly. I was also responsible for the census, for resettlement schemes and for liaising with missions. At all events, I wore at least 30 different 'hats', in addition to dozens of unofficial ones such as player/manager of the local football team. This 'poobah' role begged the question of district officers being 'jacks of all trades and masters of none' and in a sense this was a valid criticism. However, in the peculiar condition of ruling vast areas of Africa on a shoestring budget, it was probably the best, if not indeed the only, option then available.

District officers were both communicators and coordinators, providing not only the essential link between governors and governed, but also between the numerous and varied departments of the government. Their main qualities were the time-honoured virtues of integrity, intelligence, hard work and sympathy allied to linguistic ability, tact and, above all, a sense of humour. In addition to the war heroes already mentioned, there were also distinguished anthropologists, artists, authors, engineers, scientists, mountaineers, photographers and ornithologists, not to speak of amateur architects, archaeologists, horticulturists, brilliant linguists, naturalists, herpetologists, entomologists and lepidopterists.

Their tastes were as varied as their talents, and their eccentricities became more pronounced the longer they stayed in the bush. Like me, most of them had favourite projects since they could not do everything, and they naturally concentrated on what aspects of the work appealed to them most. Some loved the clearcut routine and meticulous planning and staff work of the Dar es Salaam secretariat and spent most of their working lives there, while others preferred the Sanders of the River life of the outstation. The ideal career, perhaps, was a blend of them both, and the most successful officers normally served in several different colonies before reaching the top as governor.

There were those who, like John Young, laid out wonderful gardens, others who planted forests. Some specialized in constructing roads, others studied tribal histories and customs; some shot elephants, others photographed them; some had obsessions about tax collection, cassava reserves, tie-ridging, manure — you name it. No one was bored.

The eight provincial centres, which included Tabora and Tanga, provided a compromise between capital and bush. In such places, an administrative officer could combine safari with a rather more sophisticated social life based on the inevitable club. This, catering as it did for several hundred European officers and their families, was able to provide facilities for team sports like cricket, rugby and golf — the Kasulu course was exceptionally good for an outstation. More important, there were normally excellent cottage hospitals and primary schools.

Later in 1957 I was to spend a year at the beautiful hill station of Arusha, capital of the Northern Province on the lower slopes of Mount Meru (as high as Mont Blanc) as provincial public relations officer. I was therefore fortunate during my 13 years' service under British rule from 1948 to 1961 to have had the experience of serving at all three levels of the administration. After *uhuru* on 9 December 1961 until my final departure 12 years later on 19 December 1973, I served exclusively in Dar es Salaam, although travelling a great deal upcountry, as indeed did almost all my peers. Our role was now that of staff officers and advisers rather than as rulers. Indeed, December seems to have been a significant month for me. Early in that month in 1953, soon after

Lady Twining's visit on 2 December, I suffered a serious nervous breakdown, which led to my speedy removal first to Tanga Hospital and later to Ocean Road Hospital in Dar es Salaam. It must have been a great shock to Susan and our respective families.

I was flown home after a week or so and happily made a complete recovery *en route*, coming to my senses as we flew over Rome. I was, however, left in hospital for a month or so as a precaution against a relapse. The Colonial Office doctors would not let me return to duty until I had my full entitlement of six months sick leave in addition to the six months vacation leave, so I spent the whole of 1954 on leave in Europe.

The English doctors attributed my illness to malaria and poor diet, aggravated by the famine and air crash. Zumbe Hemedi Sonyo reckoned that Zumbe Swalehe Saidi of Mgambo, who had allegedly been sticking pins into my earth effigy for some time, had bewitched me. Only the prayers of the faithful at Kideleko saved me from a worse fate. I had lost a lot of weight and was down to nine stone. Childhood memories of Ireland, my native Guinness and the love of my family and friends hastened my recovery. The Zigua proverb holds that famine brings misfortunes (*gumbo dina malema*), yet this traumatic experience at the age of 29 not only spelled the end of my youth, but in a strange way it also enriched my spirit. It relaxed me and gave me a greater feeling of a shared humanity with all those around me, which transformed my life.

Such a setback in the prime of life is a humbling experience. It gave me plenty of time to meditate on my personal insignificance in the scheme of things, which strengthened my spirit and made me more sympathetic to others in distress. I felt grateful to have recovered and been passed fit to return to my beloved Africa. I was emboldened by wonderful letters of encouragement and support from my governor, Sir Edward Twining, my provincial commissioner, Harry Gill, and above all from my parish priest, friend and mentor, Father Neil Russell. This was to say nothing of the great help given by all my friends, especially David Brokensha, Sam and Jean Humphries at Korogwe (friends from Nzega), and John Allen, deputy provincial commissioner in Tanga and his wife

Wink. My sudden illness had inevitably given them all a great deal of trouble, packing up and storing our possessions, looking after Susan and the children, and arranging their journey home, all of which they undertook cheerfully and uncomplainingly. Harry Gill, the provincial commissioner, also had to make arrangements at short notice to replace me and continue the administration of the district as quickly as possible.

If life is full of proverbial ups and downs, this was certainly my deepest down. However, fortified by Bunyan's comforting words, 'He that is down can fear no fall,' I determined to pick myself up and continue what then seemed a very real struggle for health, work and happiness. As for Tanganyika in general, and Handeni in particular, this unfortunate episode only served to strengthen my affection for the people, so many of whom had now become personal friends. It also confirmed my regard for the colonial service, whose imaginative compassion extended not only to the subject peoples in its charge, but also to those in its own ranks, whom it did not desert in their hour of need.

13

A Change of Direction, 1955–56

I t was with some trepidation therefore that, having finally been passed fit for tropical service by the colonial office doctor in Dublin, I made my way to the port of London on a cold January evening and embarked on the British India ship SS *Uganda*. My recovery was to some extent speeded by financial considerations, for after the statutory vacation leave and sick leave were up, one moved on to half pay and then no pay, fairly rapidly culminating in no job. So it was what was known in the army as a make or break situation.

It was also lonely. As the children were only five and two, Susan herself had not been too well and we were being posted to the secretariat in Dar es Salaam. For the first time it had been decided that I should go ahead on my own and the family would follow a few months later after I had settled into my new job, found a suitable house and so on.

This was a fairly normal procedure in the colonial service at that time, which of necessity often imposed a considerable strain on family life. Some stations were too unhealthy for small children, especially if they or their mothers were delicate, and others were unsuitable for older children and teenagers because there were no suitable schools. Mothers often faced an invidious choice between their husbands or their children. Some women, especially those brought up in the country, took to life in the bush stations like a duck to water, creating beautiful homes and gardens, playing

147

tennis and golf, going on safari or busying themselves teaching local girls to knit or sew. Others used to urban life in Europe or America found this existence incredibly boring and had to resort to coffee mornings or bridge parties enlivened by gin and tonics. It was remarkable that so few marriages came to grief.

Generally, women preferred larger stations where health and education facilities were better for their children, and the men — particularly younger ones — preferred bush stations where their job carried greater responsibility and their lives were more adventurous. As couples grew older and their children went to school in the hills or to England, they tended to gravitate towards Dar es Salaam and the provincial centres. There life was more ordered and work more routine, with reasonably regular office hours, tarmac roads, electric light, good clubs, sports, banks, shops and cinemas, or sometimes even railway stations, seaports and airfields.

So, after the upheaval of the year 1954, we were setting off for a completely different existence, which in retrospect probably suited us much better. Counting war service, I had already served more than ten years 'in the bush' and got to know the people and their language well, while Susan too had spent a childhood at Bangalore in India and now had the added responsibility of bringing up two small children.

Meanwhile, my voyage proceeded peacefully and uneventfully, with the usual rough seas and dark skies of the Atlantic and the Bay of Biscay succeeded by the sunnier and kinder climes of the Mediterranean and Red Sea. We swam and played deck tennis, ate good meals, read books and slept. We stopped briefly at Suez, Port Said and Aden — where I bought a magnificent silk dressing gown for my old Handeni friend Zumbe Hemedi Sonyo.

It was a wonderful feeling to sail slowly back into Dar es Salaam's beautiful harbour and to be given a warm welcome on the quayside by Bill and Phyllis Cadiz. They kindly had me to stay for a week or so in their comfortable bungalow a few minutes walk from the secretariat. It was they who had first had Susan and me to stay on our arrival at Tabora seven years before, so I felt instantly at home and even more so when they insisted I had a few minutes siesta after lunch every day.

Later the Cadiz's passed me on to my old friends from Kibondo, the Risleys who lived in the Oyster Bay seaside residential area five miles north of Dar es Salaam on the Bagamoyo road. Their own home was on the Msasani road. I spent a pleasant few days with them while collecting my kit and slowly getting unpacked and installed in an old German bungalow on Garden Avenue with the help of Abdulla Mselemu who had arrived from Handeni to look after me. The bungalow was officially a 'bachelor' quarter, which I had been temporarily allocated pending the arrival of my family. It was convenient, for it was only about ten minutes walk from my office in the secretariat on the harbour front, and even nearer to St Albans church and Chez Clos, a little French café where I often had my supper.

Early in February 1955 I took up my duties as assistant secretary of legal affairs in the attorney general's department in the old German two-storeyed wooden secretariat building with wide verandas and a dark red corrugated-iron roof. I was the schedule officer in the department to whom all routine official correspondence came in the first instance. I was responsible for sifting it out and 'minuting' the various letters upwards, sideways or downwards as required.

This was indeed another world from the healthy open-air front line of the *boma* with its daily — if not hourly — close contact with 'the people' for whom we were responsible. This was a world of real civil servants, a mini Whitehall of 100,000 files on every conceivable subject dating back to the archives of German rule at the beginning of the century.

This was a place at which we all arrived punctually at our desks at 7.30 a.m., took an hour off for lunch from 12.30 to 1.30 p.m. and went home around 4.30 p.m. in time for tea and a sail, swim, tennis or golf. We were all in uniform, immaculately dressed with white shirts and shorts and white stockings like the crew of a warship in tropical waters.

We were all paid on the same salary scale according to age and seniority and our salaries were published for all to see in the Annual Staff List. A weekly official gazette showed the dispositions of the administrative officers staffing the 56 districts, the eight provincial headquarters and the secretariat plus those on leave or seconded for special duty — a grand total of 300 officers in all.

This élite corps was responsible under the leadership of the governor and the distant direction of the Colonial Office in Whitehall for the maintenance of law and order. It was also responsible for the good governance of eight million people scattered over a vast, varied open area of 360,000 square miles stretching from the Great Lakes to the Indian Ocean.

At the time I arrived in the secretariat, this tiny administrative service was still 100 per cent expatriate, though by the time I left the country only 18 years later in 1973 almost the entire service had been Africanized. But that is another story. A few years earlier, women administrative assistants had been introduced to serve in the secretariat and at provincial headquarters and they played an increasingly important part in the scheme of things.

Slowly I began to see things from the territorial rather than the district point of view and my district map was replaced by one of Tanganyika. The whole vast office seemed frighteningly efficient; everything seemed to run like clockwork and the highest standards prevailed. Whenever possible, incoming letters were answered, or at least acknowledged on the same day, and woe betide the junior officer who was caught with an unanswered letter on a file a couple of weeks later.

In marked contrast to the *boma*, where the famous 'open door' policy held sway, everything possible was done to keep members of the public out of the secretariat; people with a grievance were advised to send in their complaints in writing only using the telephone as a last resort. My suggestion that we invite a German woman in Dar es Salaam involved in a complex dispute over a hotel once owned by her father, now in the possession of the custodian of enemy property, to my office to discuss the case in person, was viewed with horror.

There were compensations. My chief, Mr (later Sir) Arthur Grattan-Bellew, was an intelligent and charming man. He was a fellow Irishman descended from the great Irish statesman and orator Henry Grattan, whose statue stands to this day in College

Green, Dublin outside the old Parliament building — now the Bank of Ireland where he had his greatest political triumphs. He was the attorney general responsible for introducing new bills or ordinances as they were called locally into the legislative council, and also for criminal prosecutions in serious or difficult cases heard in the High Court.

His assistant, my immediate superior, Solicitor General Sir James Henry, was a baronet in his own right whose father, though a Roman Catholic, had been the first Chief Justice of Northern Ireland and, according to my own father, 'the handsomest man' he had ever met. His son took after him with a magnificent head like a statue hewn from granite and classical features. They were both exceptionally kind and helpful to me in every way and excellent 'role models' in the modern idiom. They worked extremely hard and demanded the highest standards in everything. Grattan-Bellew had been a Japanese prisoner-of-war while James Henry had won the Military Cross for bravery in the London Irish Rifles and later became Attorney General in Cyprus at the height of the troubles there. My own duties were concerned mainly with quasi-legal matters such as immigration, enemy aliens, custodian of enemy property and so on, and I was secretary of both the Immigration Control Board and the Immigration Appeals Tribunal — my first experience of taking the minutes of meetings.

My most macabre task was to ascertain from Mr Dawson, the commissioner of prisons, the precise times, dates and places of execution of prisoners condemned to death for murder, whose appeals for clemency had finally been rejected, and prepare black-edged death warrants for the governor's signature. Among other things, this involved, getting the grim documents stamped with the great seal of Tanganyika embossed by an extraordinary looking antiquated contraption kept under lock and key in the strongroom by the chief clerk, the redoubtable Mr Freddy Steel. He was a genial kind of clerical regimental sergeant major who ruled typing pools, dispatch sections, secretaries and clerks with a rod of iron. He had virtually run the office for a dozen or so years and was treated with great reverence by all ranks.

He was responsible for the elaborate filing system, including the red secret files, the blue confidential files and our own personal files, which we were never supposed to see. In the nature of things, files occasionally got mislaid or lost and were then listed in a vital 'lost files file'.

When that too disappeared for a few days, a real panic set in. Indeed, files could really get one down and one of my wartime predecessors in the secretariat took all the files in his office out into a motorboat one day and threw them overboard into the deep waters of the harbour. The authorities did not regard this as normal behaviour and, allied to the fact that this eccentric fellow also kept a horse in his bathroom, it was decided to retire him on medical grounds. 'Peace hath her victories no less renowned than war' — and her casualties too.

The purely legal work of the department was carried out by the legal draughtsman John Summerfield, later chief justice of Bermuda, and a brilliant team of young crown counsel, one of whom, John Samuels, had been at Wadham College, Oxford with me. Another, Paul Fifoot, was a nephew of the famous Oxford don who had given such memorable lectures on the interpretation of statutes on the first Devonshire course.

Most of my routine work was connected with immigration and I was in daily personal contact with the principal immigration officer, Mr Sinclair, an elderly, quiet, courteous man nearing retirement whose son became a celebrated humorous novelist, and his delightful assistant Charles Barrow. I used to have frequent correspondence over illegal Arab immigrants with legendary characters like Colonel Hugh Boustead, the British political agent in the Persian Gulf who was stationed in Abu Dhabi.

My charming and highly intelligent secretary Mrs Margaret Grant was a great help to me. Having worked in both the immigration department and the police special branch, she could deal with many problems by herself, leaving me merely to sign the letter. She was one of the fastest shorthand typists in the country and, like Athmani at Handeni, though on a higher level, could in an emergency take dictation straight onto the typewriter. She later became a family friend and her grandsons are my godsons.

Since my official duties inevitably concerned disputes and differences of opinion in relation to foreigners, I had to deal with the few diplomats then accredited to Dar es Salaam. Historically, the USA had always had a consul there and a consul general in Nairobi. The Belgians had a consul general (then M. van Gorp) with a consul in Kigoma because of the vital rail link with the Belgian Congo. A Netherlands consul looked after the interests of the numerous Dutch sisal planters, businessmen and missionaries.

It was nearing the culmination of a long drawn out dispute over a Dutch firm arguing with the customs over import duties that I was asked to draft a letter to the Netherlands consul for the chief secretary, the formidable Sir Robert de Stapledon, to sign. In a mischievous moment, I could not resist quoting in the letter, an old English seventeenth-century ballad dating from Admiral Blake's wars against the Dutch Admiral Van Tromp, which my father had taught me long ago. It went:

> In matters of Commerce
> The fault of the Dutch
> Is giving too little
> And asking too much!

With the benefit of hindsight I can now see that this was not a very wise, still less diplomatic, course of action, as my subsequent memorable interview with the chief secretary underlined when the fateful letter, suitably amended, was finally signed by the great man and dispatched. A few weeks later, however, my morale was restored when he congratulated me on a long paper he had asked me to prepare, which he proposed to send unaltered to the governor.

The governor, Sir Edward Twining, whom I had met upcountry, was a rather remote figure to junior officers in Dar es Salaam because his office was 100 yards away in Government House and he never set foot in the secretariat. One really only saw him on ceremonial or social occasions like the Queen's Birthday celebration or an investiture.

His minutes on the files were always typed or written in red ink so that they stood out boldly and normally ended the argument. A rather tedious problem was sent up to him one day to which to everyone's surprise he minuted laconically:

CCL

EFT

Governor.

Officials were flabbergasted, for the letters CCL did not appear in the usual civil service code, such as PA = put away, BUF = bring up on file, and FYC = for your consideration. Enquiries of His Excellency's private secretary elicited the response that CCL meant 'couldn't care less'.

Slightly more original perhaps than the old chestnut of a chief secretary minuting his comments on what he considered an absurd proposal by one of his staff — 'Round objects', to which an apocryphal governor had added: 'Who is Mr Round, and to what does he object?'

Lord Curzon, the famous Viceroy of India, had summed up a similar situation in Calcutta at the turn of the century with the delightful comment, 'Whilst not particularly interested, on the whole I agree with the gentleman whose signature resembles a trombone!'

Of such was the stuff of secretariat life — the ability to master the facts of any given situation and set out the pros and cons clearly, concisely and if necessary persuasively. Priorities were to pay great attention to detail, to have a tidy desk and a tidy mind, and have essential facts and figures at one's fingertips. One had to fit in with the rest of the government team and above all have a sixth sense about what is really urgent and what can wait.

A few administrative officers really loved the work and were born staff officers; some moved effortlessly around the world from secretariat to secretariat and often ended up as chief secretaries or even governors. Twining himself had said to me at Handeni, 'You must spend some time in the Secretariat, my boy. Or do you fancy yourself as a Sanders of the River?'

Both sides of the service were of course complementary and equally important. As with the fighting services, few officers reached the top without experience of the front line, the field and headquarters. Similarly, few officers became governors or chief secretaries without serving in several different colonies so that they could bring a wider experience and a broader vision to their tasks. Some high-flyers were also seconded to the Colonial Office or even the United Nations headquarters in New York.

Outside the office my big excitement was meeting the young president of the recently formed Tanganyika African National Union (TANU) for the first time. Julius Nyerere, then 33 years old, was a schoolteacher at St Francis College in Pugu, a top Roman Catholic secondary school in the hills west of the capital run by Irish Holy Ghost Fathers led by Father Lynch.

Julius Kambarage Nyerere was the son of Chief Nyerere of the small Zanaki tribe who lived at Butiama in the Musoma district of the Lake Province on the eastern shores of Lake Victoria. That he was the son of a chief from a small tribe was to assume great significance in the years ahead. Afters studyingt at the iGovernment secondary school in Tabora, where his headmaster was Father Richard Walsh of the White Fathers' Mission — yet another Irishman — he preceded to Edinburgh University via Makerere College of East Africa in Kampala.

He had not long returned from Scotland when he was elected the first president of TANU on its formation on 7 July 1954 — the seventh day of the seventh month, hence the Swahili symbolism of *saba saba* (seven seven) — since independence a national holiday.

So, when I first met him soon after my return early in 1955, he was still relatively unknown, and I do not recall having even heard of him when stationed upcountry. It was my old KAR friend Fraser Murray whose right arm had been so tragically blown off in my presence in 1944 who introduced me to him at the Cosy Café, just off Acacia Avenue in the centre of the city.

Fraser Murray, who had read law at Balliol College Oxford, had opened a private practice in Dar es Salaam and, being sympathetic to the cause, had been appointed TANU's legal adviser the previous year. He had told me that I must meet Nyerere — a brilliant man who would be well-known one day and he kindly invited me to supper at the Cosy Café to meet him. Run by a delightful

Indian known only as Mr Red, the Cosy Café was then one of the few public places where people of all races could mingle freely and that doubtless was why Fraser selected it for our venue.

I was instantly attracted to Julius Nyerere. His charm, warmth and intelligence, combined with passion, sincerity and a delightful sense of humour, made him an ideal champion of the African cause at that critical phase of Tanganyikan history. It was a joy to sit with him and Fraser on the veranda of the somewhat dilapidated old place in the warm African night with a faint sea breeze to keep us cool as we sipped our brandy and cokes and discussed everything under the sun until the small hours.

At that meeting, which was the first of many, I sensed that I was in the presence of a man of destiny, whom it was a great privilege to have met. I was later to have the honour of serving him for the first 12 years of his country's independence.

He so inspired me with his account of urban poverty in Dar es Salaam that a few days later, assisted by Abdullah, I started a soup kitchen outside my home in Garden Avenue in my lunch hour. Starting disappointingly with two or three beggars, it swelled to hundreds in a few weeks as news spread that some crazy *mzungu* (European) was giving out free food. I reluctantly had to call a halt to it because of police protests and diminishing funds.

When I asked him what, in his opinion, was the biggest influence on the lives of Africans in Dar es Salaam, to my surprise he replied 'witchcraft'. To this I retorted, 'No, I don't mean upcountry tribal Africans; I mean the new educated city dwellers,' to which, with a smile, he gravely answered yet again with the one word, 'witchcraft'.

We were soon on Christian name terms and my personal relationship with him was to prove a tremendous asset in the difficult years that lay ahead leading to independence and beyond.

Behind his infectious laugh and smiling eyes was an indomitable spirit totally dedicated to his country. He never found time to learn to drive a car, swim or even take a proper holiday, yet such was his zest for life and enthusiasm that he continued to make his work his hobby and relax in the midst of his labours.

Like Kipling's hero, he could 'walk with kings' without losing

156

'the common touch'. He combined the true humility, dignity and simplicity of an African chief with the intelligence and sophistication of a scholar. He was totally disinterested in wealth and the trappings of fame and never lost touch with his beloved *wazalendo* (heirs of the soil).

Soon after the failure of the soup kitchen, I began to feel the need for more active contact with African people, for the secretariat was the epitome of a colonial ivory tower, tied up with miles of red tape. Indeed, I wrote on a charming postcard with a photograph of the old German secretariat building a message to my mother dated 4 April 1955, 'This is where I spend one-third of my life!' I also told her that I hoped to spend Easter at Handeni, weather permitting.

I particularly wanted to meet young educated Africans — then mainly school certificate level, Standard 12 — since there were few graduates and few educated women around. So, I started a small discussion group of young African civil servants in their twenties who met once a week at tea time on Saturdays at my home. Their leader was a young Chagga called Henry Maeda who worked for the government chemist. Some of them brought their friends from time to time and the average attendance was about a dozen. They came for tea and stayed on for beer and sandwiches. I loved these meetings, they were the highlight of my week. I had seldom had an opportunity to meet the young intelligentsia upcountry and then only in my official capacity, so had no idea what they really thought about life in general and the move towards self-government in particular.

As I have already mentioned, some of my senior colleagues had an aversion to educated Africans, particularly those from Christian missions whom they thought less honest than Muslims and too big for their boots. They also quite sincerely felt that to socialize with locals after working with them all day put too much of a strain on their wives and families.

Even then, I thought this attitude odd given that the much vaunted aim of the British government in Whitehall and of colonial governments in East Africa and elsewhere was to educate local people and prepare them for self-government as soon as possible. The delightfully eccentric British, however, were not people to let such apparent contradictions stand in their way.

Be that as it may, the group gradually built up and met every week for the next six months or so. Always polite, very shy and diffident, if not a shade suspicious at first, they slowly unbent and began to confide their problems as individuals and as a section of the community, their hopes and dreams to each other and to me.

They were predominantly Chagga (from Kilimanjaro), Pare, and Bondei (from Tanga Province). Highly intelligent, sensitive and determined, they were the cream of Tanganyikan youth, the future leaders of a free nation. Acutely sensitive myself, I was only too conscious that my efforts to 'cultivate' these young men would be highly disapproved of in certain influential European quarters — both official and unofficial. For the latter, the 'commercials', as they were called, were more reactionary than even the most die-hard colonial official and moved narrowly between their elegant offices and homes and the Dar es Salaam Club, and the yacht and gymkhana clubs. Indeed, amazing as it may seem today, all the clubs, plus the leading hotels and restaurants were open to whites only. Even Indian potentates like the Aga Khan and the Karimjee family confined themselves to their own luxurious mansions.

At our weekly meetings everything was discussed, even danger-ous subjects like the colour bar, religion and sex. Sometimes I read a favourite poem to them and recall that they were so taken with Sir Henry Wooton's famous poem, *Character of a Happy Life*, that they insisted I translate it into Swahili for them.

I can see them now, relaxed on the veranda in their immaculate white shirts, shorts and stockings, with their bright brown eyes and intelligent faces sharing the thrill of acquiring new knowledge, sharing varied experiences, exchanging cross-cultural confidences. Their friendship and trust alike were to prove invaluable in the difficult days ahead.

For me the days of *bwana mkubwa* (Sir) were nearly over and the days of *mwenzangu* (my friend) had begun. It was not a moment too soon either, for the whole top-heavy archaic colonial superstructure designed for an earlier age slowly began to collapse.

I had planned to return to Handeni at Easter to lay the ghosts of the past and to exorcize the demons that had so grievously troubled my spirit. As Easter approached this visit became ever more important to me and, indeed, I doubted whether my recovery would ever be really complete until I had made it.

Some time before, I had bought a second-hand Morris Mini-Minor which, while suitable for running around in Dar es Salaam, was not ideal for long upcountry safaris. However, they were tough little cars, easy to handle and I had already managed to drive to Utete in the Rufiji district, more than 100 miles south of Dar es Salaam for a weekend, though not without difficulty.

However, as I planned to go to Handeni via Morogoro on the old main road — 250 or so miles each way — I did not anticipate any great difficulty. Abdulla came with me so that he could visit his family at Magamba. We had an excellent journey up, stopping for lunch at the old Acropol Hotel in Morogoro on the way. I stayed at the UMCA mission at Kideleko where I received a warm welcome from Father Neil Russell and all my old friends, the highlight being an emotional reunion with the congregation at church on Easter Day. I paid a courtesy call on my successor at the *boma*, Steve Stephenson, an old friend; nothing seemed to have changed — I might have been away for the weekend. We drove out to Magamba, repeated the hard-boiled egg routine with Zumbe Hemedi Sonyo and presented him with the *maridadi* (smart) silk dressing gown from Aden, which he at once wore as a kind of ceremonial robe. Sa'Mokiwa, the faithful retainer, brought the tea as usual. Two ladies came in and curtsied one by one; nothing had changed here either.

We discussed the usual topics, the rains and crops, the jealousies and petty intrigues of other chiefs and headmen, and the changing political situation in the country as a whole. The nascent political excitement in the capital had hardly reached Handeni district and few people had heard of Julius Nyerere. Little did they know that within half a dozen or so years Tanganyika would be an independent country and their own lives would never be quite the same again.

On Easter Monday afternoon, I set off again to return to Dar es Salaam. Accompanied this time by a Dr Harris, who was a lecturer at the School of Oriental and African Studies in London and a Swahili scholar. We had an eventful journey. Although I fully realized that the Mini-Minor was not an ideal safari car, even I was surprised when the steering wheel literally came off in my hands. The vehicle veered wildly off the road at about 50 miles an hour, jumped over a shallow drain and ploughed through a maize field for about 30 yards before mercifully coming to a halt. It was all over so quickly, we had no time to be scared. With the help of a few kind locals, my passengers and I managed to drag the car back onto the road. We were relieved to discover that no damage had been done and that everything seemed to work. We stuck the steering wheel back onto its rod and drove very slowly at about 15 miles an hour down the main road for 50 or so miles to the blessed sanctuary of a garage in Morogoro. Mechanics soon repaired the car properly so that we were safely home by the late evening. Certainly, poor Dr Harris had got more than he bargained for. I never again ventured far from Dar es Salaam in such a broken-down old yoke — as the Irish say.

Shortly afterwards, an expensive simultaneous interpreting system was installed for the Legislative Council (LegCo) in Karimjee Hall. Its laudable object was to ensure that members of the council whose knowledge of English or Swahili was limited could be fully conversant with the proceedings, which had hitherto been conducted in English only. This far-sighted move by Twining laid the foundations for extending the franchise in the run-up to elections, responsible government and ultimately independence, which was to dominate the dramatic events of the next few years. The ideal of a multiracial, multicultural, multilingual democracy was largely translated into fact during that exciting transition period.

It was also well argued that even those members who did speak English or Swahili reasonably well were happier expressing their deepest thoughts and feelings in their mother tongue.

The wheel came full circle of course when, after independence, Swahili succeeded English as the official language of Parliament and all proposed legislation was drafted and introduced in that language. Meanwhile, volunteers were called for and, after a preliminary test in the Tanganyika Broadcasting Corporation's

(TBC's) studios, I was duly selected to join the distinguished Coastal Swahili scholar Sheikh Kombo in the LegCo interpreting team. We normally worked in the late afternoons and evenings after office hours, for which we were paid a modest allowance. We occasionally worked in the mornings, as well as during the state opening of parliament, when the governor would lay down government policy for the future, and the subsequent debate on his speech.

We had a microphone each and two pairs of headphones as we listened intently and monitored each other. Ideally, each interpreter should have a reverence and love for his own language with an equal respect and love for the other, qualities equally essential in translations of written words to which Kombo and I were to turn our hands in the following year. Generally, it is slightly easier to interpret and translate from a 'foreign' language over to one's mother tongue, though this did not invariably follow.

As we gained experience, we began to enjoy this novel if arduous task, which we both found rewarding. It gave us a bird's-eye view of the rapidly changing political scene and enabled us to meet the principal players during interludes at the bar in the lovely botanical gardens in which the building was situated.

I felt I possessed a certain 'flair' for this work and enjoyed being thanked by members for helping them express themselves in their own languages and fully understand the often complicated proceedings. For the first time since my arrival in Dar es Salaam, I felt a real sense of achievement. I was thrilled when the Governor congratulated me on the Swahili interpreting in LegCo as I shook his hand on arrival at Government House for a sundowner in mid-September; he even called me by my first name when I left — a rare honour in those formal days.

In retrospect, I was lucky to be in the right place at the right time. Interpreting gave me my first real break in the secretariat and shaped my future career in Africa and elsewhere. By the end of the year I had been seconded to the public relations department, where I was to spend five of the happiest years of my life until the eve of *uhuru* in 1960. Here, as editor in chief of government Swahili newspapers, I had an opportunity to use my increasing knowledge of Swahili for Swahili radio broadcasts, lecture tours and rural publicity campaigns and, later, arranging Tanzania's participation in international exhibitions, organizing training for students overseas and film making. These activities took me from Dublin to Rome, from Prague to Tel Aviv and from Stockholm to Osaka. They continued even after my return home in 1973, for I spent the next 14 years doing publicity and fund-raising work for the Cancer Research Campaign in London.

The brilliant photographer John Mitchell-Hedges, son of the explorer, used to say when he was chief photographer to the Tanganyika government that 'he was paid for indulging in his favourite hobby'. To a lesser extent, this applied to me also, for I too was fortunate enough to be totally absorbed in a fascinating challenge, many of the responses to which I was privileged to be able to create and carry out personally. Such a dream job far transcended the normal civil service concerns with promotions, transfers, pensions, office hours and pay slips, and gave me the feeling of playing a small but vital role in shaping the destiny of a people — and a much loved people at that.

Every day was a fresh adventure; time flew by; letters from home normally unread until the evening were sometimes left until the weekend — when the week ended. So much had to be done; so little time remained — a paraphrase perhaps of Cecil Rhodes's dying words, 'So much to do, so little done.'

14

Public Relations, 1955–56

B y the end of September, Susan and the children had rejoined me and we were allocated a delightful modern bungalow on the Msasani road in Oyster Bay. It was only 200 yards from the beach and next door to our old friends the Risleys, who had so kindly had me to stay soon after my return from leave at the beginning of the year.

The pattern of my social life changed dramatically. Dropping Lucy off at the Oyster Bay school on the way to work in the morning and taking the whole family to the beach after work in the afternoon became the order of the day. This was not to speak of shopping expeditions to Reliable Stores at the Oyster Bay shopping centre to fill the boot of the car with crates of Tusker beer, in addition to other necessities. Being five miles away from the office, one's work did not revolve around one's home in the same way it had done upcountry, especially at Handeni where we had literally lived beside, if not above the shop. This meant that one could choose one's own friends to invite to the house who were not necessarily official colleagues, leading to a more relaxed life style.

We worked on Saturday mornings all the time I was in Africa, so a curry lunch on Saturday followed by a siesta and swim was a favourite means of entertaining friends. They were splendid lunches — the best I ever ate with the possible exception of war-time Ceylon. The menu seldom changed, being the usual careful balance between hot, spicy dishes and cool coconuts and fruit, supported by copious draughts of ice-cold beer.

Dar es Salaam was not only considerably hotter than the majority of upcountry stations, but also far more humid and quite uncomfortable in the hot season. Apparently it was very healthy, for sweating was said to be good for you and many of the White Fathers missionaries lived into their eighties and nineties.

On Sunday mornings we would go to the Anglican church of St Albans. It was presided over by Archdeacon Edmund Capper, a fine UMCA priest who had served much of his time in the diocese of Masasi in the Southern Province. He was awarded an OBE for his excellent work during the hurricane at Lindi while he had been archdeacon there a few years earlier. Later, before independence, he arranged for St Albans to become a collegiate church with himself as the first provost. We went to the English service, which in those days meant a mainly European congregation. A few years later, a fine modern church, St Nicholas, was built at Ilala for a largely African congregation, which celebrated the traditional Swahili Mass there. It was sited close to the existing small convent of the sisters of the CSP, one of whom, Sister Magdalen, we had known at Kwamkono in Handeni district. Susan went to stay with her for a weekend once, but complained that it was very noisy.

As Ilala was close to the centre of the African quarter of the city, with a football stadium (where the Sunderland and Young Africans' clubs played regularly), the Amana cinema and a large market, it was an unlikely setting for a convent. It had, presumably, been established in a more tranquil setting many years before.

As the children grew bigger they were able to attend the excellent Sunday school at St Albans while we were in church. On Sunday afternoons we sometimes went on picnics on beaches further afield, like Msasani Bay or the rocky fastness of Leopard's Cove on the edge of the old Msasani sisal estate.

At 7.00 a.m. on Mondays, I would set off again for the office, often accompanied by Robin Risley. We used to share our cars and the school runs so that one car could be left for our wives on alternate weeks. As the sun rose over the Indian Ocean and we drove past the white beaches of Oyster Bay through avenues of scarlet acacia, we would marvel at the cool beauty of the morning.

We dreamt of what millionaires might give to share a week in the pleasures we had free all our lives.

In the cool season, sleepy gardeners would be out with their watering cans and hoses to revive the faded flowers on the margins of dew-dappled lawns. The narrow tarmac road wound its way past Ras Kazone lighthouse, down Kingsway's line of red tiled two-storey commercial mansions and behind tall hedges of cedar or cypress. It went past the mangrove swamp, over the Selander bridge into Sea View and on to the final straight of Ocean Road, shady and cool with swaying casuarina trees. The sea and sky, calm and blue, shy white breakers caressing the rocks and the sand. Five miles in all, 15 minutes in time, few journeys to work on earth could fill one with such calm sublime feelings before tackling the tasks ahead. Even the traffic flowed smoothly only slowing down to cross the bridge.

Soon, I left my office on the top floor of the old secretariat building and moved into a little cluster of ramshackle wooden huts 50 yards or so to the north, which housed the public relations department. Nestling under the palm trees, hundreds of these temporary buildings had been erected during and just after the war to accommodate the overspill from the original German-built government buildings, as departments proliferated in response to growing demands.

The director of public relations, Ken Dobson, himself a senior district commissioner, was a tall, dark, handsome man with a shy smile and a twinkle in his eye. He was quiet, serious and conscientious. As the quintessentially English grandson of the late Victorian poet laureate Austin Dobson, one could never have imagined him doing anything mean or dishonourable. He gave me a warm welcome, though he regarded me as impulsively Irish and felt it his duty to 'rein me in' from time to time when excessive enthusiasm got the better of me. He and his brilliant wife Barbara remained good friends for many years and Susan and I used to visit them after their retirement to the quaint address of Priors, Jackass Lane, Keston, Kent.

Ken Dobson had recently been in bed for weeks with a slipped disc in his back. He still found it painful to sit down for too long at a desk, so had a high sloping wooden stand installed in his office at which he used to stand for hours on end perusing various photographs and mysterious charts and plans. He also liked conducting interviews in this position, which I found off-putting.

Jay Lennard was the deputy director. He had served in Cyprus with the famous author Lawrence Durrell who wrote *Bitter Lemons* there and was more or less a professional information officer. He was soon to be succeeded by Paul Wren, another district commissioner.

The chief press officer Alan Neville, an experienced journalist who had worked for the *East African Standard* in Nairobi, was a thin, dark, rather gloomy looking man. His highest accolade was to call someone a 'good egg'. I had a grudging respect for him after he had kicked me out of the St Albans choir during an evening service for singing out of tune.

Chief photographer John Mitchell-Hedges, whom I have already mentioned, was aided and abetted by one of the best fast bowlers in Dar es Salaam. This was the splendid bearded and turbaned Sikh called Mohinder Singh. A cheerful team of African darkroom assistants led by the diminutive and long-suffering James, who rumour had it was bawled out and even thumped occasionally by John on bad days only to be rewarded with cans of beer and sent home early when the sun shone, also helped him.

I got on very well with John and his team, nicknamed him *Simba* (lion) and teased him unmercifully, which was risky because he was a former public school heavyweight boxing champion. However, he got his own back by saying, 'Randal, as a public relations officer, you would make a damn good lavatory attendant.'

My main interest, however, was in the Swahili newspaper section run by a delightful 30-year-old Mnyamwezi from Nzega district called Joseph Yinza, to whom I took an instant liking. His chief was my old friend Mtemi Humbi Ziota of Mwakarundi chiefdom, so we had something in common. He and his team of five or six public relations assistants edited the government monthly newspaper *Mambo Leo* (Today's Affairs). It is the oldest Swahili newspaper in East Africa and was started by the education department in the 1920s soon after the establishment of the

Mandate so schoolchildren would have something interesting to read in their own language. It circulated mainly in Tanganyika, but was also read elsewhere in East Africa. It sold 60,000 copies a month for the nominal price of I think 20 cents, and was famous for its poetry, which was the main reason for its popularity.

The department also published a free Swahili weekly called *Habari Za Leo* (Today's News), which was a rather boring recital of local news. Ken Dobson made me a senior public relations officer in charge of all Swahili press and radio, and allied activities such as producing leaflets and arranging stands at agricultural shows. He said that the government had slowly begun to recognize the vital importance of the Swahili press and radio in disseminating information to the African population in the run-up to responsible government and independence, though it was not foreseen then how rapidly events were to move. This was an exciting task and one for which I felt I had been well prepared since my arrival in Mombasa on 12 December 1943, just 12 years earlier.

By the beginning of 1956 the stage was set for the countdown to *uhuru* on 9 December 1961, as the pace of change began to accelerate in a most extraordinary way. Sir Edward Twining had written soon after his arrival in 1949 that, 'Independence is not regarded as a practical possibility for at least another generation.'

The population consisted of 8,000,000 Africans, 80,000 Asians and 22,000 Europeans who had originally been represented in LegCo by four, three and seven members respectively. However, Twining's speech at the opening of LegCo on 20 April 1955 introduced equal racial representation for the first time with the *kumi* (ten), *kumi*, *kumi* formula as each race was allocated ten seats in the council. Women were also chosen for the first time. The reconstituted council consisted of the Speaker, 31 ex officio and nominated members and 30 new representative members. Adding 14 unofficials (including six members of the executive council) to 17 experienced senior officials had made up the government's strength of 31. Though rudimentary, the 1955 constitution, represented a great advance for Tanganyika and I think even Nyerere realized this as he wanted TANU to take as much advantage as possible of the chance to air its point of view in the chamber.

Another important factor had emerged. With the founding of the United Nations after the Second World War, the old League of Nations mandates were converted into UN trust territories. As such, UN visiting missions subjected Tanganyika to regular inspections. These missions paid three-yearly visits and wrote fairly critical reports, which encouraged African aspirations given that they were generally resented by the British administration, which pointed out with justification that some of their more vociferous members were drawn from states not renowned for their own good government.

While the first mission in 1948 raised a few eyebrows, the second in 1951 hardly caused a ripple. The third in 1954, led by John Reid of New Zealand but dominated by the radical views of the US member Mason Sears (who ultimately put his name to the controversial report that even the chairman refused to sign), played a vital role in the drama about to unfold. Indeed, the founding of TANU in July 1954 and the visit of the mission in September of the same year laid the foundations for the first embers of organized African political opposition to the white paternalist colonial government.

Twining had done a splendid job of putting Tanganyika on the map, attracting foreign investment and developing the economy needed for an improved infrasctucture. His good work was recognized in 1954 by a two-year extension to the usual gubernatorial span of five years. By his own standards, he now saw himself as a bit of a liberal, if not a radical. He dreamed of a multiracial state evolving slowly but surely, but with a British pilot still safely at the helm as the ship sailed into hitherto uncharted waters. He was encouraged in his views by Alan Lennox-Boyd, Secretary of State for the Colonies from 1954 to 1959, a big man the Africans nicknamed Bwana Kilimanjaro, who became a personal friend.

Both men had enlightened views on race and did much by personal example and inclination to break down the petty colour bars and outmoded social customs of the time by including Africans in all official guest lists and inviting them to stay in their own homes. Both men, however, reflected the attitudes and values of that post-war period — they were traditionalists and monarchists, as were

168

most of their administrative officers. They felt a natural affinity with the African aristocracy rooted as it was in the soil of peasant farmers and strengthened by its quasi-religious role as rainmakers and mediators between the living and the dead.

It was not surprising therefore that the original four African unoffical members of LegCo had been chiefs — Abdiel Shangali from the Hai division of the Chagga in Mount Kilimanjaro, David Makwaia from Sukumaland, Harun Lugusha from Tabora district (hereditary), and Yustino Mponda, a *liwali* (mayor) from the Southern Province. The best educated was the handsome young David Makwaia, Chief Kidaha as he was also known, who had been at Lincoln College, Oxford and spoke perfect English. Twining and many others thought he was ideally suited to bridge the gap between governors and governed.

Twining sincerely believed that his policy of multiracialism was accepted by the overwhelming mass of the people of Tanganyika. From his point of view, Nyerere and his helpers were only representative of a small minority of disaffected educated Africans living mainly in Dar es Salaam, Tanga and other towns, who would have to be either won over or broken. The chiefs, on the other hand, were part of the Establishment, were respected by rulers and ruled alike, were relatively rich in their own right and, like members of any Establishment, had a vested interest in maintaining the status quo.

The old Swahili proverb that 'the flag follows the wind' (*bendera hufuata upepo*) began to tell when even the most conservative chiefs slowly realized that there was a new spirit abroad and that things would never be the same again. Chief Tom Marealle, a graduate paramount chief of the Chagga whom Twining sent to address the UN Fourth Committee in 1957 as a counterweight to Nyerere, surprised people by asking for independence in 15 years. Nyerere himself could only ask them for independence in 12. Like the Duke of Wellington, he must have been astounded by his own moderation.

Back at the lower-level, frontline public relations department under the palm trees lining Dar es Salaam's harbour, a sense of urgency was apparent as the time-honoured unhurried routine of

169

the courteous and efficient old civil service rapidly gave way to unprecedented pressure for political change. Hitherto, the presentation of new colours to the sixth battalion of the King's African Rifles, the state opening of Legislative Council and the annual visit by a Royal Navy warship were what generated press releases in English. They were used mainly by the *Tanganyika Standard* and illustrated with excellent photographs taken by John Mitchell-Hedges and Mohinder Singh.

Indeed, the annual naval visit was the social highlight of the Dar es Salaam (cool) season. The protocol never varied. The governor and the admiral called on each other, entertained each other's officers in Government House and the wardroom, while naval teams took part for a week in a wide variety of sporting contests ashore. Salutes were fired, bands played and guards of honour were inspected. Best of all, the ship was open to the public, vast numbers of whom, children especially, swarmed aboard each afternoon for the time of their lives.

By tradition, each year John himself got up at 6.00 a.m. to take a splendid photograph of the warship coming into Dar es Salaam through the narrow harbour entrance at Kivukoni, which would duly appear prominently displayed on the front page of the *Tanganyika Standard* the next morning. I shall never forget the incredulous look on Ken Dobson's face as he picked up his paper and saw no warship. He at once sent for John and enquired angrily: 'What on earth has happened? Where is the picture of the warship?' 'No invitation to the party on board, no photograph' snapped John as he walked out of the office.

People had not only begun to criticize the government openly in increasingly strong TANU speeches across the country, but had also begun to challenge the policies themselves, calling for elections, more equitable representation and higher expenditure on African education. To add fuel to the flames, the publicity given to the report of the latest UN visiting mission meant that the government was coming under ever-increasing pressure at home and abroad to speed up progress in all directions.

To ensure that the literate population as a whole was kept democratically informed of the gist of these attacks on the govern-

170

ment and, more important, of its rebuttal where necessary, it was decided to set up an independent Swahili press and radio as soon as possible. I was given the task with faithful Joseph Yinza (who had been there for years) as my right-hand man. We rapidly recruited a team of bright young Standard 10 and 12 boys as cub reporters and got to work.

By the beginning of March we had launched a new eight-page weekly and called it *Baragumu* after the traditional Bondei cattle horn used to summon people to important meetings or to warn them in times of danger from enemies or natural disasters. It sold for 10p (one penny) and proved an immediate success throughout the country. Initially, we printed 20,000 copies a week, but this circulation rapidly increased and had risen to 30,000 a week by July — about half that of the long-established monthly *Mambo Leo*.

I have kept three of the early issues, numbers 6, 9 and 11 dated 5 April 1956, 26 April 1956 and 10 May 1956 respectively. I am glad to see that they carried the 50 per cent of advertising needed to finance newspapers. The front pages were beginning to print items of foreign news and Princess Margaret's forthcoming visit was featured on 5 April, while Kruschev's visit to England appeared on 26 April. Page 2, the leader page, contained an article (by me) under a picture of a *Baragumu* headed 'The *Baragumu* Blows'. Pages 4 and 5 consisted of a centre-page spread of about six photographs. They featured the opening of a new aerodrome at Kilwa in Southern Province, a KAR military parade at Iringa in the Southern Highlands Province and the opening of the new Voice of Tanganyika radio station in Pugu Road, Dar es Salaam respectively. Page 6 was devoted to local news items and radio programmes, page 7 to letters to the editor and the back page (page 8) to sport.

A letter from Ifakara on 10 May complained that there were not enough pages in the newspaper and he could read it all in a few minutes. An earlier letter criticized a fellow reader from Kahama district for writing a letter in English. A letter from B. V. Kantabenie of Tukuyu strongly defended TANU against an earlier attack from a reader in Bukoba, whom he warned not to talk to himself like a parrot but to consider carefully the future of his country. Referring to immigrant races in Tanganyika, he pointed out that Tanganyikans studying in the USA did not call themselves Americans. The paper was tabloid size, about 35 × 25 centimetres. These three issues of *Baragumu* faithfully mirrored Tanganyikan society in 1956 when it was poised to take off on its exciting journey into the unknown.

They carried news of Stanley Matthews, the legendary English footballer, coming to play in Dar es Salaam. They also carried a photograph of Edmund Fondo, the famous football commentator in action at the Ilala Stadium. They had photo profiles of Voice of Tanganyika radio stars David Wakati, Elli Mbotto, Steven Mlatie and the lovely Hadija, and a review of the Swahili film *Dawa Ya Mapenzi* (The Love Potion) starring Rashidi Kawawa and showing at the Empress cinema on 28 April — a world premiere. It was all there.

Soon after the launch of *Baragumu* on 1 March, we launched the first daily Swahili newspaper in Tanganyikan history and called it *Mwangaza* (Dawn). After starting tentatively with a modest circulation of 2000 a day in Dar es Salaam, it rapidly doubled and redoubled this figure to reach 8000. After I arranged to fly it to Zanzibar, Mombasa, Nairobi and even Kampala, it peaked at 10,000 copies a day. It was initially published as an evening paper at only five cents a copy. It was a four-page tabloid printed on white paper as opposed to the buff-coloured weekly.

I still have the issues of Wednesday 9 May and Thursday 10 May 1956. There was only room for a couple of pictures in each issue. The 9 May one shows the new radio station on the front page; the 10 May issue carries a photograph of Queen Elizabeth II and Winston Churchill at a Commonwealth Prime Ministers' Conference in London on an inside page. An article in *Baragumu* estimated that 250,000 people now listened to the radio, though not all of them had personal radio sets; many relied on the public loudspeakers installed in the Kariakoo market in Dar es Salaam and similar sites elsewhere. Very cheap 'saucepan radios' were now entering the local market and becoming increasingly popular.

By March, I was editor in chief of all three newspapers and of the Swahili radio news bulletins, and greatly enjoyed my new role as a journalist working round the clock. I was still interpreting in LegCo and translating all the governor's policy speeches, so I was kept pretty busy. Until then all printing was done by the Government Printer under the supervision of a wonderful Scotsman called Arnold Wylie who played the bagpipes at the Caledonian dinners on St Andrew's Day. However, pressure of work became so great there that the *Tanganyika Standard* under the direction of Nobby Clark took over the printing of *Baragumu*. I was thus rushing around town from press to press — three miles apart — at all hours of the day and night putting my papers 'to bed' and learning the arcane secrets of the 'stone' and other elements of the old-fashioned printer's lore. The type for Monday's *Mwangaza* had to be set up on the Sunday and all the proofs read and corrected, so for more than a year I worked seven days a week and loved it.

I was infected by the unique atmosphere of the printing presses and found the hustle and bustle exciting as we raced to meet our deadlines. I got to know all the printers, compositors and proof-readers personally, as well as the managers, editors, subeditors and reporters. Alan Nihill, the manager of the *Tanganyika Standard*, was a special friend. He was also president of the Irish Society and used to sing 'Paddy McGinty's Goat' at the annual St Patrick's Day dinner.

If all went well, the great moment when the wet sheets of the paper began to roll off the presses would come at around midnight. The papers then had to be folded, put together in the right order and the finished newspapers packed up and placed in waiting vans for distribution and delivery to airports, stations, news agents, shops and government departments.

Nocturnal panics sometimes ensued when copy was late or the machines broke down. For the first time I appreciated the real meaning of 'stop press'. Arnold Wylie prided himself on keeping calm and good-humoured throughout. If people became agitated he would tell them about the major in his regiment who lost his nerve during the British retreat to Dunkirk in 1940 and whose friends consoled him by saying, 'Don't worry Jock, the worst thing

173

they can do is bloody well shoot you.' This normally restored a sense of proportion.

Printers took great pride in their work and had marvellous camaraderie — they never let one down. I was privileged to work with them. The atmosphere was so electric that I never felt tired while there and shared the daily thrill of getting the paper out on time. My former secretary and friend Margaret Grant worked as a proofreader at the *Tanganyika Standard* in the evenings. She needed to earn extra money to enable her to educate her son Graeme and daughter Jean at private schools in the United Kingdom, so it was nice to work with her again and drink cups of tea in the small hours.

Perhaps I may be forgiven for quoting extracts from a letter I wrote to my parents on 7 May 1956 — the day after my thirty-second birthday — when Susan and I had been asked to dinner by the Twinings at Government House.

I was rung up by the secretary on Thursday and told that HE and Lady Twining would be very glad if Susan and I could dine with them on Sunday evening, 6 May, so I involuntarily said down the telephone, 'That's my birthday, what great fun!' That this remark was passed on to the Twinings was obvious, when they both greeted me with 'Many happy returns of the day' on entry. There were only five other guests, one young couple and three young men and I was placed on Lady Twining's right where I found a parcel on my plate which on opening was found to contain a delightful model of a giraffe about six inches tall as a birthday present from HE and Lady Twining so I was greatly honoured.

After dinner, at which I noticed five servants waiting in scarlet and gold liveries, Twining took me aside to a remote sofa in the corner of the drawing room and we had one of our 'chats' like the old days at Handeni and Lushoto and I was again carried away by his enthusiasm and inspired leadership coupled with his broad and human approach to people. He congratulated me on my work with the Swahili newspapers and on my speech at the St George's Day dinner the previous Saturday. He said he hoped to put me in a new more important job in the autumn. I would be in charge of all Swahili radio programmes and propaganda, which he said would become of 'decisive political importance in the next 12 months now that a quarter of a million Africans are estimated to listen to the wireless every evening!' He opens the new radio station, which has a more powerful transmitter, tomorrow afternoon. He said he saw no reason why I should not be put in complete control of the Swahili newspapers (which I am loth to leave) and the radio and that his advisers had recommended me as the most suitable officer for the job. He said he wanted someone who was *sympathique* and in his opinion I was.

He also said that if I agreed to take on the job I would remain in the Administration but be seconded to the new independent Tanganyika Broadcasting Corporation. However, he said he made no promises but wished to 'sound me out'. I told him as usual that I was delighted to serve where he considered I was of most use. He is very thrilled about Princess Margaret's visit and is building another wing at Government House to accommodate her. She will travel with a personal retinue of 12, including a hairdresser, two valets and three ladies-in-waiting!

All in all I had my best week for many years. This dinner came eight days after the greatest personal triumph of my life, the speech I made at the St George's dinner in Dar es Salaam, the great occasion of the year when the Governor makes his major policy speech. I was very nervous during dinner and afterwards when the Governor and two other speakers were making long speeches. When my turn came, I stood up in my tails and medals and faced the 200 guests. They included the Governor, Chief Secretary, members of the Legislative Council and heads of all the big firms. I suddenly felt in top form. To begin with, I abandoned my written speech and spoke extempore for two or three minutes. Encouraged by tremendous bursts of applause, I told some Irish stories, such as 'I dreamt that I met the auld devil and these were the words that he said: if you never will drink when you're living, how on earth can you drink when you're dead.' I ended by reading my prepared speech, which I had in any case learned by heart, and reading the second verse of The Mountains of Mourne:

> I saw England's King from the top of a bus
> And though we saw him he didn't see us.
> And though, by the Saxon, we've long been oppressed,
> I cheered him, God help me, I cheered with the rest!

I sat down to tremendous applause and the Governor and the President of the Society raised their glasses to me. I was overwhelmed by the utterly unexpected reception and tasted for a few minutes complete triumph as many I knew and many I'd never met before insisted on shaking my hand with congratulations!

I meditated on the triumphs and disasters I had met with in Dar es Salaam within the short space of two and a half years. I don't think I could ever make a speech like that again – I felt in some way inspired.

The reason I made this speech was that the presidents of the St George's (English), Caledonian (Scottish), Irish and Welsh societies of Tanganyika all customarily spoke on this occasion. I happened to be vice president of the Irish Society when the president fell off his horse the same afternoon and hurt his neck. He telephoned me at about teatime and asked me to deputize for him. Hence, my unexpected appearance. I drafted the speech in my bath, struggled into the grand clothes and drove off to the New Africa Hotel before I had time to start worrying about it. The excellent food and drink did the rest. If, as my father used to say, 'Every dog has his day' – this was certainly mine.

One of the joys of my new job was not being tied to a desk. Within limits, I could move around Dar es Salaam as much as I liked. Being not strictly confined to broadcasting studios and printing presses, I could keep a finger on the pulse by maintaining close contact with emerging TANU leaders; I made friends and influenced people as much as I could. Wherever possible, I tried to get my existing African friends and contacts from Handeni or from my little Garden Avenue study group to introduce me to their friends or to people I wished to meet. I normally took one of my trainee reporters with me and found this a great advantage because we worked as a team constantly exchanging ideas. The members of the public we approached on the street to ask their views on our newspapers were less alarmed when they saw a European apparently talking in a friendly way to a fellow African.

The Dar es Salaam taxi drivers were particular friends of mine and, like taxi drivers the world over, were avid newspaper readers and gossips. It never ceased to thrill me to see them poring over the latest issue of *Mwangaza* while waiting for a fare. They also had a delightful argot of their own, which they used to good effect when confronted by road hogs or other drivers of whom they disapproved in some way or another. One of their favourite expressions, which I sometimes copied playfully to their great amusement was *nenda zako kenge wewe* (get to hell out of it, you monitor lizard).

I dropped in regularly for a chat and a cup of tea or glass of Fanta or Coke with Julius Nyerere and his faithful followers. Their modest office was in an old house in New Street (now Lumumba Street) near the great dusty square of Mnazi Mmoja (one coconut tree originally) in the heart of the city. It reminded me slightly of the maidan in Calcutta and divided the ancient and modern cities of Mzizima and the Zanzibar Sultan's Haven of Peace.

Here stood the famous Arnautoglu community centre endowed by Greek sisal millionaire George Arnautoglu. It was run by a dynamic and popular community development officer called Jimmy McGairl, who inspired thousands of young Africans to attend a wide range of adult education classes, indoor games and Saturday night dances. Africans gave him the rare tribute of referring to his surname only with no *Bwana* in front of it. Few Europeans in those days ever ventured as far as Mnazi Mmoja and

McGairl would jokingly refer to people he knew as having never been west of Kassum's (a well-known store on the margins of the modern city).

When I called at the TANU office I was invariably greeted by a cheerful green-shirted choir of the TANU Youth League singing *mwingereza, rudi nyumbani* (Englishman go home) to a catchy tune. I often joined in to their amusement. As a friend of Nyerere's, I was always treated as an honoured guest. Indeed, never at any time during the often-tense period before *uhuru* was I ever treated there with anything less than warm friendship and courtesy.

Julius's younger brother Joseph Nyerere ran the TANU Youth League in Dar es Salaam and also became a good friend. He was an excellent tailor and once gave me a present of a shirt. Oscar Kambona, then a close friend of Nyerere and organizing secretary of the party, was often there with his cheerful assistant Elias Kisenge from the Pare district, and the redoubtable Bibi Titi, the founder of TANU's women's section who was a real firebrand and feared no man. She was widely quoted as saying in her speeches, *kila nikiona bendera ya kiingereza natapika jamaa* (whenever I see the English flag I want to vomit) — a sentiment that did not endear her to my more conservative colleagues.

It was interesting to note that as the Indian National Congress had been founded by an Englishman called John Hume — a member of the élite Indian Civil Service (ICS) in the 1880s at Bombay, so had TANU's parent body, the Tanganyika African Association (TAA). It had been founded in 1929 by no less a person than the great governor Sir Donald Cameron (1925–31) himself, when he had built the New Street House where TANU started its own activities in 1954.

We travelled widely outside Dar es Salaam to meet people, to explain our new initiative to the upcountry administration, to improve the circulation of our newspapers and, sometimes, even to write stories and take photographs ourselves. We covered the opening of the new aerodrome and pier at Kilwa in the Southern Province for *Baragumu* and did a feature on Bagamoyo, 50 miles north of Dar es Salaam, for the same newspaper. We flew to

Zanzibar, Pemba and Tanga in an attempt to extend the circulation of *Mwangaza*. While at Tanga, I called on the famous Swahili poet Shabaan Robert; he worked in the Land Office there and his superiors told me that he was extremely idle. Then a courteous man aged about 40, he always wore the traditional coastal Swahili dress of a spotlessly clean white *kanzu* with an embroidered *kisibau* and an embroidered white *kofia*.

He kindly invited me to a poetry party on the following Saturday afternoon at 4.00 p.m. This was to take place at his house by the sea at Minazini on the Pangani Road south of Tanga. It was a most memorable occasion. He lived in a traditional coastal house surrounded by sighing palms and built of wood and palm fronds. It had a cool, wide veranda that caught the sea breeze and one could hear the sound of the surf in the background. Here, about 20 poets, all young or middle-aged men, sat solemnly drinking sherbet and eating *mandazi* (cakes) while they took turns to stand up and chant their beautiful classical Swahili poems, in the same way that Elizabethan poets chanted theirs.

The Swahili people are renowned for their poetry, which is unequalled by that of any other people in Africa. There are large numbers of poems written in Swahili, mostly in the Arabic script, but in modern times also issued in booklets printed in Roman. There are many long poems, some of them written as early as the eighteenth century. Some are epics in the Utenzi metre (four lines of eight syllables), the longest comprising thousands of stanzas. Many describe heroic deeds of past wars. Some have a distinctly religious bias, for Swahili culture is Islamic and largely confined to the coastal cities of Zanzibar, Dar es Salaam, Tanga, Mombasa, Malindi, Lamu and Kilwa, where the purest Swahili is spoken. There is a slight difference between the Swahili spoken in Zanzibar and Mombasa. Poets are found among the common people on the East African coast who celebrate their daily lives with the topical verse that appears in *Mambo Leo* and is usually composed in response to daily events. It is normally written in short stanzas of four-line quatrains in the *shairi* (poem) metre of 16 syllables, and can often be written in stanzas of only three lines.

Shabaan Robert's poetry party gave me the idea of getting

Mambo Leo to sponsor a poetry competition in honour of Princess Margaret's visit to Tanganyika later in the year. The subject would be to welcome the Princess and the winner would not only receive the then princely sum of £25 but would also have the honour of reading his or her poem aloud to the Princess in the Arnautoglu Hall. The winner would also personally present it to her — complete with English translation afterwards.

I was thrilled when one of my young reporters, Kitwana Chumu, an 18-year-old Standard 10 Mzaramo boy from the seaside village of Mji Mwema (Good Town) a few miles south of Dar es Salaam over the Kivukoni ferry, warmly invited me to spend a weekend at his home. It was an almost unprecedented invitation at that time. With Susan's understanding agreement, and not without some slight trepidation, I duly set off.

Kitwana and I set off after work on a Saturday afternoon bound for the idyllic fishing village of Mji Mwema. It was only about ten miles away and not far from Mboa Maji where Susan and I had stayed at Mr Smith's little beach hotel on local leave from Kasulu towards the end of 1949 — seven years earlier. On arrival at the village at about 2.00 p.m., we were given a warm welcome by a curious but very polite crowd of villagers, including many children. Kitwana's father Mzee Chumu was the muezzin of the village mosque whose duty it was to call the faithful to prayer five times a day and, as such, he was able to get away with inviting an *mzungu* guest. I was in fact the first European ever to be invited into an African home there.

Chumu introduced me to his wife and to several boys and girls all younger than Kitwana. We sat down to the midday meal on the veranda of the traditional Swahili house with a roof of palm leaves and a courtyard in the rear. We had rice and fresh fish from the sea, caught that morning, followed by oranges and coconuts. We ate with our right hands in the usual manner and they laughed at me because I found the rice so hot that I took a long time to finish my meal. After lunch we went for a long and refreshing swim with the village boys followed by a trip to the coral reef in the family *ngalawa*. I had seldom felt so completely relaxed and happy.

In the evening, Kitwana took me to the Seaman's Bar where I

stood the cheapest round of drinks in my life — 20 Tangawizi (local ginger drinks) for a shilling. In African households at that time, the men and women ate separately and the children waited on their parents. Naturally, the boys and girls slept in different little dormitories; indeed the teenage girls were more or less shut up and used to stare at me with shy smiles from their tiny window.

Taking no chances, I had brought my own camp bed, which I managed to squeeze into a corner of the boys' bedroom beside the faithful Kitwana and his brothers on their brightly coloured purple and yellow sleeping mats. Fanned by the warm sea breeze and lulled by the waves, we slept like logs. I was slightly embarrassed by the apparent complete absence of any lavatory facilities, but soon realized that the Indian Ocean itself was the local loo to be entered individually, invisibly in the decent obscurity of the night.

After an early morning swim with Kitwana at 6.00 a.m. in the cool waves emblazoned by the soft colours of the shy sunrise, I washed and shaved in the courtyard. I had a fairly basic shower bath by mixing the boiling water from one *debe* (four-gallon drum) with the cold water from another by means of a kind of large ladle called locally a *kwata*. I would pour the result over my head, not always very satisfactorily to the obvious amusement of my unseen giggling audience.

Another long sleepy day ensued doing nothing and doing it well, as they say in Ireland. We swam, ate, talked and attended a preliminary *ngoma* before a circumcision ceremony. I felt quite put out when a yacht with some rather boozy, scantily-clad Europeans on board trespassed into our sea space and shattered its Arcadian tranquillity with their loud music.

As always, I was glad to get home to the family and the relative luxury of our government bungalow. By now, the archaic liquor laws, a survival of the nineteenth-century Congo Basin treaties, had long been abolished and district officers no longer had the humiliating duty of issuing patronizing permits to enable 'educated' Africans to buy liquor in public places. It would still take a few years, however, before most Africans felt at ease in the grander European hotels like the New Africa. The 'sacred' English clubs — a uniquely British institution — were for the most part still confined to Europeans, if not Anglo-Saxons, for excellent Italian and Greek clubs were established during this period.

It was then that I discovered the Princess Bar at the south end of Mnazi Mmoja and proceeded rather gingerly at first to entertain my reporters and other African friends there in a relaxed convivial atmosphere. At first, I too felt strange and out of place there, often the only white person present, and knew what it was like to be stared at and subjected to a quizzical or disapproving gaze. However, I knew it was my duty to overcome these racial barriers and, as usual, as one begins to get to know people and make friends, their colour fades away. Now that the 'boot was on the other foot' I had a far greater understanding of the plight of the Africans catapulted into alien cultures at home and abroad, often patronized, snubbed and sadly sometimes even insulted by rude or ignorant Europeans.

My knowledge of Swahili was a priceless asset; without it I doubt whether I would have ever come to be accepted in the Princess Bar and elsewhere in downtown Dar es Salaam. Again and again, a proverb, a joke, a riddle or even quotation from a popular song or poem would defuse a potentially touchy situation when the conversation — fuelled by alcohol — had turned to a delicate political issue.

Very occasionally, I too was abused or insulted. I remembered the old golden rule — 'never lose one's temper' — and left it to my companions to silence my tormentors. *Subira huvuta heri* (patience brings happiness) and many other equally wise Swahili proverbs, on which I was brought up in Africa, have stood me in good stead all my life and I still find myself muttering them when the underground train breaks down in London.

My first visit to Zanzibar since stopping there briefly in 1948 *en route* to Dar es Salaam was delightful. Sheikh Yahya Alawi, the information officer, was enthusiastic about the distribution of *Mwangaza* and *Baragumu*, which were already popular there and he took me around the town and showed me the sights. These included the Beit-el-Ajaib (Palace of Wonders), which housed the secretariat where Sultan Barghash had installed the first lift in

Africa in the 1860s (still clanking along well), the Stone Town, the Sultan's palace with its beautifully carved wooden doors, and Livingstone's house.

I called on Father Tom Dix, the UMCA priest there, who showed me around the beautiful cathedral built in coral by Bishop Steere, the famous Swahili scholar, towards the end of the nineteenth century on the site of the old slave market. The unusual barrel vault roof is quite an achievement for a non-architect.

Sheikh Alawi also took me to tea with the Arab nationalist leader of the Zanzibar Nationalist Party (ZNP), Sheikh Ali Muhsin. He was a charming and scholarly man who lived in a country villa with a garden surrounded by a stone wall. He had been partly educated in Paris and was the founder and editor of the Swahili newspaper *Al-Falaq* (Dawn).

In the Beit-el-Ajaib I called on the British administrative secretary Lord Oxford and Asquith, a descendant of Prime Minister Asquith, and was amused to note that the hereditary peerage was represented in the colonial service. The whole island smelled of cloves, which, combined with the fragrant sea breezes, made a heady elixir. The old Sultan Seyyid Khalifa drove out of his palace gates every evening in his red Rolls-Royce for a short tour of the surrounding countryside, politely applauded by a group of his subjects. The Al-Busaid dynasty from the Gulf state of Oman, of which Muscat was the capital, had ruled Zanzibar since Sultan Seyyid Said had established a cool summer residence there in 1833. For centuries, Zanzibar had been a great Arab trading centre and headquarters of the notorious slave trade where Indian and Persian traders also played a key role.

British influence too had slowly been gaining ground during the second half of the nineteenth century. Incursions into the East African mainland had culminated in the establishment of the British East Africa Company, the protectorate and the construction of the Uganda railway, immortalized by the book *The Maneaters of Tsavo*. A consulate was opened in Zanzibar and the famous consul Sir John Kirk helped the missionary explorer David Livingstone prepare for his last African journey.

In 1890, a British protectorate was formally declared and a

183

British Resident appointed. Even after Kenya became a crown colony, a ten-mile coastal strip remained part of the Sultan's dominion and the British government paid him a token annual rent for the lease of it — a sum still paid to his unfortunate descendant in exile in England today.

I flew north for 20 minutes or so to the spice island of Pemba — also in the Sultan's dominions though ruled by a British district commissioner — where the scent of the cloves was almost overpowering; the entire island was one vast clove estate. It was also, as I mention earlier, famed for its university of witchcraft. It felt delightfully rural after the over-heated urban sophistication of Zanzibar, where Arabs from Oman and Persians had settled as long ago as AD 1200. I spent a night at the resthouse at Chake Chake, the main town on the west coast not far from the *boma*.

Back in Dar es Salaam after my coastal newspaper safari, I found excitement growing over the Suez crisis, which dominated global politics in 1956. Earlier in the year, dynamic young Egyptian revolutionary President Gamal Abdel Nasser, a tall handsome man idolized by almost the entire Arab world, had done the unthinkable and nationalized the Suez Canal. The Western world was left completely stunned by his audacity. At the same time, it thrilled and encouraged the Arabs, to a lesser extent the Africans and, I suspect, subject peoples everywhere.

It was certainly the first major outside event to grip the imagination of the African population and hence our Swahili readers. Circulation of the newspapers increased considerably and I worked late at night to translate British Prime Minister Anthony Eden's speeches during the climax of the Suez crisis, which coincided with the Hungarian rising against communist rule in Budapest, brutally suppressed by the Red Army.

British, French and Israeli armies and air forces had unwisely invaded Egypt in an attempt to win back control of the canal. However, this highly controversial operation was hurriedly abandoned after a few days in the face of unexpected combined Russian and US diplomatic pressure, with a great 'loss of face' all round.

If the fall of Singapore to the Japanese in 1942 had heralded the collapse of the British Empire, then the ignominious withdrawal from Suez in 1956 must surely have been the coup de grâce. I certainly felt at the time that things could never be quite the same again, and one could sense a definite change in the mood of people in Dar es Salaam. They had begun to realize that their erstwhile imperial masters had feet of clay.

The young bloods in the city, the famous *wahuni* (hooligans), the local equivalent of the teddy boys of London or tsotsis of Johannesburg but rather gentler than either, incorporated the Suez Canal into their racy local slang. They did this with such expressions as *alani* (hello), *taabu tu* (nothing but trouble) *nalia mfereji mkuu wa Suez* (I am crying for the great canal of Suez) *taabu tu*. A sexual innuendo is included in the double entendre. Another example of this argot was a young housewife saying to her friend, Alani. *Taabu tu! Mume ninaye akili hana. Taabu tu!* (I've got a husband but he has no sense. It is such a problem) — and so on *ad infinitum* — the great verbal craze raged in the bars, squares and alleys of the vibrant city.

15

Star of Freedom, 1956

After several months of feverish preparations, the Queen's younger sister Her Royal Highness Princess Margaret duly sailed into Dar es Salaam harbour in the royal yacht *Britannia* on Monday 8 October 1956. It was the first royal visit since the end of the Second World War and, as such, was eagerly awaited. It was carefully planned so that the Princess could meet as many people as possible. In fact, during the 11 days of her visit before leaving for Nairobi on 18 October, she travelled nearly 2000 miles by land and air and saw or was seen by over half a million people on ceremonial occasions and official tours.

In a sense, her visit crowned Sir Edward Twining's distinguished governorship and finally put Tanganyika on the map. At the same time it gave Africans the romantic dream that she had been sent by the Queen as a herald of forthcoming independence, which they felt could hardly now be long delayed. This view was epitomized by the 28-verse winning poem in the competition in her honour, entitled *Mtukufu Margaret* (Her Royal Highness Princess Margaret), the last line of each verse of which repeats the refrain, '*Karibu mwenye nemsi nyota ya uhuria*' (Welcome your Royal Highness star of freedom).

The first day of the visit was an undoubted success. The entry of the royal yacht into Dar es Salaam harbour was spectacular. The *Britannia* sailed slowly past thousands of cheering schoolchildren on the beaches at the harbour entrance. It was escorted by two warships, a flotilla of yachts from the yacht clubs and by *ngalawa* (outrigger canoes) and *mashua* (rowing boats) from Msasani and

186

other coastal fishing villages — all gaily bedecked in brightly coloured flags, pennants and palm fronds.

At precisely 10.00 a.m. the yacht was safely tied up at the new deep-water berths the Princess was shortly to open. While the bands of the Royal Marines and the King's African Rifles played and the 21-gun salute boomed, the Governor and Lady Twining went aboard to greet her. After naming the new berths the Princess Margaret Quay, the Princess drove off on a ceremonial drive through the streets of the capital to Government House. Any nascent fears that her welcome might be less than enthusiastic were soon dispelled as 100,000 people lining the beautifully decorated streets supported by at least 60 *ngoma*s gave her a memorable welcome.

A state banquet at Government House on the Monday evening was followed by a royal *baraza* at 11.00 a.m. the next day at the old airport on Kilwa Road south of the city attended by a record crowd of 60,000 people. The old *liwali*, the traditional Afro–Arab mayor of Dar es Salaam, made the first address of welcome and presented Princess Margaret with a beautifully carved old Arab camphor wood chest. There were then more speeches and presentations of gifts. These included a trumpet and a royal stool from the local Wazaramo tribe, a prayer mat, initiation drums, a lovely silver carved Arab dagger (*jambia*), a tray and a ceremonial mask from the people of the Southern Province who were represented here. Her Royal Highness was sadly unable to visit every single province in the short time available. I attended the *baraza* and was presented to the Princess in my somewhat unusual role as vice president of the Irish Society of Tanganyika.

Tim Harris, the district commissioner of Dar es Salaam, played a major part in planning and organizing the royal tour in Dar es Salaam in general and the royal *baraza* in particular. I first met him at Wadham College, Oxford, of which he was also an alumnus, and he visited me there on his leave in spring 1947 when I was on the first Devonshire course. Tim, who had been invited to a private lunch at Government House, had been so taken with the youthful beauty and charm of the Princess that he told me he was 'torn between his lust and his patriotism'.

It was he who told me how two very senior officers had invited him to dine at the Dar es Salaam Club with their wives who were so boring, complacent and snobbish that he 'suddenly felt an overwhelming desire to jump on the table and shout "bugger"!'

The district commissioner of Kisarawe, Trevor Griffith-Jones, was also present and in charge of his tribesmen who had descended in force from the Pugu hills west of Dar es Salaam. He too was an old friend and at one time our next-door neighbour in Oyster Bay. The royal visit was a newspaperman's dream and the first challenge to our recently established Swahili press, not to mention the international press corps of more than 50 strong. Our small staff, superbly assisted by the printers, responded magnificently, working round the clock to produce special editions (*toleo maalum*) of the newspapers, all three of which broke their circulation records. These special editions were lavishly illustrated by John Mitchell-Hedges's and Mohinder Singh's marvellous photographs and the front-page headlines surmounted by two crowns.

The highlight of the Princess's visit to the Arnautoglu Hall on the morning of Thursday 11 October was the Swahili poetry competition run by the monthly *Mambo Leo* in honour of her visit. More than 700 entries were received from all over Tanganyika, many of quite outstanding quality judged by a select panel of experts under the chairmanship of the great uncrowned poet laureate Shabaan Robert. A young Tanga fisherman called Mwidau Ulenge won first prize with his heroic 28-verse poem to which I have already referred. He was unanimously judged to be the winner of the 500-shilling prize with the honour of reciting it in person to the Princess and presenting it to her afterwards.

Sheikh Kombo, my colleague in the LegCo simultaneous interpretation box, and I were given the tough task of translating the poem into English so that Her Royal Highness would have at least some idea of what it was about. We both found it an exciting and challenging test and it kept us busy for several hours a day for a week. However, we derived a great deal of satisfaction from the result, which, together with the original, was beautifully printed in gold letters on white vellum and presented to the Princess by the proud young writer after he had chanted his poem to the some-

188

what bemused young lady. She had of course followed the English version on a more modest copy and the recitation made in deep silence was received with rapturous applause and the obvious delight of the Princess on its conclusion. It took about a quarter of an hour to read and the hundreds of guests, including the press, were suitably impressed.

The next morning's English *Tanganyika Standard* carried the story on its front page under the inch-deep headline 'Ode to a Lovely Princess'. The African intelligentsia were astonished that such a young unknown could have produced the brilliant winning poem; it was even unkindly suggested that the poem had been written by Shabaan himself, who had been unable to compete because he was chairman of the judges. Given the tradition of anonymity in Swahili poetry, this theory is not that far-fetched. None the less, I prefer to think of this lovely twenty-fourth verse being conjured up under the stars by a young fisherman dreaming of romance and distant lands:

Beti mia za ndorosi, Ningekupa maulia,	A necklace of a hundred verses I would have given you in queenly style,
Za upeo wa ususi, Katika kutunga nyia,	In composing innumerable songs.
Kila mrembo Paris, Wivu angekulilia,	Every bejewelled Parisian would be jealous of you.
Karibu mwenye nemsi, nyota ya uhuria.	Welcome, Your Royal Highness, Star of Freedom.

This poem takes pride of place in Shabaan Robert's anthology *Almasi Za Afrika* (African Diamonds) published in Tanga four years later.

The next morning the Princess left Dar es Salaam to tour other parts of the territory, which of course our newspapers continued to cover. Her flight round the country started with the Southern Highlands Province, where she attended a *baraza* at the provincial capital Mbeya. The next day, *en route* to the picturesque capital of the east Lake Province Mwanza, she stopped off for a midday *baraza* at Tabora, my old provincial headquarters in Western Province. At a spectacular *baraza* in Mwanza, she watched a wide variety of tribal dances and processions of snake charmers, as well as other traditional ceremonies that included parades of porcupines and pythons.

There was also a splendid nocturnal regatta of 100 illuminated canoes on Lake Victoria at Mwanza, which featured in an excellent illustrated article in our weekly paper *Baragumu*.

While in the Lake Province, the Princess lunched at the Mwadui diamond mine with its owner and discoverer, the reclusive Canadian geologist Dr Williamson who had presented the Queen with a superb diamond as a wedding present. From Mwadui, she flew on to Arusha, capital of the Northern Province, where she stayed at the charming little Governor's Lodge. After more *baraza*s with the colourful Masai and Wa-arush tribesmen, she continued on to Moshi, 50 miles away by road. She entered the great Chagga vastness of Mount Kilimanjaro — at 19,314 feet Africa's highest mountain (the shining mountain) covered with eternal snow — to be greeted by the *mangi mkuu* (paramount chief) Thomas Marealle. She then left for Nairobi and her tour of Kenya.

16

A Tale of Two Cities: Dublin
and Rome, 1956–57

lthough the royal visit had no immediate political results apart from the general sense of peace and wellbeing it engendered, in retrospect it somehow seemed to have rung a bell for the last leap to independence. At all events, from then on the pace of political progress accelerated remarkably, aided and abetted in no small measure by the increased readership of Swahili newspapers and the growing popularity of broadcasting.

Ironically, though the more conservative colonial establishment originally conceived of Swahili newspapers and radio as weapons to counter TANU propaganda and set the record straight by clarifying government policy and recording government achievements in the best possible light, as often happens it had the opposite effect. The British tradition of a free press shone through to some extent, even with a paternalistic government, and I did all I could to encourage our readers to express their views in the correspondence columns and to report TANU political speeches as objectively as possible. In this approach, I was greatly assisted by the failure of most of my immediate superiors fully to comprehend the mysteries of colloquial Swahili and the fast changing urban slang so fashionable in those days.

Indeed, my linguistic hobby — for such it was — was an enormous advantage at that time, for it enabled me not only to deal with African politicians and trade unionists, but also to establish my own credentials as an expert in revolutionary African politics, especially in Dar es Salaam. I was asked to represent the chief secretary at all TANU meetings in Dar es Salaam between 1956 and 1960. I had to intercede with the general secretary of the Postal Workers Union, the fiery J. D. Namfua who was planning a Christmas strike; and visit the Tanganyikan students at Makerere University in Kampala who were allegedly disaffected.

Early in 1957, I set off for Uganda, visiting Mwanza and Bukoba *en route*. For the first time, I sailed across the great inland sea of Lake Victoria Nyanza. It took about 12 hours and when the wind blew it got quite rough, which surprised me. The Bukoba administration lent me a Land Rover with a driver who took me to Kampala, stopping briefly at Masaka on the way. Makerere, the University College of East Africa and at that time its only university, was on eye-opener. I had never before seen hundreds of young East African students concentrated in one place with such splendid buildings and facilities situated in lovely grounds on a hill outside Kampala — like Rome built on seven hills. Most of them then were young men turned out in blazers, ties and white shirts, who wore the scarlet gowns of their parent university, St Andrew's in Scotland, during lectures and meals.

I spent a few pleasant days there staying in one of the student halls of residence. I had a chance to get to know some of the Tanganyikan students informally, in addition to the more formal meeting that had been arranged in a lecture room one afternoon to enable them to air their grievances. For the first time, I met the leading Chagga artist Sam Ntiro, then a lecturer in the arts department and later to become Tanzanian high commissioner to London. He introduced me to his clever young Chagga pupil Elimo Njau, whom I found charming and amusing. Mrs Trowell had built up an outstanding art school at Makerere and I spent a fascinating afternoon being shown round by her and seeing some of the original impressionist style paintings and sculptures on display. The Ugandan sculptors were particularly outstanding. Sam Ntiro arranged for me to meet Dr Wilfred Chagula, a cheerful Msukoma from the Lake Province — another lecturer destined to become vice-chancellor of the University of Dar es Salaam.

A Tale of Two Cities: Dublin and Rome, 1956–57

A friendly Mhaya student from the Bukoba district who occupied a neighbouring room kindly acted as my 'bear leader'. He accompanied me to meals and one evening took me out with some of his friends to the Hollywood nightclub in Kampala. His name was Michael Ngirwamungu. On my return journey, he asked me to give him a lift to his home village near Bukoba and try to explain to his old father, a peasant coffee farmer, why he needed about 200 shillings each term to meet his minimum college commitments, which I duly did. About 15 years later, I had the sad duty of helping to carry him, badly injured, out of a terrible car crash near my house in Oyster Bay and rushing him to hospital in my car, only to find him dead on arrival. He himself was a doctor.

Back at Makerere in 1957, I met Tanganyikan students for a couple of hours and heard their complaints, which, as with students everywhere, were mainly about money and their inadequate allowances. I think there were about 100 or so present, but I do not suppose all of them came.

I started off with a short introductory talk in Swahili. This appeared to amaze them, but it gave me a psychological advantage and enabled me to make my meaning crystal clear, which is essential when money matters are under discussion. I reckoned that if after 14 years in East Africa I did not speak Swahili far better than they could speak English, then I should not be where I was.

I listened, I hope patiently and sympathetically, to their various points, which I promised to bring to the attention of the chief secretary and the director of education in Dar es Salaam on my return. We then had a frank exchange of views on political matters and they ended by bemoaning the lack of higher education opportunities overseas for Tanganyika students. I replied impulsively that I was shortly going on leave to Dublin and would see if I could get any scholarships for them there.

Until that moment, when I was inspired by the enthusiasm of the cream of Tanganyikan youth, I had not thought much about higher education abroad. I saw it more as a matter for the education department. On thinking about it, however, I felt that seeking scholarships in Ireland would be an interesting 'holiday task', for our inordinately long vacation leaves could at times become a bit

193

boring. Also, as far as I knew, no Tanganyikan had ever studied in Ireland, though Trinity College had a long tradition of teaching Nigerian students.

I felt that it would be courteous to inform the education department of my intentions and, though they seemed less than enthusiastic, they grudgingly agreed to my proposals. In retrospect, their attitude seems eminently reasonable, for they must have thought of me as an interfering outsider. At least, they did agree to most of the students' requests, which I relayed to them and considerable increases were duly made to their grants and allowances, which was the main thing.

It seemed shameful that Ireland — my native land — had done so little for African students. I hastily conferred with my compatriot Father Richard Walsh, the education secretary for the White Fathers in Dar es Salaam, who was enthusiastic and supportive. As headmaster of St Mary's Roman Catholic secondary school in Tabora, he had been Julius Nyerere's headmaster and had been a tower of strength to him in the formative stages of his career.

He suggested I consider approaching Dr John Charles McQuaid the formidable Roman Catholic archbishop of Dublin and ask him for help and advice. He added jokingly that no Catholic, not least a priest, would dare go near him but, as a Protestant, I might just pull it off.

Arriving in Dublin in midsummer after a short stay with Susan's family in Gloucestershire, England, I lost no time putting this rather ambitious project into action. My father's old friend Lord Wicklow, who had so kindly helped me to arrange a retreat at Glenstal Abbey three years earlier, now arranged for me to meet the Archbishop in his palace at Drumcondra.

My own family kindly introduced me to General Sir Charles Harvey, assistant managing director of Guinness, which was by far and away the richest and most important company in the Republic of Ireland at that time. He invited me to lunch in the director's dining room at the St James' Gate brewery. I started with Guinness and, fortified by an excellent lunch of salmon and stout, found Sir Charles a sympathetic listener. Before going to see him I had prepared a memorandum on the importance of higher education for Africans in Western countries, which I had sent in advance to both him and the Archbishop. His board had already considered the memorandum and I was thrilled when Sir Charles told me before I left that the company had agreed to offer five scholarships for African students from Tanganyika. Each was worth £300 per annum, one to be given each year for five years and tenable at Trinity College, Dublin and University College, Dublin alternately.

Emboldened by this success, a week later I went to see the Archbishop. On being ushered into his book-lined study, I felt apprehensive when he asked me to sit down and said, 'Well, Mr Sadleir, what can I do for you?' I expanded a little on the views already expressed in my memorandum, stressing the urgent need to educate African Christians in the West, rather than leave the field wide open to the highly efficient communist proselytisers of eastern Europe. I ended by telling him of the wonderful work done by Irish missionaries in general and by the Holy Ghost Fathers at St Francis College at Pugu in Tanganyika in particular. I also told him in passing of the generous offer made by Guinness.

He replied at once that he would give a scholarship worth £400 per annum to University College, Dublin forever. Not only that, he would send me to Rome in August with an introduction to his friend Sir Marcus Cheke, the British minister to the Holy See, with a request that he arrange for me to see the Pope. He said he felt that the issues raised in my memorandum were of great importance and should be studied by the Vatican; he sent Sir Marcus Cheke a copy of the memorandum, which he asked him to get translated into Italian and sent to the cardinal secretary of state.

I got on very well with Archbishop McQuaid, who had a great sense of humour beneath his grave, austere exterior, greying dark hair, sallow ascetic face and piercing eyes. He seemed amused at my cheek in going to see him at all. I could not resist telling him that my great-great grandfather, Provost Franc Sadleir of Trinity College, had been a close friend of the then Roman Catholic Archbishop Murray who had invited him to preach in the Catholic pro-cathedral in about 1845, the only Protestant clergyman ever to do so. He looked suitably amazed.

I also visited both universities, which welcomed the plan warmly and promised full cooperation. They also agreed to provide a substantial number of other places for Tanganyikan students should funds be forthcoming. The Dublin newspapers gave excellent publicity to the scheme under the headline 'Irish scholarships for Africans'. The *Irish Times* carried a photograph of Sir Charles Harvey with the caption, 'Sir Charles Harvey, Assistant Managing Director of Guinness in Dublin, who organized the company's participation in the new scholarship schemes whereby African students from Tanganyika will be able for the first time to attend universities in Ireland.'

This 'holiday task' gave me a great sense of satisfaction in that, in some small way, it brought together two of the great loves of my life — Ireland and Tanganyika.

I duly set off for Rome where Father Walsh had kindly arranged for me to stay at the headquarters of the White Fathers — Padri Bianchi — on Via Aurelia close to the walls of the Vatican palace. There I found a letter awaiting me from Sir Marcus Cheke, who not only gave me a splendid lunch but also arranged for me to attend a semi-private audience with Pope Pius XII. This was to be held at his summer palace of Castel Gandolfo in the Alban hills outside Rome, to where he retreated in the 'dog days of August' to escape the heat.

After lunch, Sir Marcus gave me a lift back to the White Fathers in his Rolls-Royce with the Union flag flying, which I much enjoyed. The next day, escorted by one of the White Fathers, I drove out to Castel Gandolfo in the late afternoon for the papal audience. There were perhaps 100 of us all told arranged around a first-floor balcony with a superb view of the lake and hills. The Pope, a frail, ascetic looking old man in white, came out of a central door about 20 yards away from us, said a few kind words of welcome in several different languages including English, blessed us and left. It was all over in about ten minutes.

Before I continued my journey back to Dar es Salaam, I had a private meeting in the Vatican with the acting secretary of state Cardinal dell'Acqua. He said that, had it not been August, the Pope would have granted me a private audience; he apologized for being such an inadequate substitute. I enjoyed penetrating the labyrinthine mysteries of the legendary palace and being escorted by Swiss guards with pikes down interminable corridors.

Cardinal dell'Acqua kindly arranged for me to visit the Tanganyikan seminarists at the Propaganda Fide College in Rome, which, propagating the faith internationally, trains young men for the priesthood from the four corners of the earth. It is sad to think that the infamous Nazis distorted the noble Christian concept of spreading the faith in such a twisted manner as to give it a pejorative meaning ever since. The young budding priests were delightful and gave me a warm welcome as they proudly showed me round the college and invited me to their rooms. I met one or two of them a few years later after they had returned to Africa as ordained priests.

Back in Dar es Salaam, I received a warm welcome from Father Walsh and TANU, a letter of congratulation from the Governor and the splendid news that Christopher Kahangi and Maulidi Ntamila had been awarded the first Dublin scholarships to University College and Trinity College respectively. The crusade had begun.

17

The Cock's Trousers: A Northern Dream, 1957–58

I already had a general love for Tanganyika, but was about to
develop a particular affection for the Wachagga who lived on
the lower slopes of Mount Kilimanjaro, which I had first
gazed at in wonder from the top of the New Stanley Hotel in
Nairobi soon after arriving there as a soldier in December 1943.
The British regarded them, with the Baganda in Uganda and
Kikuyu in Kenya, as one of the most intelligent tribes in East
Africa. Strangely, this view was attributed to the banana being the
staple diet for all three peoples; indeed, the Chagga were said to
cook it in 50 different ways, not to speak of the excellent drink
mbege made from it.

Be that as it may, I incline to the view that, unlike the majority
of their fellow men, these three peoples have the good fortune to
live in cool, green, fertile lands with excellent rainfall and an
assured water supply. Food grows in abundance there and their
gentler environment is more conducive to the leisure that is an
essential prerequisite to cultural pursuits. All three had thus been
able to develop widespread cultivation of coffee and the resultant
cash had made them relatively prosperous — hence their predom-
inance among students at Makerere and elsewhere.

Therein hangs a tale that for me had always epitomized the
spirit of the Chagga people. Soon after being posted to the
Northern Province as the first provincial public relations officer
(PRO) in September 1957, I was invited to spend a night in a

village in Machame on the western slopes of the mountain by one of my small staff called Alfred Moses. It was a Saturday night and, encouraged by my happy visit to Mji Mwema, I readily accepted, and again brought my own camp bed. There could hardly have been a greater contrast from the sleepy coastal village. I snuggled down under three blankets near the embers of a campfire and slept soundly to the music of running water and the breeze in the banana groves. At 6.00 a.m., Alfred's mother woke me up and handed me a wooden mug brim full of home brewed *mbege*. When I expressed surprise at the early hour of this unexpected sunriser, she replied with the immortal remark: 'The cock hasn't put his trousers on before the Chagga starts drinking.' This quizzical comment was an allusion to the traditional African 'clock', whereby the first cockcrow — at about 4.00 a.m., was followed by the second cockcrow at 5.30 just before dawn. It compared well with one of Tolstoy's peasant characters in War and Peace who says to his cunning neighbour, 'I can see right through you, and six feet under you.'

With people like these, one can understand why the Northern Province with only four districts — Arusha, Masai, Mbulu and Moshi — possessed a far greater influence than its size and population would suggest. Within its boundaries were some of the most advanced and backward people in the territory, ranging from the Chagga and the Meru to the Masai, Wa-arush, Iraq and Sandawe — the latter living entirely from hunting and collecting honey, nuts and berries. Their primitive clicking language was difficult to understand. They lived in the hilly Mbulu district to the south at Babati where a Masai-like pastoral people, the Barabaig, also dwelt. The main tribe, the Iraq was a handsome race with such slender figures that it was difficult to distinguish between the males and females. They claimed to have trekked south from the Middle East many hundreds of years before and their language was unusual in having totally different stems for singular and plural, for example *he* (man), but *rho* (people).

To these ethnic curiosities were added a colourful collection of European settlers attracted by the excellent climate, fertile soil and beautiful scenery. Many of these settlers grew coffee in Arusha and to a lesser extent Moshi, while others grew the best wheat in the country at Ol Molog in West Kilimanjaro. A handful of white farmers also grew wheat at Oldeani in the north of Mbulu district. They were a microcosm of the Europeans in the White Highlands of Kenya, though with nothing like their political influence. A handful of South African farmers eked out a precarious existence growing wheat and maize at Sanya Juu behind Mount Meru.

The crowning glory of the province, however, was the majesty of Kilimanjaro and Meru (14,979 feet). This is not to mention the magnificent game parks of Lake Manyara, Tarangire, Ngurdoto and the unique Ngorongoro crater, the so-called eighth wonder of the world, which even then had begun to attract large numbers of international tourists. Further west, it bordered on the great Serengeti plains, roamed by vast numbers of wild animals as far as the Lake Province. It included the Olduvai Gorge where Dr Leakey had discovered Homo Zinjanthropus, two million years old, the first man in the world whose skull was on display in the King George V museum in Dar es Salaam.

It was thrilling to be sent to such a wonderful place with rather vague instructions to do all I could to improve relations between government and people. I was under the general supervision of the provincial commissioner Mike Molohan, a former Irish rugby international, and his deputy, my old friend Robert Robertson with whom we had stayed at Tabora in 1948.

During the ten or so months I was in the province, I was able to try out my pet ideas for bringing government closer to the people, ideas the government later adopted for the whole territory on my return to Dar es Salaam in 1958. Moshi was the obvious area on which to concentrate. It was densely populated with a million people living in banana groves (*migombani*) and coffee small-holdings (*vihamba*) on the fertile slopes of the mountain. This was where they cultivated the excellent Arabica coffee the Catholic missionaries introduced at the end of the last century. Thanks to the government, local authorities and Catholic and Lutheran missions, Moshi had universal primary education and the highest literacy rate in the territory. The Kilimanjaro Native Cooperative Union (KNCU) was probably the most efficient and progressive cooperative organization in Africa. A district commissioner called Sir Charles Dundas, a Scots baronet, started it in the 1920s to enable Chagga coffee growers to compete on equal terms on world markets with the European growers.

A First World War fighter pilot Mr A. L. B. (Ben) Bennett DFC, who was general manager for years and later adviser to the KNCU, carried the task on splendidly. Such was the devotion of the Chagga to these two men and their gratitude for their services that they bestowed unique Chagga titles on them both. Dundas was given the title *Wasaoye-o-Wachagga* (Elder of the Chagga) and Bennett that of *Mbuya-o-Wachagga* (Friend of the Chagga). Indeed, so greatly loved and admired was Sir Charles Dundas that when he left Moshi for the last time by train to Tanga and ship to Dar es Salaam, the Chagga reputedly hired a band to accompany him on board ship and serenade him on his journey. As the boat sailed into Dar es Salaam harbour a day or two later, the band apparently struck up God Save the King. History relates that the Governor was not amused.

Bennett was at the peak of his career when I arrived and always gave me his help and support. His pride and joy was the recently opened building in Moshi that housed the KNCU headquarters. Not only did it accommodate all the cooperative headquarters' staff in splendidly equipped modern offices, but it also housed a fully residential KNCU commercial college. There was also an excellent multiracial hotel, the KNCU Hostel. It had beautifully furnished bed-sitting rooms with bathrooms attached and a top-floor scenic restaurant with wonderful views of the mountain.

Because it gave me such a good opportunity to meet the hand-picked young students of the college and many other interesting people who stayed or dined there from time to time, I never stayed anywhere else in Moshi. So important was Moshi in my work that I normally spent about a week every month on safari in the district. I would be based either at the KNCU Hostel or the Kibo Hotel at Marangu, a delightfully old fashioned establishment run by an elderly German, Mrs Bruehl, 20 miles or so from Moshi and 6000 feet above sea level.

Marangu was one of the most beautiful places in Tanganyika

and the headquarters of the Vunjo district led by Chief (*Mangi Mwitori*) Petro Itosi Marealle and Paramount Chief (*Mangi Mkuu*) Thomas Marealle, installed in 1951, who lived in Moshi itself. It was also the centre of the tourist trade — such as it then was — and the base for climbing the mountain. A second excellent hotel, the Marangu Hotel, run by Mr Bennett's sister-in-law a couple of miles away from the Kibo, completed the tourist trade infrastructure and climbers took off on a trek through the rainforest on the first stage of the 36-mile walk to the summit.

A river with a spectacular waterfall ran under a little bridge between the two hotels. Ice cold waters ran down the mountain and fed the Marangu Hotel swimming pool, perhaps the coldest in which I have ever swum. A glowing carpet of pink wild flowers covered the green verges of the road making Marangu a sylvan paradise from which from time to time one caught tantalizing glimpses of the snow-clad glory of Kibo and the black rocky fast-ness of Mawenzi, speckled sometimes with a hint of snow. The mighty mountain seemed to cast a spell on everyone. The Chagga had known since time immemorial that the gods dwelt there, so would never desecrate such a holy place. That Europeans should wish to climb to the top seemed stupid, pointless and profane.

Like all goddesses, the mountain hid her beauty coyly, some-times for days at a time behind wispy veils of gossamer tinged with the rainbow colours of the sky. The brooding spirit of the mountain, which seemed to follow one nearly everywhere one went in the Northern Province, never looking exactly the same constantly fascinated me.

Another feature of Marangu was Nicholas Marko's bar, a short walk from the Kibo Hotel. I often went there after dinner for a chat and a drink with the locals, who kept me up to date with the latest intelligence, political and otherwise. The regulars included teachers, local government and cooperative officers, nurses and coffee farmers, and the conversation was always lively and amusing. As in Dar es Salaam, though usually the only European present, I was invariably treated with great courtesy. The latest hits from the Congo provided excellent background music.

The tarmac road ended at Marangu, but a branch district road continued north for another 50 or so miles around the mountain. It led to the Rombo chiefdom in the Roman Catholic sphere of influence and its cheerful chief, John Maruma, became a good friend of mine. Far from the madding crowd, it was perhaps the least developed part of the country at that time. Chief John was incredibly hospitable and it was impossible to visit him without being invited to a meal at almost any hour of the day (or night) accompanied by large quantities of Tusker beer. I remember marvellous open-air lunches when Chief John would call out to one of his retainers, *lete sanduku lingine* (bring another case [of beer]). It was just as well that drink driving had not become a big issue in those days, though, as one normally had the road to oneself, it was not perhaps so important.

With the exception of dedicated teams of guides and porters based around the Marangu hotels, whose profession it was, hardly any Chagga had climbed the mountain purely for pleasure. Apart from anything else, few of them would have been able to afford the cost of the climb, which included fees for the huts and extra protective clothing like boots and gloves. Also, for that matter, the European concept of a holiday had not entered the local culture.

However, with support from the Chagga chiefs, Ben Bennett who promised financial sponsorship, and the Moshi police who promised clothing, I planned to take a small party of volunteers from the KNCU College to the summit. We would go over the 1958 New Year holiday and I eagerly looked forward to the adventure.

The following year in Dar es Salaam, I started a series of study tours to enable the emerging class of educated young Africans to begin to participate in experiences previously pursued only by Europeans. I remember being shocked to discover that young African graduates had never been to Government House, never been on board a ship, or inside a hotel, never really been in the inside of anything — a state of affairs I determined to alter as soon as possible. Even as late as 1957, the African inhabitants of the UN trusteeship territory of Tanganyika were still being treated as second-class citizens in their own country.

Back in Arusha, I established my two-room office in the new Town Hall building in the main street not far from the provincial headquarters. I was allocated a pleasant bungalow a few hundred yards away, from which I could walk to work each day over a footbridge across the river, if I did not need my new car, a grey Peugeot 203. I had brought the faithful Kitwana Chumu with me from Dar es Salaam as my PR assistant and proceeded to recruit locally a young Chagga typist called Robert and a bright 17-year-old ex-Standard 8 Mwarush youth called Loanyuni as our local guide and interpreter. Alfred Musa, with whom I stayed in Machame, was a Standard 12 student on holiday employed temporarily. Robert could be sullen and temperamental, but he was a brilliant typist who could take dictation straight onto the machine and he rarely made a mistake.

It was a wonderful feeling to be back upcountry again with a small independent command and no one breathing down one's neck. Best of all, it was fun to be opening a brand new office and carrying out an unprecedented task to which I could devote as much or as little time and energy as I pleased. We started with virtually empty rooms and had to build up the office from scratch. I enjoyed choosing carpets and furniture, and getting a typewriter and stationery. After a week or so we were all set and ready to go. The arrival of out telephone marked the kick-off.

My director in Dar es Salaam and the PC gave me a free hand. The original ideal was to have a PRO in each of the eight provinces, starting with me as a kind of guinea pig in the key Northern Province. In the event, so far as I can recall, I was the first and last provincal PRO and a short-lived one at that. Though I had a successor for a few months, the experiment was not extended.

Also in the main street were Arusha's two famous hotels. The New Arusha displayed a board announcing that it was exactly midway between Cape Town and Cairo, and the Safari Hotel boasted an unusual copper topped bar to which a baby elephant had been led in for a drink in a recent Hollywood film *Hatari* (Danger). Mount Meru overlooked the pretty garden town beyond the golf course and the main road to Nairobi to the north. The streets in the residential areas were lined with purple jacarandas and the well kept gardens displayed a profusion of tropical zinnias, petunias and marigolds mixed with the roses, hollyhocks, ferns and carnations of England. At 5000 feet above sea level, the climate was perfect after the sultry heat of the coast and the early mornings were a delight with dew-dappled lawns, mists and a nip in the air, mingled with the fragrant scent of cedar hedges. Six miles down the main tarmac road to Moshi — to the east behind the Natural Resources School at Tengeru — lay Mrs Gladys Rydon's fabulous garden overlooking Lake Duluti. It was the most beautiful garden I ever saw in East Africa.

A mile or so further on and on the other side of the road lay the West Meru middle school. It was a particular favourite of mine, not only because it was so easy to visit but also because an outstanding team of teachers had made the naturally lively Meru teenagers a joy to visit. Little did I think then that 14 years later one of the brightest 16-year-olds in Standard 8, Nicephori Sandu, a pilot in the air force, would fly me from Dar es Salaam to Mwanza. I was also amazed when another student Kitomari, now deputy governor of the Bank of Tanzania, recognized me at a reception given by the Tanzanian high commissioner in London 35 years later. Such rare encounters are part of the joy of living.

Another Meru schoolboy who lived in a village nearby and who was to make himself a name was Sam Hagai. After independence, he reverted to his tribal family name of Sarakikya, but at that time he was a 19-year-old Standard 12 Tabora government schoolboy. When we first met soon after my arrival in Arusha, he was waiting to go to England to attend the Royal Military Academy at Sandhurst, one of the first two Tanganyikan cadets ever to go there. He once invited me to his modest home, apologizing that the only furniture was a table and bed. He was an orphan whose father had been a policeman, hence his determination to become a soldier. He had a temporary job in Arusha — about ten miles away — for his vacation and no transport save for an irregular and costly bus service.

On the spur of the moment, I invited him to stay with me during the week to assist with this problem and also help a little with his English. He accepted at once and he came the next day to spend a few weeks with me, the first of many African guests. He was delightful company, Susan was in England with the children, and we got on very well indeed. I recall him being an avid reader of Jane Austen's novels.

Each Sunday evening he would return from his home with a large sack of delicious avocado pears, which he said with a smile was 'all he had to give'. His presence in my home caused a stir at the time among my white neighbours and even my faithful old cook Juma looked slightly surprised, but said nothing. When I took him to my usual pew in church rather than leave him at the back with the servants, I could not help but notice strange looks from some of the white settlers in the congregation.

There was a happy sequel to this 'racial' episode. When I was next on leave in England in the autumn of 1960, Sam Hagai sent me an invitation to his 'passing-out' dinner at Sandhurst and booked me a room at the Duke of York Hotel in Camberley. There was a dinner in formal evening dress followed by a boxing match against Oxford University, which I think Sandhurst won because of the excellence of their Gurkha and Thai cadet boxers. Sam's company commander told me how well he had done on the course, where he had distinguished himself in athletics, winning the mile race in the recent triangular contest with the French and Belgian military academies. I also met the other Tanganyikan cadet — a Nyasa called Alexander Gwebe Nyirenda, who was destined to make his name a year later on 9 December 1961, Independence Day, when he symbolically planted the new Tanganyika flag on the peak of Mount Kilimanjaro. This feat was recognized by a special issue of postage stamps.

When I went to settle the bill at my hotel the next morning, I was told that Mr Hagai had taken care of it. The wheel had come full circle. After the unfortunate army mutiny of 1964, then stationed at Tabora Captain Sarakikya, as he had then become, was promoted immediately to brigadier and later to major general in command of the army. On retiring some years later, he successively became ambassador to Ethiopia and Nigeria, and high commissioner to Kenya. I was honoured to be the only European guest at his wedding in the Lutheran church in Dar es Salaam.

✳ ✳ ✳

Back in Arusha in October 1957, the Governor arrived for a few days with Secretary of State for the Colonies Alan Lennox-Boyd. Twining's new private secretary Brian Eccles, who had been district officer in Pemba before becoming private secretary to His Highness the Sultan of Zanzibar, accompanied them. He was to become a close friend. Lennox-Boyd, whose wife was a Guinness, had heard about the Dublin scholarships from several different sources and thanked me personally for my efforts to get them.

There was a feeling of urgency and expectation in the air. After the independence of the Gold Coast — renamed Ghana — on 6 March 1957, all Africa seemed to be racing for freedom. It was no longer a question of 'whether' but 'when'. Tom Mboya, the Kenya trade union leader, had a summit meeting in Arusha with Rashidi Kawawa, the secretary general of the Tanganyika Federation of Labour (TFL). Rashidi asked me to drive them around, which I was delighted to do because it gave me a chance to get to know Tom Mboya, the dynamic young Luo leader then at the height of his fame. They lunched with me at my home and I recall Mboya's enthusiasm over his recent visit to the USA when he returned with dozens of scholarships for Kenyans to attend US universities. He told me after lunch that it was relatively easy to persuade workers in large factories to strike against anonymous employers but that attempts to get domestic workers to go on strike inevitably failed because of the close personal relationships that existed between servants and their masters. Mboya, who might well have become a great Kenyan leader had he lived longer, was tragically assassinated in the centre of Nairobi a few years later, soon after Kenyan independence, while walking out of a chemist shop.

I performed much the same transport service for Julius Nyerere in Moshi. He too was staying at the KNCU Hostel and wanted to entertain the district organizer of the New York branch of the Ladies' Garment Workers' Union, whom he had met on a recent short tour to the USA. She was a brilliant young woman called Maida Springer who was becoming very interested in African affairs and was to play an active part in organizing African trade unions. Nyerere had met her the year before while staying with the Mary Knoll Fathers on the Hudson River. She had great energy and drive and a delightful sense of humour. When she called on me in my office in Dar es Salaam several years later and I asked her whether she was busy, she replied, 'I'm so darn busy that I haven't even time to divorce my goddamn husband!'.

The year 1957 was nearly over. My father had a stroke and was dying in Dublin. By the time I got a delayed telegram on Christmas Eve to say that he had died on 21 December, he had in fact already been buried. My DC at Kahama in 1948, now a Lutheran missionary in Moshi, Donald Flatt and his wife Ruth kindly had me to stay for the night on Christmas Day and could not have been kinder. I saw no point in cancelling the mountain climb in the new year and decided to do it in memory of my father, a great walker, who would have approved. Our party of ten or so, including a marvellous old guide, set off from the Kibo Hotel on the morning of New Year's Eve. I persuaded Sam Hagai — already an experienced climber — to join us. The party included Jubilate Munisi, David Marealle and Jackson Kessi, with whom I have kept in touch intermittently ever since.

We set off through the tropical rainforest with rushing streams and moss and lianas trailing from tall trees. It was cool in the shade and colobus monkeys played in the branches. We spent the first night in the Bismarck (now Mandara) hut just above the forest. It was cold, but still reasonably comfortable and civilized with a few birds flying around. As we continued the next day to Peter's (now Horombo) hut, the last vestiges of animal and vegetable life disappeared off the face of the dreary lunar landscape. Then came the tough trudge on a stony path along the 'saddle' between Mawenzi and Kibo to the Kibo hut at the foot of the final scree. We had now walked for three days and covered more than 30 miles. The real climb through snow and ice to the crater and the summit lay ahead. It was bitterly cold as we lay in our bunks at Kibo hut and snatched what little sleep we could. It was customary to wake up at the ungodly hour of 3.00 a.m. and attempt to reach the peak as the sun was warming up a few hours later. Cynics said the reason for this was that if one could see clearly what lay ahead no one would go on.

Nevertheless, inspired by the guide and Sam Hagai, we set off in freezing cold and bitter wind, using our ice axes to cut steps and crampons to help us along. For the first time we were really climbing and we encountered deep snowdrifts; the guide said the snowfall was heavier than usual. I remember feeling exhausted and thirsty and eating snow to stop feeling sick. Munisi lost a glove and has had frostbite on his hand ever since. The stench of sulphur from the volcanic crater was overpowering and we felt dispirited and enveloped in a cold Stygian gloom.

It was all worth it, however, when at last we reached the summit and the golden rays of the sun broke through the morning mists to reveal an unforgettable view beneath; we were aware of standing literally on the top of the great unknown continent itself. This Olympian feeling was accentuated by a feeling of light-headedness brought on by altitude sickness.

We then scampered down the mountain half-running, half-walking, shouting and singing. Wearing crowns of immortelle flowers we had picked on the mountain heights, we were filled with the physical glow of health and the sense of relief and achievement. We reached Bismarck hut by the evening of the fourth day. The next morning, we raced down the forest glades and returned safely to the Kibo Hotel a few hours later. We demolished the great feast that kind Mrs Bruehl had prepared for us and knocked back a case or two of Tusker beer before driving back to Moshi in the evening. We had all enjoyed the expedition tremendously and, in my case, it was the best possible remedy for the sorrow I inevitably felt after my father's death.

Back in my office I finished plans for a publicity drive in the province so that no one should be in any doubt whatsoever that the government's policy was to prepare the territory as quickly as possible for a viable independence as laid down by the UN charter. We would go neither too fast nor too slowly, but would continue the present steady progress based on the sound economic development needed to finance each step forward.

For a start, I decided to attack centres of civilization, namely the secondary, middle and even primary schools, where convenient, by talking to them and bombarding them with attractively produced posters and leaflets. Specialist training schools such as the natural resources school in Tengeru and the game college at Mweka were also included, and I made a point of visiting every police unit and prison, whose captive audiences were particularly appreciative.

I made friends where possible with some of the intensely individual white settlers, several of whom I already knew, like David and Pat Reid. I had attended their wedding at Ranchi and had stayed with them at Ol Molog on West Kilimanjaro where, on their splendid farm cut out of the forest, they grew not only wheat but also prize beans for export to the Netherlands.

I joined the Arusha Club and played for the rugby football and cricket teams. Bowling off-spinners, I once took a hat trick that culminated in the dismissal of my bank manager Mr Steele with a ball that bounced twice. The club's Chagga barman, Coleman, was a great character who kept secret medicines for members suffering from hangovers and took tops off beer bottles with such an elegant flourish that they invariably hit the ceiling with a cheerful thud.

I was invited to attend regular meetings of the predominantly Euro–Asian Arusha Chamber of Commerce and Agriculture and had a particularly fruitful relationship with its director, Mr Dick Alkin. Robin Thorne, from whom I had taken over Handeni district in 1951, was DC Arusha when I arrived and, to my delight, I found that Paul Digges La Touche had been promoted to assistant commissioner of police for the Northern Province.

On Chagga Day, the anniversary of the *mangi mkuu*'s installation, the police band at Moshi played the Eton Boating Song in honour of their old Etonian DC, Brian Hodgson, whom I had first met at Tabora. All the guests were then treated to an open-air banquet of *kidari* (breast of goat, a Chagga delicacy).

Inevitably, most of my work was concentrated in the densely populated Moshi district where, with splendid secondary schools, Roman Catholic seminaries and large numbers of middle and primary schools, people were relatively well educated. I particularly liked and often visited the government secondary school at Old Moshi and the Holy Ghost Fathers' secondary school at Umbwe in Chief Abdiel Shangali's Hai division in Machame in West Kilimanjaro. At Arusha, the Lutheran Ilboru secondary school a short distance from my bungalow, was a home from home and I was sometimes invited to take English classes there. Apart from courtesy calls on the district commissioner, I rarely visited the headquarters of the Masai and Mbulu districts, though I often stayed with the Irish Pallotine Fathers at Karatu in the north of Mbulu district near Oldeani, and talked to the boys in the middle school there. I once took a party of them to spend Sunday in the nearby Ngorongoro crater and, like me, they were all thrilled with this Garden of Eden where animals and men had coexisted so happily since the dawn of time.

Some European farmers grew wheat at nearby Oldeani, includ - ing the Irish Olympic hurdler Bob Tisdall. Also at Oldeani was the quaintly named Paradise Bar where Frank Reynolds (the DC Mbulu), Kitwana Chumu and I once spent an evening admiring the epicene beauty of Iraq youth. The combination of wild scenery with a good climate gave one an extra elixir of life and I felt a daily *joie de vivre* seldom equalled elsewhere. The clear starlit nights, the crisp morning mists, the gaiety and charm of the people cast a spell over the denizens of this enchanted land.

Sadly, the northern dream was drawing to a close. I was recalled to the political drama fast unfolding in the sultry heat of Dar es Salaam and slowly drove away. Daydreaming with vivid images racing through my mind, I recalled the pink flamingos and tree leopards of Lake Manyara; the grandeur of Serengeti, Tarangire, Ngorongoro and Ngurdoto; the Masai plains; and the fantasy of Lake Duluti. I remembered the misty pools of Lake Momella; the white rhino and mourning elephants;* the stately beauty of the Masai and Iraq; the laughter of smiling Chagga and Meru schoolchildren; and the grave enthusiasm of youth. Towering above all was the cold glory of the mountain.

---

* Popular belief holds that when Mrs von Trapp, the Austrian owner of Momella farm West Meru, died after having lived there for many years, a herd of elephants of which she was very fond trumpeted mournfully outside her house.

18

Step by Step to Freedom, 1958–59

Early in 1958, I returned to Dar es Salaam after a year's absence to resume my delightfully unpredictable duties in the public relations department headquarters. It was a thrilling time to be there. The last of the great governors of the old school, Sir Edward Twining, was about to leave after nine years, to the sadness of many and the relief of a few who felt that he had outstayed his welcome. He had spent the last few months in triumphal farewell tours of the territory. He collected an enormous quantity of gifts, some of which, displayed in the Arnautoglu Hall shortly before his departure, were inspected by the secretariat wag Willy Wood, who told me, 'There had been nothing like it since Warren Hastings left India.'

Twining's view of a gradual move to independence along idealistic (if somewhat unrealistic) multiracial lines, was widely shared by most Asians and Europeans and by many of the older and more conservative Africans, including most chiefs. It was also supported by a majority of senior government officers and, in an ideal world, might conceivably have served Tanzania better in the long run.

My own opinion then was that, in the light of the existing circumstances and if serious civil disturbances were to be avoided, there was no alternative but to hand over to an African majority government as soon as we could safely do so — a view that ultimately prevailed.

Showered with gifts and honours, Twining finally sailed out of

212

the harbour on 16 June to an emotional farewell of bands playing and crowds cheering. Soon after his return to England, he was made a peer as Baron Twining of Tanganyika and Godalming in the county of Surrey. He duly took his seat in the House of Lords as one of the first life peers whose son, though given the courtesy title of Honourable, would never succeed to the title of hereditary Lord.

His departure marked the end of the colonial era, accompanied as it had been latterly by the Suez crisis, Princess Margaret's visit and Ghana's independence, to say nothing of the rapidly increasing influence of Julius Nyerere and his TANU party.

A month later, his successor Sir Richard Turnbull* flew in and was sworn in at Government House on 15 July in a ceremony I witnessed. I had met him once before at the Hartebeest Club in Oxford in 1951. I was then attending the second Devonshire course and he was provincial commissioner of the vast northern frontier district of Kenya. As chief secretary of Kenya, he had masterminded Operation Anvil, which had rounded up many of the Mau Mau Kikuyu freedom fighters in Nairobi and heralded the final collapse of the rebellion. Several TANU leaders told me that they feared they might soon be thrown 'out of the frying pan and into the fire'.

There could scarcely have been a greater contrast between the two men. Twining, a scion of merchant princes, chronicler of crown jewels, regular soldier and lover of ceremony, was great of stature and an expansive, witty bon viveur. Turnbull, the scholarly Scot, opera lover, Kenya DC par excellence, fluent Swahili speaker, admirer of Somalis and slim, keep-fit enthusiast, was shy and austere. Twining was a romantic idealist with a warm heart; Turnbull was a down to earth realist with a cool head. Both were highly intelligent, lovers of Africa and totally dedicated. It was an honour to have served them.

Little did we think on that cool July day on the green lawns of Government House that Turnbull would be the last governor of Tanganyika and its first (and last) governor-general. Still less did we think that, within weeks, he would have accepted the inevitable, turned Twining's policy upside down, compromised with

---

* He died on 21 December 1998 aged 89.

TANU, celebrated constitutional changes and sent the country racing to independence. This was exactly the opposite of what Nyerere and his friends had expected of him.

Since, from 1955 to independence in 1961, I translated all the governor's speeches to LegCo and all the broadcasts to the nation I got to know both men extremely well and admired them for their distinctive qualities. I had, of course, known Twining for much longer and, having spent Christmas 1952 with him and his family at Lushoto, had a slightly closer personal rapport with him. Lady Twining was particularly kind to me. Having helped with her improved latrine campaign in Handeni shortly before her final departure, she conferred on me the dubious distinction of director of the Dar es Salaam Red Cross. I had never forgotten her kindness to Susan at Kasulu in February 1950 shortly after Lucy was born.

The Hansard report of the debate in LegCo on 10 June 1958 quotes my old chief Sir Arthur Grattan-Bellew, now chief secretary, as saying:

> For internal work it is really I think more a question of getting a man who has an aptitude for it. And he must know Swahili very well indeed and know the country. We have had a notable success with one administration officer ... the praise that has been given to that Administrative officer, a provincial Public Relations officer is very marked. Praise unsolicited from members of the public and from institutions. ... That officer has been brought to Dar es Salaam because it is the Headquarters of the Department, to carry out some very important publicity work of a territorial nature and the Northern Province will of course get the benefit of that as well as other parts of the country.

Such was the official background to my untimely recall to the capital. It was clear that the government had at long last realized the gravity of the political situation and decided even before the arrival of the new governor that something must be done at once if the growing unrest was not to deteriorate further into riots and possible bloodshed. The awful example of Kenya was ever in our minds.

At all events, Chief Secretary Grattan-Bellew sent for me personally a few days after the LegCo debate and gave me just a week to draw up plans for the improvement of government relations with the African public in general and those living in the Dar es Salaam area in particular. In brief, the plan included:

(a) radio political broadcasts by the Swahili programme *Majadiliano* (debate);
(b) study tours – of Dar es Salaam area suitably modified for external publicity on 'meet the people tours';
(c) PR offices in African areas – the opening and running of the Livingstone Street office by the PR department not far from the TANU office in New Street, and the opening of a police information centre in Msimbazi;
(d) lectures and talks to schools, police units, prisons, training schools and African study groups throughout Dar es Salaam and Eastern Province in general; and
(e) constant close liaison with Swahili press, trade unions, and political leaders.

This outline plan was duly approved a week later and was in full swing by the time the new governor arrived in mid-July 1958. It was in fact a refinement of schemes already successfully tried out experimentally in the Northern Province.

The radio weapon was perhaps the most important, for its influence was out of all proportion to the number of listeners, perhaps ten to each radio set. Its voice carried the stamp of authority and a reputation for veracity. Its emotional appeal, interspersed with popular music, had a special attraction for the still large numbers of illiterate people.

Acting as government goalkeeper, I invited prominent African leaders from all walks of life to join me for an hour once a week for a live broadcast with no holds barred. No subjects were prohibited and the spontaneity and frankness of these discussions made them instantly popular, not only in Tanganyika but also throughout East Africa. I was delighted when, fearful of their subversive content, the Portuguese colonial government in

Mozambique jammed the transmissions. For the first and last time in my life, I had a large fan mail of dozens of letters a week from all over East Africa; and I was thrilled to have my voice recognized when filling up with petrol on leave in Nanyuki in northern Kenya. The programme ran for a year and the TBC estimated that it had 80,000 listeners each week. With the sole exception of Julius Nyerere, nearly every prominent figure in African political life, including the future vice-president Rashidi Kawawa and the trade union leader Michael Kamaliza took part.

Best of all I greatly enjoyed the broadcasts myself, with the cut and thrust of Swahili debate spiced as it was with proverbs, riddles and laughter. There were no particular topics for the day, just a general free for all with some extremely awkward questions raised. It was invariably conducted with the greatest courtesy and good humour. It was without precedent at that time.

The study tours started almost at once. They too were close to my heart and were to some extent a coastal equivalent of the Kilimanjaro climb. Once a fortnight, a dozen or so African politicians, trade unionists, journalists and other people with a place in public life were taken on a study tour of Dar es Salaam to gain an insight into how the capital was run. A typical tour might start with a visit to Government House — hitherto inaccessible to all but a select few. It would then continue to the Criminal Investigation Department (CID), with a revealing visit to the finger-printing department, before a well timed visit to the brewery to inspect one of the country's most vital industries. This would be followed by a chance to sample the finished product in the general manager Alan Bailey's office.

Indeed, Alan and his convivial sales manager Pat Pearson were a tower of strength as they always welcomed the inclusion of the brewery in almost all the study tour programmes and a cool pint of their excellent Tusker beer in the heat of the day guaranteed the success of every tour. It created a relaxed atmosphere — a prerequisite to developing new friendships and good relations generally. One of the first things the Germans did at the end of the last century was to install this excellent brewery; they had obviously got their priorities right.

A lunch of curried chicken followed in the Cosy Café with an hour or so for the visitors to discuss what they had seen in the morning. We would spend the afternoon in the office of a local private newspaper *Mwafrika* (The African) before moving on to the TBC's broadcasting studios, where some of the participants would record messages to be broadcast to their home districts.

A typical cross section of participants might include a politician, a student on holiday from Makerere University, a trade-union official, a probation officer, three journalists, a young African policewoman and a female clerk from the technical institute.

From time to time, we varied the itinerary. We might include a tour of the harbour in a police motor launch, a visit to a Union Castle liner, an inspection of the US destroyer the USS *Bigelow*, where Rear-Admiral Stephan would welcome them, and a day trip to the historic town of Bagamoyo. The general idea was to take the lid off the capital and find out how it worked. I hoped that participants would meet people, get to know each other and generally grow in confidence, as they slowly emerged from a kind of ghetto of second-class citizens. I never ceased to be surprised at how ignorant many educated young Africans were of how a country was run, where their taxes went and what government entailed — no matter who was at its head. I hoped that these informal tours would to some extent remedy this, in addition to giving them a sense of the economic aspects of life in the capital.

Another project Tim Harris, DC (later PC) Dar es Salaam, and I often discussed was the importance of bringing the government to the people by opening a PR office in the heart of the African city, with a complementary police information centre nearby. After looking around for a few weeks, we found a couple of rooms to let. They were in a typical Swahili house next to a popular charcoal seller's shop on Livingstone Street in the centre of the Kariakoo area, which seemed ideal. We promptly rented the property, decorated and furnished the rooms, and moved in.

At a slightly different level, we were following Tim Harris's example of moving his *boma* from its historical position in the European shopping centre in Acacia Avenue to a building in Ilala near the football stadium where Sunderland and Young Africans fought it out every Saturday. Better still, for about six months in that fateful year, Tim was director of public relations and this was a great help in getting the chief secretary to approve our schemes in record time. From the day the Livingstone Street office opened, it was extremely popular with the young literate residents of the town. It supplied this vitally important section of the community with valuable channels of communication with the central government through the written and spoken word.

The police information centre run by my Chagga friend Inspector Lyimo — later to join one of my own courses for African information officers — also fulfilled a vital role in dispelling popular anxieties and fears about the work of the police. At that time, the police were nicknamed *ndugu mchana* (brothers by day) because they were believed to be enemies at night, when it was thought they went around arresting people anonymously.

A long-held superstition that policemen sometimes killed people and sold their blood to European hospitals, where it was used for making a special medicine (*mumiani*),* engendered atavistic fears. The noble Red Cross symbol on the side of ambulances was regarded as especially sinister and there were cases of ambulances being set on fire for this reason. Earlier, a policeman had been brutally murdered by a panga-carrying mob shouting *mumiani* against the wire railings of the railway line at Buguruni beyond Ilala.

The fourth plank was the well-tried programme of lectures and talks to schools and other centres of learning, which we had pioneered with some success in the Northern Province. Over the next few years, this scheme was to be successfully extended throughout the entire territory until, by independence, I had spoken at nearly every secondary school, teacher training centre, institute, seminary and prison in Tanganyika. So, the educated élite at least were fairly well informed. I continued to maintain close liaison with the Swahili press and with political, trade union and business leaders, many of whom I met almost daily.

Before the end of June 1958, this plan had been drawn up, sub-

---

* *Mumiani* is (a) a medicine made from blood and (b) the men (in this case police) who allegedly kill to get their victim's blood. European doctors were presumably considered to be an essential link in the chain.

mitted to the chief secretary and approved, even before the arrival of the new governor, Sir Richard Turnbull. I am sure it was one of the first papers he was shown after his arrival in mid-July and I have no doubt that he too gave it his blessing. Certainly, by swimming with instead of battling against the tide of public opinion, he wasted no time in transforming a dangerous political situation.

He sent for Nyerere within days of his arrival and disarmed him by asking for his support and cooperation in preparing the nation for independence. Furthermore, in a radio broadcast in English and Swahili on 20 August, one month after his arrival, he announced that the first LegCo elections due to take place in September 1959 in the Dar es Salaam, Southern, Central, West and East Lake constituencies, were to be brought forward to February. I translated the broadcast into Swahili and accompanied the Governor to the TBC studios for the recording the next morning. I gave him as much encouragement as I could, but parts of the Swahili broadcast had to be repeated a few times because he had a slight stutter and hesitated with unfamiliar words.

When he opened the new LegCo session on 14 October, he declared that 'the inclusion of elected representatives in the Legislative Council was a major step towards self-government'. However, he said that he was glad to note that the territory's major political leaders were agreed that, although the executive and legislative were likely to be predominantly African when self-government was attained, the rights and interests of minority communities in Tanganyika must be secured.

The political situation grew more tense when TANU's raised hopes were frustrated by the inevitable delays in constitutional advance. By now, Nyerere was almost a national Messiah and vast crowds attended his increasingly emotional rallies across the length and breadth of the land. In Dar es Salaam, weekend meetings at Mnazi Mmoja, Msimbazi or at the old airport on Kilwa Road were attracting crowds in excess of 50,000. These would be preceded by hours of curtain-raising *ngoma*; the TANU Youth League's green-shirted choirs would sing patriotic songs, often conducted by Joseph Nyerere, and local TANU leaders would make 'warming up' speeches. Whenever possible, I would attend the Dar es Salaam meetings and everyone knew I was there representing the government, as well as the Swahili newspapers. I normally took a couple of young reporters along with me to cover the story for our newspapers and to help me check difficult or inaudible passages in the oratory, which was often interrupted by tremendous applause. TANU always reserved a seat for me right up front so that I had an excellent view of the proceedings.

As a rule, the only other Europeans present were Special Branch police officers and journalists from the English press, none of whom could fully comprehend the nuances of the colloquial Swahili used on these occasions. On at least one occasion, Nyerere found himself in serious trouble with the authorities when some of his expressions were misunderstood. At a meeting in London many years later, he publicly thanked me for putting the record straight and saving him from possible prosecution. In one of his speeches he had used the words *kutawaliwa ni fedheha* (to be ruled is a disgrace) as a rhetorical reproach to his own people, only to have it hurled back in his face, incorrectly translated as 'we are ruled disgracefully', a treasonable utterance, breaking the criminal law. From time to time, there were similar but less dramatic misunderstandings, any one of which was potentially explosive in the tense atmosphere prevailing.

Nyerere mesmerized the crowds with his powerful oratory; now quietly good-humoured teasing friend and foe alike with his earthy parables and inimitable laugh; now gravely guiding his people towards the 'promised land'; now passionate and angry as he railed against the injustices suffered by his compatriots.

He loved to compare the English invader with the camel that, invited into a kind man's tent for a rest from the heat, stood up and walked off with it. He orchestrated the vast crowds gently, chiding them one moment, reducing them to fits of laughter the next. He would arouse their anger, educate them gently about economics and at times delicately approach an awkward subject, perhaps involving local TANU leaders in some malpractice or other. The vast crowd would seize on the point and let out a great roar of *pasua*, which literally translated means cut or chop, but in this context meant something like 'go for it', 'let's hear it', or

220

'expose them'. I made short written reports to my director after each meeting, which were passed straight to the chief secretary and sometimes shown to the governor as well.

Alarmed by outbreaks of civil disobedience in some areas and inflammatory speeches by minor TANU leaders in others, the government banned TANU meetings in some provinces and instructed expatriate civil servants not to 'fraternize' with members of the party. TANU's supporters, misunderstanding the British civil service tradition of observing strict political neutrality by not allowing civil servants to join political parties, saw this as a colonial government ploy to 'do them down'.

Given that non-fraternization had last been associated with the behaviour of allied soldiers towards defeated Germans in occupied enemy territory after the Second World War, it seemed a singularly inappropriate way of dealing with TANU and I personally treated these instructions with the contempt they surely deserved. I did better. A few months later, when the ban was at its height, I gave a party for Julius Nyerere and his brother Joseph in my new home at 22 Mzinga (Beehive) Way. It was on the extreme northern edge of Oyster Bay near the old fishing village of Msasani. The party was a great success and when the news that Nyerere was there spread to Msasani, half the village turned up in my little front garden to cheer him.

I hurriedly sent up to Reliable Stores for more beer and a most memorable 'rout' developed. I had the pleasure of introducing Julius to my mother, who had come to stay with us after my father's death, and Joseph Nyerere later danced with her. One or two of my more 'sticky' friends felt unable to accept the invitation.

Ironically, it was during this most critical period that I got to know Julius Nyerere and his family best. His wife Maria was not entirely at ease in English and always made a beeline for me at mixed parties, knowing that I would talk to her in Swahili. His mother ran a small shop in the suburb of Magomeni, in the house where Julius then lived and I always dropped in for a chat and a glass of beer or Coke when in the area. She never liked me to have more than one beer and did not sacrifice her principles for profit.

In February 1959, I asked Julius for a cup of tea at our old haunt the Cosy Café. Over it, Julius said, 'You know, Randal, you had better tell your bosses that if they won't grant us responsible government, the colonial administration will break down. We will see to that, we can do it. I mean it.' When I duly reported this conversation to Chief Secretary Arthur Grattan-Bellew, he commented, 'another of Mr Sadleir's remarkable conversations with Mr Nyerere in a teashop'. Next day, in changed mood, Grattan-Bellew sent for me because the Governor apparently wanted to see me himself to find out some more.

According to Judith Listowel in *The Making of Tanganyika*, this was the first warning Sir Richard Turnbull had received that the political situation had changed completely since he last addressed LegCo after the elections of 14 October 1958. His speech on 17 March 1959 was charged with special significance, for overwhelming TANU pressure was building for him to persuade the British government to grant responsible government by the end of 1959 and to announce it on that occasion. Nyerere came to see him several times to try to press home the point. According to Judith Listowel's excellent account, the pressure on Turnbull mounted in the days before the LegCo meeting, when European and Asian leaders such as Lady Chesham, Derek Bryceson and Amir Jamal joined Nyerere in trying to persuade the governor of the dire consequences of failing to heed their advice.

Turnbull, for his part, offered constitutional progress in the shape of four unofficial ministers (later increased to five under pressure), which Nyerere realized was a substantial step forward, for it marked the end of a purely civil service government. He also appreciated Turnbull's goodwill and understanding and admitted to him that the changes to be announced on 17 March were fair and reasonable. His fear was that he would be unable to explain them to his followers and that the country would suffer widespread and serious disorder.

Both men were understandably anxious. Turnbull knew what an emergency meant because he had recently been through one in Kenya and was well aware of the suffering it inflicted, especially on the weak and innocent. At that time, the British government's policy was still geared to slow and steady progress with a tentative

222

timetable for independence in 1970, which meant responsible government in 1963/4. On the evening of 14 March, Nyerere, Jamal and Bryceson returned and the chief secretary was also present. They admitted that their original demand for an unofficial majority in the Council of Ministers was not a practical possibility and they felt that the introduction of five unofficial ministers, of which three would be African, would be just sufficient to allay African disappointment and to prevent disorderly demonstrations.

On Monday afternoon, 16 March, Nyerere made a personal call on the Governor to reassure him that all would be well. The country was tense, the colonial government feared there would be civil disobedience (*kugoma*, literally to go on strike). Fortunately, the naturally peace-loving and well-disciplined Africans obeyed Nyerere's call for calm.

The next day, through streets lined with police and security men Turnbull drove to LegCo to make his critical speech. After making his offer of five unofficial ministers, he went on to tell them that the date of responsible government depended on two things — the people's ability to operate the substantial executive changes outlined that day in a workmanlike manner, and the maintenance of law and order in the territory.

He went on to give a solemn warning that the growing lawlessness of the past 18 months must stop. He referred specifically to deliberate campaigns to damage the dignity and integrity of the courts, to hamper and obstruct the police in the execution of their duty of bringing offenders to justice, and to encourage disrespect for lawfully established authority. He mentioned noisy demonstrations outside law courts conducted with the intention of causing the authorities to set free persons who had been placed in lawful custody. He also spoke of attempts to hold unlawful courts and to impose unlawful fines, as well as the intimidation of those who refused to take part in these illegal proceedings. A powerful debate followed for several days, which Sheikh Kombo and I interpreted to the best of our ability. There was a definite change in the atmosphere both in the House and in the city. People were slowly starting to realize that things were on the move. Nyerere wound up the debate by saying that TANU had agreed to accept these

223

proposals — however inadequate — provided certain clarifications were made. 'The clarifications were made and we are accepting these proposals as a challenge to the people of Tanganyika.' He went on to say that there cannot be any government without civil servants and that in his opinion 'we will need the expatriate civil servants even more than we need them at present'.

This step forward in relative harmony was only possible because of the increasingly friendly relationship between Turnbull and Nyerere, bred from mutual respect and trust. TANU demands had only partially been met, yet public opinion had been calmed. The scene was now set for the next stage to be reached by constitutional methods. More important still, save for one or two isolated incidents, this milestone had been reached without bloodshed or riot. The tragic death of a policeman in the *mumiani* incident at Buguruni and the accidental death of a Mluguru tribesman in an unfortunate incident in Morogoro district could have happened anywhere at any time. Tanganyika had set a peaceful example to her neighbours.

Like a well-trained horse, Tanganyika now raced to independence, accelerating rapidly as it moved from walk to trot, to canter and finally to gallop past the winning post on 9 December 1961. It seemed incredible even then that things could go so fast. In retrospect, the critical period, the period that was to shape the entire process, was over the next nine months. This was between Turnbull's LegCo speech on 17 March 1959 and his announcement to LegCo on 15 December 1959 that the government intended to grant 'responsible government' after the forthcoming general election in September 1960.

Various factors combined to create a completely changed political climate; they were both internal and external. In Tanganyika, Sir John Fletcher-Cooke had succeeded Sir Arthur Grattan-Bellew as chief secretary soon after the Governor's March LegCo speech. He was one of the most brilliant men ever to serve Tanganyika, having been in the élite Malayan civil service before being taken prisoner by the Japanese — an ordeal he vividly describes in his book *The Emperor's Guest*. He was probably the only civil servant who could begin to match Nyerere's intellectual passion, and the duels between them in the LegCo debates were a pleasure to witness, if not always easy to translate in the rapid cut and thrust of argument, mockery and repartee.

Nyerere's personal and political stature grew by the hour at home and abroad and he succeeded in uniting the Africans as no one had ever done. Prominent Europeans like Lady Chesham and Derek Bryceson, leading Asians such as Amir Jamal Mahmoud Rattansey and Sophia Mustafa also threw in their lot with him. Great chiefs like Nassoro Fundikira of the Nyamwezi, whose installation I witnessed at Tabora in 1948, Tom Marealle and Adam Sapi, as well as the Chagga and Hehe paramount chiefs who led the chief's convention, which Twining once dreamed of turning into a local House of Lords, had slowly begun to see which way the wind was blowing. That Nyerere, like Mandela, was himself the son of a chief, greatly strengthened his hand in dealing with the chiefs who, since time immemorial, had been the temporal and spiritual leaders of their people.

Better still, in the recent elections TANU had literally 'swept the board' against the multiracial United Tanganyika Party (UTP) and the extremist African Congress Party led by his erstwhile colleague Zuberi Mtemvu. Twining had virtually sponsored the UTP at the end of 1955 in a move to offer a more moderate alternative to TANU. Its leader, Ivor Bayldon, was a pleasant middle-aged Southern Highlands settler who ran a successful motor business and garage in Mbeya. He was an honest and honourable man with rather woolly ideals. These were mostly borrowed from the idealistic European leaders of the Capricorn Africa Society. Among them were visionary war heroes like Colonel David Stirling (one of the legendary Stirling brothers who had formed the Special Air Services (SAS) regiment in North Africa) and my old friend Robin Johnston, the RAF Ace from Kahama now farming in West Kilimanjaro, who was their Tanganyika representative. His friend Derek Bryceson, whom he introduced to me in Dar es Salaam in 1955 as the 'chief oath administrator', was also with Capricorn before he joined Nyerere.

Mtemvu, whom I had known well when he worked at TANU headquarters, was a renegade consumed by personal ambition. He

225

thought Nyerere's constitutional approach too slow and cautious for such exciting days and, helped by ill-wishers and malcontents abroad, pursued an openly socialist policy, which got him only 53 votes in the election. Always good-natured and cheerful, the electorate did not take him seriously. His final eclipse came after independence in 1962 when, standing against Nyerere in the presidential election, he polled only 21,279 votes against more than a million for Nyerere.

Thus, inside Tanganyika, Nyerere and TANU reigned supreme, while in the world outside events were moving in their favour. After the British elections in October 1959, a new colonial secretary, Iain MacLeod, had been appointed in England to succeed Twining's friend Alan Lennox-Boyd. These men differed as much as Twining and Turnbull. MacLeod, a shrewd and realistic politician who had been a Bridge international had relatively radical views for a conservative and was determined that Tanganyika at least should move peacefully towards independence. Lennox-Boyd, a more patrician figure was to some extent inevitably associated with the old Twining regime.

When MacLeod and Nyerere finally met for the first time towards the end of 1959, they took an instant liking to each other and soon became friends. Nyerere was impressed by MacLeod's radical views and felt there was a man he could trust to give all possible support to his plans for speedy constitutional progress. With both the Governor and the new Secretary of State on his side, things were really looking up.

At all events, at that time in Dar es Salaam one could feel an excitement and growing sense of urgency in the air. Decisions taken in Whitehall and Government House were gradually filtering down to the frontline operators in the districts and the by now vitally important public relations department and TBC. By July 1959, Turnbull's first full year as governor had laid the foundations for ultimate self-government in a little over two years.

It was no longer if but when independence would come. Paternalistic ideas of postponing the evil day for the greater good of the territory's inhabitants had perforce been speedily jettisoned. The old target of independence in 1970 had vanished before our eyes. It was clear that there was an immense amount of work to be done if the territory was to be anything like ready to govern itself in the next two or three years.

In my sector, the five-point plan for improving relations with the African public, drawn up at such short notice in the previous year, was pursued with redoubled vigour. Broadcasts, study tours and lectures were intensified; certain parts of the plan such as lectures to schools and visits to police units and prisons were extended throughout the country and entailed extensive safaris. In Dar es Salaam, the centre of gravity moved from departmental HQ on the harbour front to the Livingstone Street office and the newspaper offices where our papers were printed.

At the same time, the department's entire internal and external publicity systems were overhauled. Emphasis was placed on the selection and training of African public relations officers and other personnel and on arranging for them to take a greater part in the department's activities, such as attending press conferences and going on safari, both — amazing to relate — for the first time.

I, personally, was haunted by the extraordinary perception of an independent Tanganyika, which so many ill-educated people held. They seemed to harbour a dream of a future utopia in which the large houses of Europeans and Asians would be up for grabs. Bank notes would be printed in vast quantities, money would be readily available from the banks, and taxes would be abolished or reduced. Protected game would be freely hunted; one would be free to gather firewood and charcoal in the government forests and tiresome agricultural regulations such as tie ridges and famine reserves would be abolished.

While doubtless an exaggeration, this is less far-fetched than it might seem. It reminds me of a well-known Irish story about a Dublin sweeper who asked the Irish statesman Daniel O'Connell (the Liberator) the following question in 1829. 'What job will I do, sir, when Ireland gets her freedom?' To this, the great man replied: 'when Ireland gets her freedom you will still be sweeping this street.' Rendered into colloquial Swahili, I used it with deadly effect to pour cold water on over-optimistic and fanciful forecasts of post-*uhuru* paradise.

Nevertheless, these misconceptions encouraged me to conceive of the idea of mounting an experimental publicity campaign in Northern Province called *uhuru ni jasho* (freedom means sweat), designed expressly to explain the realities of self-government and the extra effort and sacrifice that would be required from every citizen. I chose the Northern Province for being geographically the most compact, politically the most important and, above all, the province I knew best, where I would have an entrée to key people and organizations.

That the government approved this publicity campaign at all, illustrates the extreme urgency of the situation in mid-1959 as seen from the desks of the Governor, Chief Secretary and their advisers at that time. All complacency had vanished; they had long realized that they were in a crisis situation. Given that the British are always at their best in a crisis, this was a welcome change. Our requests for money, staff and vehicles were approved almost immediately; new projects and plans were welcomed with enthusiasm and unorthodox suggestions were accepted with alacrity. Even my request for a modest 'entertainment allowance' to help cover my expenses buying beer for a constant stream of relative strangers at bars in Dar es Salaam was approved without demur.

After several visits to Arusha and Moshi to prepare the ground, the five-week campaign was duly launched in September 1959. We moved in for a week at a time to five key areas in the most densely populated parts of the two districts. These included my old favourites of Marangu, West Meru, and Kibosho where I stayed with Father Joseph Babu, the first Chagga priest on the mountain and a greatly revered figure; an appearance at Sunday Mass in his lovely cathedral worked wonders. Having regard for the fairly dull life of the average villager, even in the relatively developed highlands of Kilimanjaro and Meru, we decided that, as in broadcasting, we must not merely inform and educate but also entertain. We took a leaf from the great Roman policy of *panem et circences* (bread and circuses) with which the emperors had kept the notoriously unruly Roman populace happy for centuries.

The drill was much the same in each of the target zones. We would arrive at our base — say Marangu — on the Sunday after-

228

1. ABOVE. Zanzibar Market.

2. BELOW. Royal Baraza, Dar-es-Salaam, in honour of H.R.H. Princess Margaret, October 1956. President (Alan Nihill) and Vice-President (Randal Sadleir) of the Irish Society of Tanganyika being presented to the Princess, and the Governor, H.E. Sir Edward Twining.

3. ABOVE. Congo Crisis, July 1960. Sir Richard Turnbull – last Governor of Tanganyika – with George Rockey, Press Secretary and Randal Sadleir.

4. BELOW. Makonde Stilt-Dancers from Newala on the Mozambique Border, Southern province.

5. RIGHT. Cheerful crowds besiege the Author in his Livingstone Street Public Relations Office near Kariakoo, Dar-es-Salaam to get copies of Governor Turnbull's speech announcing the Path to Independence.

6. BELOW. Opening of Co-CABS Office Mnazi Mmoja, Dar-es-Salaam by President Julius Nyerere in 1963. Prime Minister Rashidi Kawawa and Minister for Cooperative & Community Development Jerry Kasambala also attended the ceremony. Author present as 'Back-Room Boy'.

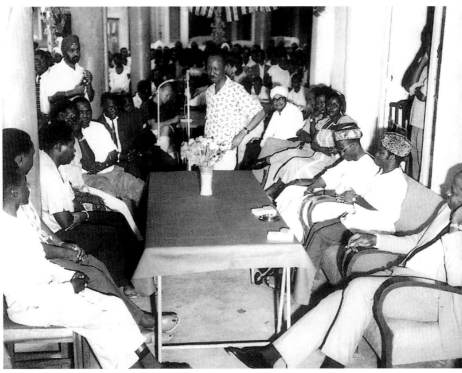

7. ABOVE. Kilimanjaro – the Shining Mountain – reflected in the still waters of the lake.

8. BELOW. Mt Kilimanjaro with Mt Meru in background from the air.

noon, call on Chief Petro Itosi Marealle and settle into our quarters at the local school. For each of the five week days, Monday to Friday, we would 'blitz' a preselected 'development zone', perhaps based on a secondary school, and launch our propaganda attack. Our 'firepower' was impressive, consisting of a mobile exhibition with coloured posters and masses of leaflets and badges (which everyone loves) for distribution at villages *en route*. A mobile cinema van led the procession playing popular music interspersed with broadcast commentaries and slogans in the Chagga language, bringing hundreds of people, mainly children, scurrying out of their dark fastnesses in the banana clumps and coffee farms to inspect this novel caravanserai. I would usually give a talk for half an hour or so at the secondary school, followed by questions, and generally managed to fit in short talks to two or three middle schools as well. In the evenings, thousands of people from miles around would come to see our film show.

The week ended on a festive note with a grand gala at Marangu. This included sports contests for all ages, a tug of war, a police band concert, a police dog-handling display, beauty competitions for girls and babies, and pop music from the loudspeaker van, a mobile publicity exhibition and a film show after dark. There were many prizes solicited from local European and Asian firms.

Our secret weapon was a light aircraft flown for the price of the petrol by a friend in Arusha. It flew low over the assembly and neighbouring villages dropping off thousands of leaflets in Swahili and Chagga inscribed with brief slogans about the challenges presented by the forthcoming *uhuru*. The leaflets were all numbered and handsome cash prizes were awarded to the lucky winners of this aerial lottery. This was more than a mere stunt, for the hope of winning a prize meant that almost every leaflet was eventually discovered in trees and fields and, one hoped, read.

Many thousands of people from far and wide attended these 'circuses'. By the time all five areas had been successfully saturated with publicity material from van and sky, and all ears and eyes assailed by radio and cinema, there were few people left who did not have a fairly good idea of what self-government involved. The posters graphically portrayed just how many bags of coffee were needed to buy a bicycle, motorbike or motorcar, and to educate a son or daughter for a year at middle school, secondary school and university.

An amusing incident occurred on my way to Marangu in a pick-up van laden with 100-kilo bags of sugar intended as prizes for the sports events. On rounding a bend on a particularly steep hill, one of the bags rolled off into a banana grove. We could not stop until we reached the top of the hill and found somewhere to turn the van and retrace our steps, which took perhaps five minutes in all. Sadly, however, it was too late — not a sign of the bag or its sweet contents could be seen. Hundreds of hands and feet moving like lightning had cleared up this manna from heaven in a few minutes and swiftly and silently returned to their homes.

I have never ceased to wonder at this phenomenon, which taught me more in a few minutes than years of study about the harsh realities of life in an African village — and a relatively prosperous one at that. I made no effort to investigate the matter, still less to report the incident to the police and was secretly pleased that this particular bag of sugar had also played its part — albeit not the one originally planned — in the *uhuru ni jasho* campaign.

This experimental publicity campaign was originally conceived as a prototype to be extended, if successful, to the remaining seven provinces, much as the first provincial PRO in the Northern Province was meant to be the forerunner of a team of PROs in all the provinces. In the event, neither project got beyond first base, for all these novel proposals were overtaken by the rapidly changing situation. From then on, a series of hastily improvised and flexible plans were the best we could do. We were no longer calling the shots.

Back in Dar es Salaam as the year drew to a close, Turnbull flew to London in November and put his plea for Tanganyika before Secretary of State Iain Macleod. Macleod not only agreed to a date being set for responsible government, but also said that he would come out and take a look at the situation for himself. There was a great sense of expectation in the air when, on the morning of 15 December 1959, the Governor drove to Karimjee Hall in his stately Rolls-Royce to make his historic statement to LegCo. More than fifty journalists and photographers awaited him while large crowds, controlled by green-shirted members of the TANU youth league, thronged the streets outside.

He began by announcing that the forthcoming elections in 1960 would have similar qualifications for all voters — the ability to read English or Swahili, an income of at least £75 a year, or being (or having been) the holder of a prescribed office. He added that, for the first time, there would be a majority of elected members. Then, he announced quietly that after the general election Tanganyika was to have responsible government.

While Nyerere naturally welcomed the announcement, he voiced his disappointment over the limited franchise. He said, 'I am extremely disappointed to hear that Tanganyika's general election next year is planned on a franchise based on literacy and income. I would still urge my friends on the other side of the house to reconsider this decision and go ahead on the basis of universal adult franchise.'

When he appeared later at the head of the steps, thousands of Africans outside the hall spontaneously broke into wild applause and started singing and waving their TANU cards. Then, they broke through police barriers and carried Nyerere shoulder high to a jeep decorated with flowers and branches. Slowly, the vast procession wended its way singing and cheering through the streets of the city. Cars, taxis and vans joined in; journalists and cameramen were swallowed up in the joyful stampede.

Having witnessed the debate indoors, I too now joined the procession. As I ran alongside the hero of the hour and reached up slightly to shake his hand and congratulate him in this moment of triumph, I became conscious of a slight sensation of loss in the right back pocket of my white shorts. I quickly realized that nimble fingers had deftly removed my prized elephant-skin wallet containing 80 shillings (£4) in notes. The irony was not lost on me. As the patronizing *bwana* sought to share in the reflected glory of his old friend, one of the 'green guards', my erstwhile friends, had with perfect timing struck his own blow for financial freedom. This was an urban microcosm of the great Marangu sugar haul a few months earlier. I wished him well as he kindly jettisoned the wallet on the beach, from where it was later recovered by the police. When, shortly afterwards, I could not resist relating the tale to Julius himself, he too saw the joke with good grace, though I suspect he found the Irish sense of humour somewhat puzzling. Two days later, on 17 December, the Colonial Secretary Iain Macleod arrived in Dar es Salaam to be greeted by crowds of Africans chanting 'One man, one vote'.

A couple of months later, on 3 February 1960 in Cape Town, British Prime Minister Harold Macmillan made the definitive speech that signalled the start of a new era in British colonial policy. He said *inter alia*, 'the wind of change is blowing through this continent, and whether we like it or not, this growth of national consciousness is a political fact.' Indeed, this speech was to herald the rapid and orderly winding-up of the British colonial empire, which had begun to unravel in Asia a decade or so before.

At a much lower level, George Baker had taken over from Tim Harris as director of public relations and promptly changed the name of the department to Information Services and his own title to controller. Both British and African bureaucrats share a love of constantly changing names of departments and ministries. In this case, it was felt that Information Services more clearly reflected the fast changing political situation. I was thrilled to be given the task of running the first African information officers' training course, which ran for a few months in the middle of the year, finishing on 6 August 1960. Some 14 young officers took part, including Police Inspector Lyimo and a hand picked selection of the cream of Tanganyikan youth, several of whom achieved distinction in future years. So eager were they to learn, so fired by a desire to serve their emerging nation, that it was a pleasure to work with them. The majority had been cooperative inspectors — carefully selected Standard 12 boys who had already gained valuable field experience with the highly efficient Cooperative Development Department. I was very proud of them. Hashim Mbita, a Nyamwezi from Tabora, later became chairman of the liberation committee of the Organization of African Unity (OAU), while nearly all the others held senior posts in the fields of diplomacy, civil service and journalism in the independent government.

I was delighted when the Treasury's newly established organization and methods branch described the course as a 'model of its kind'.

Towards the end of the course in July, the Congo army mutinied soon after that country's independence, and I recalled with grim satisfaction the critical comments of Belgian officers on board our troopship sailing from Mombasa to Colombo in March 1945. The mutiny resulted in the brutal slaughter of Belgian expatriates, including women, children, priests and nuns, in an explosion of pent-up frustration and fury. It had a chilling effect on neighbouring countries, for other colonial governments naturally feared that it could lead to eruptions of violence during the delicate period of transition to independence.

Tanganyika had special cause for alarm in view of its historical legacy of having included Rwanda–Urundi in former German East Africa, of allied Belgian troops capturing Tabora in the First World War and of its geographical proximity across Lake Tanganyika.

Soon after the mutiny began on 1 July, the Governor sent for me. He wanted me to advise him on the reactions of the African public to events in the Congo in general and to the imminent arrival of large numbers of Belgian refugees in particular. On 14 July, I worked all night on his instructions, to try to persuade local Swahili newspaper editors not to publish inflammatory commentaries about these refugees, the majority of whom were women and children. The material was not in fact published and the government was relieved.

Nyerere did not want to see lawless elements upsetting the apple cart when the country was on the whole proceeding fairly smoothly in the right direction. He warned them on several occasions that he was not going to tolerate any form of intimidation from anyone and that, if anything, TANU's attitude towards law and order would be even tougher than that of the colonial government. Fortunately, the majority of Africans heeded these warnings and the government's worst fears were not realized.

None the less, when hundreds of Belgians duly arrived by train a day or so later, elaborate steps were taken in utmost secrecy to ensure their safety and avoid any provocation that might be caused by their presence in Dar es Salaam. Arrangements were made for the train to stop at Pugu station, about a dozen miles from Dar es Salaam. The press and crowds of people gathered to wait for them at the railway station terminus in the centre of the city. Police, Red Cross workers and a host of European volunteers who had offered accommodation had descended on the tiny, little-used station and gave the demoralized, involuntary visitors as warm a welcome as was possible in the circumstances.

Being reasonably fluent in French, I was included in the official reception team responsible for coordinating arrangements and was distressed to hear the tragic stories of husbands murdered or missing and women raped. We, with the Belgian consul general and his wife, were the first to board the train. We tried to comfort the exhausted and shocked passengers as best we could, to reassure them of their safety and to explain the plans for their reception and onward flight as soon as possible to their homes in Belgium.

After they had been given hot and cold drinks, sandwiches and biscuits, their hosts drove them, with their pathetically few belong-ings, in a fleet of cars to private homes, most of which were in Oyster Bay 'far from the madding crowd'. After a day or so, they were taken in a police escorted convoy to the airport where they boarded a special Sabena aircraft for home. All this was carried out successfully and in secrecy, with no hostile demonstrations of any sort. Inevitably, the city was tense and buzzing with rumours, for it was impossible to conceal totally the presence of such a sudden influx of foreign 'tourists' with nowhere else to go.

Soon afterwards, at the request of the Sixth Battalion KAR's commanding officer, the chief secretary asked me to run a civic affairs course for the regiment. The object was to forestall a similar mutiny in Dar es Salaam. It was a job after my own heart. I thus returned to my old regiment at its splendid new Colito barracks a few miles north of Dar es Salaam for a couple of afternoons a week. It felt like old times to be back again laughing and joking with the cheerful *askari* — the sons of my brothers in arms. Nothing seemed to have changed, yet, in a sense, everything had changed. The simple unquestioned loyalties of the past had given way to the various anxieties and challenges of an unknown future.

I began each informal session with a brief outline of the current political situation with responsible government imminent and *uhuru* itself in sight. I touched briefly and frankly on the mutiny of the *Force publique* in the newly independent Congo and the tragic consequences for all concerned that had ensued. I then asked for questions, which I found extremely revealing. It soon transpired that this was not the wartime KAR I had known and loved, where excellent discipline was combined with a genuine spirit of camaraderie that bound all ranks with mutual respect and friendship. No officer would dream of eating or sleeping until his men had been looked after and the shared dangers and hardships brought them closer together. Above all, nearly all the officers and British NCOs spoke fluent Swahili in the knowledge that their lives depended on it.

I suspect that the main reason for the superb morale was that regular officers had for the most part served in the peace-time regiment for several years before the outbreak of the war and had developed a real affection for their *askari* and vice versa. They also had a superb cadre of regular African NCOs trained by the Brigade of Guards, who, in turn, imposed the highest standards of discipline and smartness.

Now, alas, all had changed. It was clear that few officers spoke the language adequately. Instead, they relied on the limited English of African NCOs and of a sprinkling of *askari*. They could just about get the letter but not the spirit of their instructions and orders across to the troops. The British army had also changed and the uncertain future of colonial regiments in itself precluded the old-fashioned secondments for six years to African regiments. There were more officers with short-service commissions who could hardly be expected to spend hours learning a language that might well never be used again. Both officers and men tended to see their respective futures apart rather than together — hence, the relatively low morale of the soldiers.

I had, of course, discussed my plans with the commanding officer and his company commanders and invited the company commanders and platoon commanders concerned to be present at all the talks. However, hardly any of them could understand much of what was going on, so it was a fruitless exercise that scarcely helped dispel the natural feeling that a 'smart aleck' civilian from government HQ had come to stir up sedition among the soldiers behind their backs. I was told to submit a confidential report to the chief secretary at once and not to send a copy to the colonel, though I did communicate the gist of it to him verbally over a farewell drink in the Mess.

My report stressed the generally low morale of the soldiers as a result of the lack of communication between officers and men. This was exacerbated by the failure of Europeans in general to speak the language fluently and I strongly recommended Africanizing officers as soon as possible if a similar fate to the Congo army was not to befall us. The colonel must have been shown excerpts from the report and been 'rocketed', for when we met soon afterwards he gave me a dirty look and ignored my greeting. My advice to Africanize the officers of the KAR was disregarded and a mutiny sadly took place in January 1964 — how sad it was to lose friends and fail to influence people.

Having upset them all I then flew home on leave in the middle of August 1960. This was shortly before Julius Nyerere, as chief minister, formed the first semi-independent government, responsible government, on 1 September 1960 — *serikali ya madaraka* — or the last major step on the road to freedom.

236

19

The Eve of Uhuru, 1960–61

It was an interesting time to be on a long vacation leave because, in anticipation of impending independence, I was offered various fairly tempting jobs in the United Kingdom on the assumption that I would not even consider staying on in Tanganyika after *uhuru*. Soon after my return in September 1960, the Colonial Office offered me a job in its information department and early, in 1961, both the Central Office of Information and the East African Office also offered me good jobs; I turned them all down. I had earlier refused a job as editor in chief of all Swahili newspapers published by the *East African Standard* in Nairobi, despite the blandishments of the friendly Major Curtis, then his Highness the Aga Khan's man in Kenya.

I broadcast three times from the BBC — once in English on responsible government in Tanganyika and twice in Swahili on Tanganyikan students in England. While visiting Dublin, I broadcast on Irish radio from the historic General Post Office on O'Connell Street, the scene of the Easter Rising in 1916. Dr Gaspar Ndaalio, then an Archbishop of Dublin scholar at University College, Dublin and later lecturer in chemistry at University College, Dar es Salaam, took part in the broadcast with me to my pride and joy.

I revisited the great Guinness brewery and persuaded its director to give us five more scholarships. I even got the redoubtable Joe McGrath, who ran the Irish hospitals' sweepstakes, to endow one more scholarship at University College, Dublin. It was fun to meet the handful of young Tanganyikans who had already started their courses and to hear their reactions to life in Ireland, which were on the whole fairly favourable after the initial culture shock. They introduced me to some young Tanganyikan seminarists studying for the priesthood with the Pallotine Fathers at Thurles in County Tipperary, of whose existence I had previously been unaware. On the rare occasions they visited Dublin, I would try to take them out for meals and a cinema, which was a great treat for them. My brother-in-law David Shackleton (kinsman of the great Antarctic explorer) was especially kind to them and took their cheerful leader Father John out to a pub in Clonsilla and home for dinner. David had never met an African before and was intrigued by Father John, who was equally fascinated by him.

It was about this time that the Pope made Laurian Rugambwa, the Mhaya Bishop of Bukoba on the western shores of Lake Victoria, Nyanza, the first African cardinal. This was a tremendous encouragement to all Catholics in Tanganyika and indeed throughout Africa.

I must confess, I had not previously realized quite how lonely life could be for a young African student far from home in a strange land and cold climate, in every sense of the word. Some, receiving only a modest allowance on which to live, had to leave wives and children behind for several years. Conditions were easier in the United Kingdom, where thousands of foreign students were well looked after by organizations like the British Council and Victoria League. Also, the universities there had many years of experience in dealing with them, not to speak of the many retired colonial servants and missionaries who often knew them personally and would invite them to their homes for Christmas and weekends.

In Ireland, it was all beginning for East African students, though West Africans, particularly Nigerians, had long had an association with Trinity College, Dublin. The Protestant Archbishop of Dublin, Dr George Sims, a distinguished Gaelic scholar, had recently opened a centre for overseas students in Dublin called Koïnonia House. I visited it once or twice, but by and large African students, or any Africans for that matter, were a rare sight in Dublin and almost unknown in the country. I once brought a few Tanganyikans down to our local town — Naas — for the day and took them into the local pub, Mrs Lawlor's famous inn. The locals stared at them incredulously, muttering 'are you from the Congo?' — where Irish soldiers were currently serving with the United Nations Force. There was no racism here, only affectionate curiosity on both sides.

While in Ireland that very cold winter, I took delivery of my pride and joy, a beautiful new grey Peugeot 403 shipped from Marseilles to Dublin, in which I hoped to drive from Cape Town to Dar es Salaam on my way back from leave. When I went to collect it from the North Wall on the River Liffey, however, I was disappointed to find the car covered in straw and orange juice, which tempered my excitement somewhat.

I, plus the new car, was booked to return to Africa on the *Edinburgh Castle*, the luxury Union Castle liner sailing from Southampton to Cape Town, a fortnight's voyage, in January 1961. Susan felt that the very long 3000-mile drive across Africa would be too much for her and elected to fly out and join me soon after my return to Dar es Salaam. That both Lucy (aged 11) and Gerald (8) were being put into English boarding schools for the first time, was another important consideration. Taking both children to their respective schools near their maternal grand-parents' home in Gloucestershire was a traumatic experience and I was grateful for a sea voyage on which to recover.

I did not know when I boarded the lovely lilac-coloured vessel at Southampton that it was to be my last sea voyage on a Union Castle ship. The rise in air travel was soon to force the famous company to close down its passenger service.

The beauty of Cape Town on arrival was marred only by the ugliness of the apartheid regime, then perhaps at its most oppressive under its architect Dr Hendrik Verwoerd. Nationwide demonstrations and rioting the previous year had culminated in the brutal massacre of 69 unarmed Africans at Sharpeville in March 1960.

As soon as I came down the gangway, I was in trouble. I leapt into a 'black' taxi by mistake, only to be politely told by the driver to get out and seek a 'white' taxi. I did not know whether to laugh or cry. Catching a suburban train at the railway station was even more ridiculous. Three different classes of platform seats and compartments in the railway carriages themselves were reserved, in English and Afrikaans, for each of the different racial groups.

The Africans I met not unnaturally looked sullen and suspicious. The whites in hotels and public places glanced at me with looks of surprise and contempt if I so much as smiled at a waiter. Giving lifts in the car to African men was frowned upon; giving lifts to women, even if they were eight months pregnant, aroused suspicion. I drove north to Durban along the 'garden route' through glorious coastal scenery. The journey took me through George, Knysna, Port Elizabeth and Grahamstown. As I drove past splendid gardens, vineyards and white Cape Dutch farmhouses, I felt the strange sensation of gliding along beautifully maintained tarmac roads through a sunlit white paradise superimposed on a seething black hell of filthy, overcrowded shanty towns, shabeens, tsotsis and grinding obscene degradation and poverty.

Superficially, it all looked wonderful and appeared to run efficiently. Many semi-skilled jobs — for example, drivers, shop assistants and policemen — were held by whites, while totally unskilled jobs and heavy manual labour was confined to Africans. I drove through black 'homelands' like the Transkei, vast native reserves where Europeans were unwelcome and spent a night in Umtata. I even passed an armoured car regiment on its way, as I learned later, to quell a rising in Pondoland.

On going to lunch with David's parents, the Brokenshas, in their flat in Durban, I complained to the black lift attendant about the extreme slowness of his lift. He replied with a big smile that I was in the wrong lift and that if I got out and changed to the 'white' lift, I would get there in no time.

I was fascinated, yet repelled, by this extraordinary land of sinister beauty and constant contradictions. The tourists' delight in the unequalled flora and fauna left them blissfully ignorant of the rumbling volcano beneath the great mountain ranges, the valley of a thousand hills between Durban and the jacaranda-lined silent streets of Pietermaritzburg, where I stayed in the Plough Inn for £1 a night. During the strict curfew from dusk to dawn, the city was left deserted, and I remember the eerie sound of my own footsteps echoing through the cool Natal night.

I soon moved north through the sugar estates of northern Natal into Zululand, whose martial people had defeated a British army at Isandhlwana, which had always held a great fascination for me. I gave a young Zulu student a lift for a hundred or so miles to the recently opened campus of the New University of Zululand. He was suspicious at first, but once he realized that I came from Britain and worked in Tanganyika, he gradually unbent and gave me a fascinating account of his life in South Africa. Indeed, before he left me on arrival at the splendid new white buildings of his university, he told me that when I stopped to offer him a lift he thought I must be a secret policeman.

Soon, I was through Swaziland, over the border and into the Portuguese colony of Mozambique. The Portuguese had ruled this colony for more than 400 years and, along with their sister colony of Angola on the west coast, were to stay in Africa longer than any other European power.

Back over the South African border and into the Transvaal, I soon realized we had returned to the harsh racist rule of Verwoerd. On reaching Johannesburg I was surprised to see a large road sign bearing the startling legend 'caution — cattle and natives crossing.' This notice even stunned the students of the new University of Dar es Salaam when I mentioned it in a talk I was giving there a few months later.

I was thrilled to be in Johannesburg at last, the great golden city that had sprung up on the Witwatersrand (White Waters Reef) with the discovery of gold nearly a hundred years earlier. It looked like Manhattan set in the African veld, with the great yellow pyramids of mine workings having a certain stark beauty in the clear sunlit air.

Here, hundreds of thousands of migrant workers came from all over the southern half of Africa — latter-day Dick Whittingtons seeking their fortunes if not in streets paved with gold, at least laboriously and dangerously digging out the gold from the great mines of the fabulous city.

I pushed on north as fast as I could, sometimes travelling 500 or even 600 miles a day, from dawn to dusk to meet my deadline. I sped through the little dorps of the Transvaal, over the Limpopo River at Beit Bridge, along the tarmac — strip roads of Rhodesia, stopping a night at Fort Victoria to spend a fascinating few hours in the Zimbabwe ruins, which have lent their name to the present successor state.

The local Europeans simply could not believe that Africans could have built such splendid palaces, temples and walls. They provided several theories pointing to the probability that Persian, Portuguese or Arab invaders must have built the city hundreds of years ago. Such theories have, however, long since been exploded and it now seems certain that a great indigenous civilization, possibly similar to that of the Aztecs, existed many centuries ago, though very little is known of it and no traces of any literature survive. The great Zimbabwe bird — symbol of Rhodes House, Oxford, vividly illustrates their artistic tradition.

As the roads got worse and worse, so the people got happier and happier. Already, I breathed more freely and in some Rhodesian hotels I noticed that Africans were allowed to drink in an annexe attached to the main building. I lunched in Salisbury, the capital, and visited the new university and the large African township of Harare, which has since given its name to the capital of independent Zimbabwe.

Soon I was racing through the last Northern Rhodesian *boma* at Mpika and with a great feeling of relief crossed the Tanganyika border at Tunduma. A few hours later I was at Mbeya, the capital of the beautiful Southern Highlands Province and reporting my safe return by telephone to my director in Dar es Salaam from the provincial commissioner's office. I returned to Dar es Salaam the following day, just on time.

I had found the long drive north through South Africa, Swaziland, Mozambique, Southern Rhodesia and Northern Rhodesia quite fascinating — at once instructive and stimulating. It helped me to place Tanganyika in a proper perspective and to view its problems in a fresh light, from a completely different angle.

So much had happened since Vasco da Gama rounded the Cape

of Good Hope in 1498 and Jan van Riebeeck established the first Dutch settlement there in 1652. Beside these venerable states, for Tanganyika to be preparing for independence seemed almost precocious. It was only 70 years or so since German rule began and a bare 40 years since the establishment of the British mandate after the defeat of the Germans in the First World War. Yet, this is not an altogether fair comparison, for more has happened in the twentieth century than in the other nineteen put together, and the sheer pace of life has got faster and faster. East Africa had been rushed from the bronze to the nuclear age in less than a century, and it was surely remarkable that it had survived at all.

During my absence, things on the political front had moved at breakneck speed. Nyerere came to London several times between October 1960 and February 1961 to discuss constitutional problems with the Colonial Secretary Iain MacLeod. The close rapport he developed with him was to prove invaluable in the delicate negotiations ahead.

MacLeod agreed at once to one of Nyerere's three requests, namely that the constitutional conference be held in Dar es Salaam. On 25 March 1961, accompanied by his wife, he duly arrived there to preside over what was to be the shortest constitutional conference in British imperial history: it lasted two days, from 27 to 29 March. During negotiations in Karimjee Hall, MacLeod agreed to Nyerere's requests that he be given the title of Prime Minister rather than Premier when full internal self-government was granted on 1 May 1961 and that full independence should be granted on 28 December 1961 (later changed to 9 December).

When the Secretary of State announced the date of independence, his words were drowned by cheers that spread from Karimjee Hall to the gardens filled with thousands of expectant Africans and into the streets of the city before being conveyed by radio to towns and villages throughout Tanganyika. It was a supreme moment in the struggle for independence and I felt fortunate to have returned from leave in time to witness it. I felt as happy as any African. This was surely the reason why we had come to Africa and we had achieved our goal.

Nyerere ended happily:

> This is the day of triumph for Tanganyika. But because of the attitude shown by Her Majesty's Government, in your person, and because of the attitude of so many helpers of Her Majesty's in Tanganyika, I rejoice to say that it is not a day of triumph over anybody. It is a happy victory for a good cause in which all are winners. One and all in Tanganyika can rejoice with us in saying 'Uhuru 1961'.

On a personal note, I was no longer centre stage. With the advent of responsible government and the imminence of independence, my work in the public relations department became superfluous. I was transferred soon after my return to the Ministry of Agriculture's cooperative development department where I was promoted to the newly created post of chief training and publicity officer responsible for all the cooperative movement's training and publicity work.

Almost immediately, from March to July 1961, I was sent on safari and ordered to prepare a report for the government on the alleged dissatisfaction within the cooperative movement. The report was duly submitted and many of its recommendations, including the abolition of honoraria for committee members, were implemented.

As frantic preparations for the independence celebrations got under way, I was placed in charge of the cooperative activities at the Tanganyika 1961 exhibition being held next to the national stadium. I was also asked to write a short history of the cooperative movement in English and Swahili for publication on Independence Day.

20

Uhuru, 1961

As far as I was concerned, Uhuru Day, Saturday 9 December 1961, was just like every other day in that I worked from sunrise to midnight putting the finishing touches to the cooperative pavilion at the independence exhibition. We had a float in the procession of floats, which was to be one of the outstanding features of the independence celebrations. Students of the Dar es Salaam Technical College had built the float for us. Their principal, Mr Crabtree, who wanted his boys to play their part, had lent us a five-ton lorry upon which the delicate wood structure featuring Mount Kilimanjaro could be mounted.

For some days, foreign notables had been arriving at the airport to be met by Governor Sir Richard Turnbull, Chief Minister Mr Julius Nyerere and a KAR guard of honour. The last to arrive was the Duke of Edinburgh, who was representing HM the Queen. Having stepped off the red aeroplane of the Queen's Flight dressed in the white tropical uniform of an admiral of the fleet, he received a warm welcome as he drove through the streets in an open car to Government House.

The climax to the celebrations at midnight on Friday 8 December was preceded by a state banquet for 300 guests at the Aga Khan's Jubilee Hall, followed by a splendid military tattoo by the KAR in the huge newly built national stadium filled with 70,000 spectators. Working on our pavilion on the nearby exhibition site, we had a ringside view of the proceedings over the arena wall. As midnight approached, a KAR guard of honour handed over the regimental colours to an African officer of the newly formed

245

Tanganyika Rifles in a symbolic prelude to the changes to come. At midnight, in complete silence, the Union flag was slowly hauled down in front of the royal box and all the lights went out. Then, a spotlight suddenly lit up the flagpole to reveal the new black and green Tanganyika flag floating proudly at its masthead, saluted by the joyful cheers of the vast crowd. It was a deeply emotional moment for us all. I felt too tired to cheer or cry, but my heart was brimming over. The next few days sped by in a dream-like euphoria of excitement, sound, heat and colour.

The following morning, before another vast assembly at the national stadium, the Duke of Edinburgh handed over the 'constitutional instruments' to Prime Minister Nyerere and Sir Richard Turnbull was sworn in as governor-general. A state ball was held in the evening and a fireworks display was mounted from the decks of the cruiser HMS Belfast, to which I managed to bring Susan. It was a magnificent display, punctuated by a 21-gun salute and the strains of the band of the Royal Marines. The ship, floodlit and anchored near the harbour entrance at Kivukoni, added a magical quality to the festivities and entertained hundreds of thousands of people densely packed around the palm-fringed shores of the harbour.

The celebrations continued with a Government House garden party. Dar es Salaam was proclaimed a city with the Duke as its first freeman and there was a state opening of the newly elected parliament. An extraordinary excitement gripped the gaily decor-ated and illuminated city as huge crowds ran hither and thither trying to catch glimpses of the principal actors in this historic pageant. Like the Edinburgh festival, it had a fringe with dozens of simultaneous activities going on all the time, not to speak of the endless public and private parties and receptions. Susan and I were among the very few Europeans invited to a ball given by TANU in Lumumba Street in honour of Jomo Kenyatta, Kenneth Kaunda, Oginga Odinga and other nationalist leaders. Jomo Kenyatta was asked to start the dancing and, selecting one of the loveliest women within range, said in a great deep voice, '*Mimi nasema, uhuru na kucheza dansi*' (I say, freedom and dancing).

I have still got the service sheet for a thanksgiving service for the independence of Tanganyika held at St Albans church at 9.00 a.m. on Sunday 10 December 1961, at which Prince Philip read one of the lessons. The rousing hymns were sung in both languages and the new national anthem, God Bless Africa, sung for the first time in the church after God Save the Queen. God Bless Africa is of course the Zulu hymn, *Nkosi Sekelele Afrika*, the battle hymn of South African nationalism, which was borrowed by Tanganyika (and several other African states) and translated into Swahili as *Mungu Abariki Afrika* to a somewhat melancholy tune.

A special set of stamps was issued to commemorate the occasion, one of which depicted Lieutenant Alex Nyirenda placing the flag and a torch on the summit of Mount Kilimanjaro at precisely the same moment as the new flag was raised in Dar es Salaam. The old LegCo had since been renamed National Assembly (*Bunge*), though it continued to meet in the Karimjee Hall.

After a week or so, I received a deputation of office messengers. They told me that, since *uhuru* had now arrived, they felt it was servile to be asked to continue to make the traditional cups of morning and afternoon tea for the officers. They asked to be excused from this menial task — a request I gladly granted because the tea was not in any case of a very high quality and was far too sweet and milky for my taste.

I was surprised when, a few weeks later, the same deputation turned up again with the humble request that the traditional cup of tea be reinstated. They were all, they claimed, greatly missing the tea in the hot weather. In any case, it was free because the officers themselves funded it to the tune of three shillings a month per head. With much merriment on all sides, I graciously acceded to their request.

As people slowly began to realize that their great *uhuru* dream of big jobs, big houses, few laws and restraints and an easy prosperous life was unlikely to be fulfilled, a strange anticlimax settled over the still decorated city. I so wished that we had had time to extend our successful *uhuru ni jasho* campaign from the Northern Province to the rest of the country, or at any rate to Dar es Salaam. Hard as we tried with our Swahili newspapers and radio broadcasts, it was clearly not enough and could always be dismissed by second-eleven TANU politicians and political agitators as merely colonial government propaganda.

Macmillan's 'wind of change' was indeed blowing strongly across Africa, sweeping away the dusty cobwebs of preconceived colonial ideas and fanning the nascent embers of African aspirations. Tanganyika's position as a ward of the United Nations — dominated by the USA and USSR — who were in complete agreement over its future destiny — was a further decisive factor.

To come down to earth again, it became increasingly clear that, now that *uhuru* had been attained, splits were developing inside the TANU party itself, with the minister of education Oscar Kambona leading a left-wing faction. He was supported by Job Lusinde and Jerry Kasambala from within the government and by Christopher Tumbo, the rather racist secretary-general of the Railway Workers' Union, from outside. The TANU newspaper *Uhuru* carried anti-British editorials and Oscar Kambona actually made an attack on Governor-General Turnbull in the Swahili weekly *Ngurumo* (Thunder).

With not enough top government jobs to go around, dozens of disgruntled young TANU and TANU Youth League members and trade union leaders began to mutter angrily that the Europeans still ran the place. This was true up to a point, especially in the commercial sector; unemployment was growing and poverty was endemic. The average European income was at least ten times higher than that of an African. Large numbers of young unemployed people inspired by the *uhuru* dream poured into Dar es Salaam and other large towns.

Workers became less polite, at times aggressive, as trade unions encouraged them to clamour for more jobs and more money. Swarms of pathetic, well-mannered and smartly dressed young men with Standard 8 leaving certificates stormed the government offices to compete for one or two junior clerical vacancies.

There was always a possibility that there would be some kind of popular reaction against 'rich' Europeans and Asians, whose very presence in their newly independent country seemed an affront to racist elements, perhaps understandably so given the circum-

248

stances. Turnbull and Nyerere, whose partnership had done so much to bring about early independence, were well aware of the danger, especially in view of the recent post-independence tragedy in the Congo. Expatriate officers — as we now began to be called — were also unsettled and nearly half of them gave in their notices to leave around this time, despite the government's efforts to retain their services for the first critical year or two of independence.

Some of the 'old school', just as racist as some of the young African hotheads, left as soon as they could, saying they were not prepared to serve under Africans. Some of the youngest and brightest officers, realizing that their career prospects were limited in independent Tanganyika, left as soon as they could to pursue other careers. They joined the Foreign Service, went to other colonies such as Aden, Hong Kong and the West Indies, to academic and professional posts, and into businesses at home and abroad.

Under the terms of the independence agreement with Britain, the government offered us all fairly generous compensation for 'loss of career prospects' in the form of lump sums of up to £12,000, which was a lot of money in 1961. At 37, I fell into this category.

To encourage officers to stay on, the government paid this lump sum compensation, soon referred to as 'lumpers', to all expatriate officers whether they stayed or left. Furthermore, Prime Minister Julius Nyerere himself wrote a personal letter to administrative officers several months before *uhuru* asking them to consider staying on to help the new government. He said, *inter alia*, 'I want to appeal to the sense of mission, which our Administrative Officers have always felt. It is your sense of mission, which has seen you through the challenge of the past. I can offer you challenges too and I don't think they are so very different from the challenges that brought you out here.'

Most of us appreciated this letter, for we all naturally like to feel needed. It also, albeit unintentionally, reinforced the views of HM Government, which, as we saw earlier, wished to maintain British influence for as long as possible.

Susan and I had little hesitation in accepting Nyerere's invitation. We decided to stay on in the country we both loved and that had been our happy home for 13 years. Our daughter had been born at Kasulu in 1950 and both children loved their African holidays. Also, since the age of 19, I had had the honour to serve with Tanganyika *askari* in the KAR in the Second World War from 1943 to 1946. The happiest days of my life had been spent there.

The challenges Julius Nyerere offered promised to be exciting, and they were. I never regretted my decision for one moment. I served for another 12 years until my final departure on 19 December 1973. I never felt that white or black rule was superior, but they were very different; each had its strong and weak points.

I often reflected on the noble ideals and high hopes that had inspired us on the first Devonshire course at Oxford in 1946. This was just after the dark days of the war when our mentors told us to go out to the colonies and help them govern themselves before transforming the colonial empire into a self-governing commonwealth. This surely was what we were now striving to accomplish.

21

Sunrise in Tanganyika: The Republic, 1961–62

On Uhuru Day, 9 December 1961, the solemn ceremonial lowering of the Union Jack to the strains of God Save the Queen signalled the symbolic sunset of British rule in Tanganyika, which had lasted for more than 40 years. As the new green and black flag of independent Tanganyika was hoisted, simultaneously on Kilimanjaro and in Dar es Salaam, where it was accompanied by the sounds of the new national anthem God Bless Africa, it heralded the dawn of a new era, the sunrise of a new nation.

As the cool golden beauty of the African sunrise is followed by the bright sunshine of the morning, so the outward and visible signs of sovereignty — stately ceremonial and cheering crowds — slowly but surely gave way to the harsh birth pangs of an infant nation. This was a nation with fewer than 100 graduates, a mere dozen African doctors and only one dentist for 12 million people. It was one of the poorest countries in the world with an average per capita income of only £20; average life expectancy was only 35 and one child in four died before the age of 15. Only half the children received any education at all and there were only a few hundred students at university. The 5000 Europeans and 100,000 Asians completely dominated the commercial, professional and technical sectors.

Such were the insurmountable problems confronting the newborn state. It was small wonder that Nyerere was soon to launch

'A war against poverty, ignorance, and disease', the slogan that became a byword in the early years of independence. It was easy to blame the colonial power — the usual scapegoat — for the distressing situation, which in this case was to some extent justified. Even at its richest, Great Britain was unable to fund development for a quarter of the globe; it therefore encouraged its dependencies to be self-financing as far as possible. In the 'appeasement' policy days of the 1930s, the possibility of the 'mandated' territory of Tanganyika (formerly German East Africa) being returned to its former masters meant that it was literally starved of imperial cash. This was quite apart from the world depression that followed the Wall Street crash of 1929.

Into this sombre picture came a real bolt from the blue. Just six weeks after *uhuru*, on 23 January 1962, the hero of the hour Prime Minister Julius Nyerere suddenly resigned in favour of his more radical colleague Rashidi Kawawa. The nation was stunned and I can recall the sense of complete astonishment with which the announcement was greeted.

For over a year Nyerere had been under considerable pressure to move faster to show that Africans were really more in control. On the whole, he had resisted this pressure in the interests of a smooth takeover from the British and of efficient government in general. He also felt that, as he sat in his imposing office surrounded by British advisers and guided by the British governor-general, he was in danger of losing touch with the masses in general and with TANU members in particular.

A great deal has since been written and said about what motivated this unusual step, but a suggestion that Nyerere was forced to resign by extreme elements in TANU has long been discredited. However, it soon became clear that he was engaged in a shrewd tactical move in the nature of *reculer pour mieux sauter*. This was borne out by the overwhelming majority he received in the presidential election at the end of the year when he became the first president of the Republic of Tanganyika on 9 December 1962 — exactly a year after independence.

In any case, Kawawa was always his man and the two worked in a close partnership. Nyerere was still the father of the nation, *baba wa taifa*, and the real force in the land. Nyerere toured the entire country asserting his unique magic on his people everywhere, listening to them and talking to them in the earthy parables they loved. Wherever he went, he rapidly regained control of TANU. From being a *mwalimu* (teacher) with a small 'm' he soon became the teacher of the nation and had the unique title *Mwalimu* bestowed upon him by popular acclaim.

Kawawa, for his part, took swift steps to Africanize the civil service. He removed his British principal secretary and head of the civil service, Kim Meek, within days. He sacked the British commissioner of police and replaced most of the expatriate principal secretaries with bright young African civil servants. He recognized the importance of getting Africans into key posts in the politically sensitive administration and police as quickly as possible.

He tamed TANU's wild young men and women by giving them responsible jobs. In February 1962, he appointed political regional commissioners to replace the eight British provincial commissioners who had been civil servants. He soon followed this by appointing area commissioners to replace the legendary district commissioners who, with the Union flag fluttering over their crenellated forts (the ultimate symbol of alien rule), were perhaps the most vital pillars of the entire structure of colonial government.

At the same time, the whole picturesque poobah image of the DC who did virtually everything single-handed was shattered overnight. A wise decision was made to appoint political area commissioners (assisted by civil service area secretaries) to run the administration, local government officers to run the local authorities and magistrates to run the judiciary. Some expatriates would joke that 'There are four or five chaps running my old district now.' They had, of course, underestimated the almost indefinable hidden mystique of the self-confident, totally detached and (almost always) completely honest and incorruptible outsider with no local axe to grind and whose very ignorance of the intricacies of local politics could be almost an advantage.

Within a few months in 1962, as these drastic changes were gradually introduced, the whole provincial administration was turned upside-down. It took time to extend effective African political control to 60 districts, now renamed 'areas' as the 'provinces' had been renamed 'regions.' In some cases, the opportunity was taken to change boundaries as well; it was certainly an improvement to divide the vast unwieldy Lake Province into West Lake and Lake Regions.

Of course, politicians who had been outstanding TANU provincial secretaries or chairmen did not necessarily make good regional commissioners and there was a fairly high turnover of these jobs for several years after independence, some involving serious abuses of power by people unaccustomed to it.

In Dar es Salaam, Kawawa created several posts for parliamentary secretaries. These junior ministers were mostly political hotheads like Rowland Mwanjisi, the editor of *Uhuru*, whose racist leaders were notorious. Another was my old friend Elias Kisenge from TANU headquarters, who, having developed an advanced stage of xenophobia, was calling in parliament for the removal of all expatriates and warning against the establishment of foreign embassies. Here again, the shrewd Prime Minister hoped to rein in some of the more vociferous critics of the government's fairly moderate policies. At that time, Rashidi Kawawa had a more ruthless streak in him than Julius Nyerere, though the latter doubtless developed the essential ruthlessness of all leaders in the fullness of time.

Kawawa, an Mngoni from the Southern Province, had all the stubborn courage of his Zulu ancestors and the boyish good looks of the youthful film star, though I personally found him less easy to deal with than the more charismatic, charming and intellectual Nyerere. His great achievement was the brilliant way in which he handled the Africanization of the government in general and the civil service in particular without causing an immediate exodus of expatriate officers, which the government naturally dreaded.

On 1 February 1962, a Ministry of Cooperative and Community Development was formed under the leadership of a new minister Mr Jerry Kasambala, formerly general manager of the Rungwe African Cooperative Union (coffee) from Tukuyu. The highly intelligent Nyakyusa people live there growing excellent coffee like the Chagga in Moshi and the Haya in Bukoba. Kasambala, an ally of Oscar Kambona, the new minister of home affairs in charge of the police, was of course an elected MP and a fairly radical politician. As a top cooperative official, however, educated like many top Tanganyikans at the cooperative college at Loughborough in England, he had his feet firmly on the ground and had an excellent grasp of finance and business in general.

He was a great big friendly bear of a man of about 35 years old, who had a good sense of humour and enjoyed a drink. He was honest and straightforward to deal with and had no airs or graces. His home, to which he sometimes invited me for a beer, was sparsely furnished with small children – spoiled rotten and running wild, which was usual in Africa. I can see Jerry now, with his shoes off and his feet up, sprawled along a settee with a glass of beer in his massive paw, roaring with laughter as he recounted some amusing story.

We quarrelled occasionally and once, when I felt (probably wrongly) that he had impugned my integrity, I lost my temper and offered my resignation on the spot. He looked startled, said he had only been joking and begged me to change my mind. We were firm friends after that. My abiding memory of him is trussed up and bandaged after a cataract operation, looking forlorn and miserable in the former Princess Margaret Hospital (renamed Muhimbili), like a caged lion, when I visited him after his operation.

It was a wonder that we did not have more rows in those exciting post-*uhuru* days. After all, our roles had been reversed with the white *bwana*s now the servants and the former colonial subjects now our masters. To some extent, I was now in my element; with my impulsive Irish temperament I had never really fitted into the élite Oxbridge circle of the British colonial Establishment and had usually felt agin' the government – a failing apparently both my last governors and, I think, my future president recognized.

Certainly, when I lunched in London with the newly ennobled Lord Twining on my last leave before *uhuru*, he asked me whether I wished to join the foreign service or stay on in an independent Tanganyika as a 'back-room boy'. Before I could reply, however, he had answered the question for me. 'You would be no good in the civil service my boy,' he said with a twinkle in his eye, for 'you're neither civil nor servile. Have a drink.'

One newly appointed junior minister was a very intelligent and charming young lady. She was Lucy Lameck from Moshi, whom I had known for some years when she worked for the KNCU. She was in fact the first woman minister and was made parliamentary secretary to our ministry. I was delighted because I had always got on very well with her. She had accompanied Julius Nyerere and Maida Springer on their visit to Moshi a few years earlier.

Lucy was a real ball of fire with a great sense of humour and a dynamic personality who soon made a big impression on the ministry. She suffered a slight sense of humour failure, however, when I was unwise enough to praise the lovely profile of the beautiful young Chagga community development officer Basilla Renju. She occupied the next-door office and bore an uncanny resemblance to the golden mask of the ancient Egyptian Queen Nefertiti. 'Keep your views to yourself, Mr Sadleir,' she snapped at me. So, the human factor was always present.

In the ministry, Africanization proceeded apace. My old friend Maharage Juma from Tanga succeeded Sandy Dyer as commissioner for cooperative development and the brilliant young Dickson Nkembo took over from my friend Robin Risley as deputy commissioner. He was later to become principal secretary to the president at State House and one of my closest friends. He always borrowed my overcoat when he was sent abroad to cold countries like Russia and Scandinavia, and told me jokingly ten years later that I would have been 'Africanized' and asked to leave years ago without my overcoat, which was in such demand.

His close friend and contemporary Cleopa Msuya, whom Susan and I had first met many years earlier at the Mziha resthouse on the borders of Handeni and Morogoro districts, soon succeeded Horace Mason as commissioner for community development. In time, he was to become minister of finance and prime minister. My fellow student on the first Devonshire course at Oxford, G. J. B. (Gavin) Green had been appointed principal secretary to the new minister and he at once got me promoted and made chief training and publicity officer to the entire ministry.

Sunrise in Tanganyika: The Republic, 1961–62

The ministry hummed with activity. As new diplomatic missions were rapidly established, offers of scholarships for Standard 12 and Standard 14 boys and girls began to pour in from all over the world. Dar es Salaam began to be transformed into a cosmopolitan capital city with new embassies springing up like mushrooms. The size of their buildings and the scale of their operations did not necessarily reflect their international status. The new government's avowedly non-aligned policy held a magnetic attraction for newcomers to the African power game. Soon, the great red banners of the communist super powers China and the USSR were fluttering menacingly in the humid air. These were closely followed by Israel's blue and white Star of David, Canada's maple leaf and the USA's Stars and Stripes — which had of course always been there but now flew from grander buildings. The Czechs and the Yugoslavs moved in too in the wake of their Soviet mentors, the Federal Republic of Germany, Belgium and the Netherlands, and the Scandinavian banners emblazoned with gaily coloured crosses all soon made their presence felt.

The Portuguese consul was kicked out and the North Vietnamese and North Koreans came, as if to balance the scales in this oh so delicate power game in which Tanganyika did it but know it was a relatively powerless pawn. South Africa was the bogeyman. All trade links with it were severed, no aircraft going to and from its airports were allowed to over fly Tanganyika, an absolute boycott was imposed on all its exports in our shops and its passport holders were banned from entry.

As the fateful year of 1962 drew to a close, the country prepared for the final severing of its ties with Britain. It had been agreed during the independence negotiations that Tanganyika would become a republic on 9 December 1962, a year after *uhuru*. Nyerere had drawn up a new constitution, which gave him powers even more sweeping than those held by the US president. He would be both head of state and commander-in-chief of the armed forces, would have full executive authority and would not even be bound to accept his cabinet's advice. He would rule for seven years.

On 9 December 1962, Chief Justice Sir Ralph Windham duly swore him in as the first president of the Republic of Tanganyika.

He received traditional gifts of a spear, a shield and a cloak from the tribal chiefs, who also anointed him. His friend and counsellor Sir Richard Turnbull, the governor-general, left to a sad farewell, the like of which had not been seen since the departure of Sir Donald Cameron many years before. The president officially moved into Government House, which had been renamed State House (*Ikulu*). However, he found the pomp and ceremony oppressive and soon moved back for most of the time to the bungalow he had built a few miles north of the capital on Msasani beach, next door to his friend Derek Bryceson. State House was soon 'fortified' with barbed wire around the perimeter of its lovely grounds. A sentry box manned by *askari* for 24 hours a day ensured strictly controlled entry.

While some expatriates looked on with amusement at this republican conversion, the need for it was to become all too apparent just over a year later. The '*Kawawa interregnum*' had served its purpose. The foundations had been laid for the Africanization of the government and the civil service, while Nyerere, freed from the reins of government, had toured the country and united people and party as never before. He had made a triumphant return to power as the nation's first president, untrammelled by links with an alien crown. Now Tanganyika had only itself on which to rely.

22

Back-Room Boy, 1962–63

I think that we were all, black and white, in a state of shock after the severance of the last direct link with the British crown on 9 December 1962. We were sailing into uncharted seas and, though there were plenty of precedents (so beloved of civil servants), including India, Ceylon and Ghana, none of them bore the faintest resemblance to our peculiar difficulties.

All we had in common was our joint membership of the Commonwealth of which HM the Queen was titular head and the English language. Our first and last governor-general, Sir Richard Turnbull, was in some respects the white hero of the hour. He had played an outstanding part, largely through his realism and his partnership with Nyerere, in bringing Tanganyika to peaceful nationhood. However, somewhat ironically, he appeared to have a more cynical attitude personally to the new order than did his paternalistic predecessor Lord Twining.

Dining with him at Government House shortly before his departure, he remarked rather sadly that the only lasting legacies of our rule were football, the bicycle and the English language — in that order. I remember feeling disillusioned. On a brighter note, he told me that 'tolerance' was the mark of a civilized man and that I should go to the Glyndebourne opera at the earliest opportunity as it would be the nearest I would ever get to heaven. So, I too was sad to see him go.

He later went to Aden as governor-general during a troubled period in its history. He took with him a select team of Tanganyika administrative officers, including my old friends Robin

Thorne, whom I succeeded at Handeni, and Tony Lee, who had travelled out with us in 1948 on the *Llangibby Castle,* and who had been with me at the Cambridge summer school in 1950. Sadly, Robin, who was financial secretary, suffered severe injuries from a letter bomb that exploded in his office.

Turnbull himself left Aden during the emergency there, before he had completed his tour of duty. He felt that the government of the day had made him a scapegoat for the failure of their policies. Be that as it may, his place in Tanzanian history is assured.

In our new Republic of Tanganyika (*Jamhuri ya Tanganyika*) — *jamhuri* from the Arabic word for republic, which hardly anyone had even heard of before — precedents were less important than those treated with such veneration in the efficient bureaucracies of the Raj. It was exciting to be working in a brand new ministry of a new state.

Development projects could be greatly speeded up because we did not have to 'queue up' at Whitehall to beg for a share of limited resources. To be fair, though, for the first few years of independence by far the greater proportion of our overseas aid came from Britain.

There was plenty of 'new money' around, often from unexpected quarters and my minister, Jerry Kasambala, and I were determined to lay our hands on as much of it as possible in this honeymoon period. United Nations experts moved in so fast that the ministries that could accommodate them often got them first, provided that their expertise bore some relation to the activities for which they were responsible.

Now my two worlds, Africa and the European world of my youth, came together. I revelled in the new capital city with the chance to meet diplomats from all over the world, to speak French, German and Russian again and to do my best to interpret Africa as best I could to the various intelligent newcomers.

Casually parked cars with CD numberplates blocked the narrow crumbling roads of the humid metropolis and the new social era of nightly diplomatic receptions began. The Americans, British, Canadians, Chinese, West Germans and Russians competed with each other to see who could throw the most lavish reception. The food and drink were so good that we could go straight to bed on returning home. Once the novelty wore off, the parties became boring because much the same set was there every evening. However, I used them shamelessly to make contacts to establish which 'key' personnel in the various embassies could be approached to give us scholarships, money or both.

The young Polish diplomats Lewandowski and Jerzy Novak were my favourites because they never came to dine without a bottle of vodka. The Yugoslav ambassador — a wartime guerrilla comrade of Tito's — often told me how frustrated he was by the bureaucrats in Belgrade. 'They take six months to answer my letters, my dear, but Moscow is much worse.' Despite these delays, he managed to get places for a few of our cooperative inspectors on the next course at the cooperative college in Zagreb and was unfailingly friendly and cheerful.

Ambassador Timoshenko of the USSR and Ambassador Ho of the People's Republic of China were oriental potentates with vast official and residential fortresses, enormous limousines and large retinues of gloomy looking subordinates. Although the Chinese ambassador spoke perfect English, he always spoke in Chinese through an interpreter, which doubtless gave him more time to think up suitable replies to awkward questions. At one of his great open-air parties for hundreds of people, we had to sit through a propaganda film called *The East is Red* for over an hour before being allowed to get a drink.

The smaller communist embassies were slightly more cheerful and relaxed, though none of them was really welcoming. They were all suspicious of visitors. A great deal of form filling and unlocking of doors took place before one could force an entry. The North Vietnamese and North Koreans were slightly more cheerful than the Chinese, although it required great devotion to duty to sit through some of the Vietcong propaganda films with their crude anti-Western 'running dog' and 'paper tiger' style content. However, we were politically 'non-aligned' and I felt it important to be totally loyal to my adopted country or get out.

✲ ✲ ✲

I had long befriended the Dar es Salaam taxi drivers whose picturesque speech I have mentioned earlier. I was delighted therefore when I heard that they were forming a cooperative early in 1963 and that they had applied to the registrar of cooperative societies for registration in the usual way. There was one snag, however, they could not agree on a suitable name for the new society — the first of its kind in East Africa and, for all I know, the world, for I have never heard of another — and they asked me to help them.

After much discussion at a long meeting in their new offices near the main taxi rank in Mnazi Mmoja, I suggested the name Co-Cabs as being simple, clear and readily understood by all. It was accepted unanimously. The ministry was excited by the idea of this unique cooperative society, which brought a new dimension to our mainly rural agricultural movement. Jerry Kasambala managed to persuade President Nyerere himself to open it shortly afterwards. This took place at a well attended and widely publicized ceremony also graced by the presence of Prime Minister Rashidi Kawawa, the Mayor of Dar es Salaam, Co-Cabs's aptly named chairman Songambele (meaning press ahead) and many other national and civil leaders. I was there as a 'back-room boy' and secretly proud of having christened it.

Meanwhile, Jerry Kasambala was pressing ahead with plans to establish our own new cooperative college at Moshi. It was to be modelled partly on the well-known college at Loughborough in England, which he and many other leaders had themselves attended. Moreover, he hoped to find a top Loughborough teacher to be the first principal of his new college. He therefore wrote to Mr Marshall, the principal of Loughborough, who had been a guest at the *uhuru* celebrations, and who had been impressed by our 'rainbow' stand at the exhibition, and asked him if he could spare a first-class man to get the college going.

To keep things moving, Kasambala planned to visit England himself in spring 1963 in the hopes both of finding a suitable principal for the new college and of persuading the British government to fund it. As I was going to be on leave at the time, he asked me to join him for some of the London talks.

I found him sitting in an armchair in his room at the Cumberland Hotel in Marble Arch, a famous wartime meeting place. As we drove in a taxi to the Colonial Office to meet the Duke of Devonshire, the then Minister of State, I felt a perverse satisfaction in my new role as a British (albeit Irish) adviser to an African minister on an official delegation to the British government. My innocent pleasure was heightened by the knowledge that, unless I had been a colonial governor, I would never in a hundred years have walked up the grand staircase and been ushered into the presence of a Colonial Office minister.

The Duke could not have been more courteous, friendly and helpful. I was to meet him again soon afterwards in the unlikely setting of the African suburb of Magomeni, where he spent an hour or so with a trowel in his hand helping to build a house in a new housing development.

There were also meetings that week with the minister for technical assistance Dennis Vosper at Carlton House Terrace and with the cooperative adviser to the Secretary of State for the Colonies, Mr Surridge. The upshot of it all was that we got the money for the college and Mr Fred Howarth from Loughborough was appointed as its first principal.

I took the opportunity to get Jerry Kasambala to agree to my returning from leave via Prague, Belgrade and Tel Aviv. I wanted to visit our cooperative students who were studying in Czechoslovakia, Yugoslavia and Israel *en route* and see for myself what their conditions were like, especially behind the Iron Curtain.

Feeling slightly apprehensive, we set off for Prague for our first trip behind the Iron Curtain on a lovely spring day in early May. The cold war was at its height and Czechoslovakia was still very much in the grip of communist rule.

Through friendships within the worldwide cooperative movement, we became the official guests of the *Ustredni Rada Druzstev*, the Czech cooperative union. Its cheerful general manager Mr Nepomucky met us at the small rural looking airport and drove us to the Hotel Flora in Wenceslas Square in the heart of the city where we were staying.

The next day, we drove down the river for a few miles to an old country house that had been converted into an international cooperative college. Here at last we found our Tanganyikan students. They gave us a warm welcome, but they were not allowed out of sight of their Czech hosts. I was amused to observe that after a few months they all seemed to speak Czech fluently. To the obvious annoyance of our hosts, I spoke Swahili to them and learned that, as I had suspected, they were well fed and looked after, but kept under very strict control and subjected to a certain amount of communist propaganda, which they took in their stride.

It was quite a relief to fly away to the slightly freer air of Yugoslavia, which, as it were, was only half behind the Iron Curtain. Belgrade's fine new airport terminal had been built by Americans and the non-aligned leader Marshal Tito was trying to get the best of both worlds and transcend his communist roots by living like a tsar with a luxury yacht and an island palace at Brioni.

I duly found our little group of students in Zagreb, took them to lunch at the Savoy Hotel and found them in very good spirits and much happier on the whole than their compatriots in Czechoslovakia. Like them, they too had mastered the local language and were able to order our meal in fluent Serbo-Croat. Flying back to Belgrade in the late afternoon, we entered a fierce thunderstorm and the plane pitched and tossed alarmingly. The passenger sitting next to me smiled and said reassuringly, 'Don't worry. Driver, he is learner!' This was apparently true, for Yugoslav Airlines had just taken delivery of new French aircraft with which they were not yet fully familiar. I was relieved when a few minutes later he 'dive-bombed' the Belgrade airport in true continental style and landed safely.

We could not fly direct to Tel Aviv, but had to break the journey for a day in Athens before continuing that evening to Israel. There we were met at Lod Airport and driven to the Hotel Samuel on the Tel Aviv seafront. Here we were based for a week as guests of the all-powerful *Histadrut*, a vast monolithic organization that seemed to embrace all the cooperatives and trade unions in the country.

I was soon satisfied that our students could not receive a better training anywhere on earth. Academic excellence was combined with a practical down to earth approach. Agriculturists and cooperative and trade union officials in particular, benefited enormously from training in conditions that provided a unique blend of the First and Third Worlds, culturally, environmentally and climatically.

Politically, too, the young State of Israel, itself not yet 20 years' old, seemed to seek influence in nascent African countries, possibly as a counterweight to Islamic Arab aspirations. Their military training was also excellent and in the early years of independence they were to play a key role in training both our soldiers and our national servicemen.

We met our students on the courses at the *Histadrut* headquarters in Tel Aviv and 'sat in' on some of their lectures. We drove up the rocky road to Jerusalem and our glimpses of the great golden crenellated walls of the Holy City shining in the sun far exceeded my wildest dreams. The Arabs still occupied half the city, divided at the Mandelbaum Gate, so we could not visit the Holy Sepulchre or Bethlehem. We could, however, see the Mount of Olives and the golden Dome of the Rock on the site of the Great Temple from the Upper Room on the Holy Hill of Zion, where 'The Last Supper' took place.

The spirit of the new Israel was perhaps best exemplified by its experiment in communal living in kibbutzim and moshavim, several of which we visited. 'To each according to his need and from each according to his means,' was their motto and certainly in their early days the more extreme kibbutzim, where people shared everything, including their clothes, must surely have been the purest form of real communism ever attempted. Human beings, however, can only tolerate such unreal forms of existence when threatened by grave natural or human disasters and, as the country became relatively more peaceful and prosperous, so did the earlier zeal diminish.

Susan and I had breakfast in a desert kibbutz near Beersheba and were amazed to eat peaches grown there and to see tables decorated with bowls of roses.

By the end of May, we were back in Dar es Salaam after a most memorable leave. I was at once given special responsibility to plan the new cooperative college in Moshi, whose principal, the Lancastrian Fred Howarth, we had just recruited in Britain. A young

Haya cooperative officer from Bukoba, Gabriel Kagaruki, was designated his deputy and duly succeeded him a few years later.

The excitement generated by *uhuru*, however, sent tens of thousands of hopeful young men and women to Dar es Salaam like so many Dick Whittingtons seeking employment and fun amid the bright lights of the capital. They stayed with their friends' relations and fellow tribesmen (*ndugu*) in the already overcrowded cramped insanitary rooms of Kariakoo, Magomeni, Ilala, Temeke and Kinondoni. Their presence naturally aggravated an already serious situation. The government did what it could to discourage this unwelcome migration by slogans and posters exhorting the public — *usiwe kupe: ji tegemee!* (don't be a tick: be self reliant!).

Nyerere felt that these job seekers were abusing traditional tribal hospitality where custom dictated that one would entertain one's fellow tribesmen forever. The proverb *mgeni siku tatu ya nne mpe jembe* (a guest for three days, give him a hoe on the fourth) also, however, obtained. No doubt, in the city a few shillings sufficed for a hoe. Needless to say, some of the visitors were only nominally job seekers and really came to have a good time in the bars and dance halls of the big city.

The inadequate took to begging and the vicious to crime and prostitution, rewarding occupations in all cities. Freedom from family, tribal customs and discipline, and the absence of elders, combined to fan the flames of detribalization and demoralization. This was exemplified in the growth of new shanty towns like Manzese, outside the city boundaries beyond Magomeni on the north of the main road to Morogoro, which was notorious for crime and prostitution.

In fact, beggars, vagabonds (*wa-huni, ma-lofa*) and petty thieves with no fixed abode became such a serious problem that the government was driven on several occasions to order the police to round them up. Thousands were moved in buses and lorries to special labour camps in the fertile Kilombero valley in the Mahenge district 150 miles southwest of Dar es Salaam to work on the large sugar plantations there. This was an ideal solution in theory, but sadly it did not work out in practice and, within a few months, most of them had trickled back to the capital.

23

Revolution in Zanzibar and Army Mutiny, 1963–64

The second anniversary of *uhuru* on 9 December 1963
heralded the unfolding of a dramatic sequence of events. It
started with the independence of Zanzibar, followed by
revolution on the island and mutiny on the mainland. It culminated in a union between the two countries four-and-a-half months
later in April 1964. The population of Zanzibar included a domin-
ant Arab landowning minority of 30,000, the descendants of the
rulers and traders who had made it an important offshore base in
the slave trade and legitimate commerce between the mainland
and Arabian peninsular. Until 1964, there were also 30,000
Asians, who were mostly traders, shopkeepers and civil servants.
The vast majority of the people, however, were the 270,000
Africans, either descendants of a mixture of Persian invaders and
indigenous African Zanzibaris or more recent and contemporary
emigrants from the East African mainland.

The Arab-led Zanzibar Nationalist Party (ZNP), headed by my
friend the scholarly Sheikh Ali Muhsin, fostered traditional ethnic
and Islamic links with Egypt, the Sudan and Muscat, with which it
had historic ties and from where the ruling Al-Busaid dynasty had
originally derived.

Its radical wing, led by Abdul Rahman Mohammed Babu, broke
with the ZNP just before independence to form the Umma Party
(the Masses). By far the largest party, however, reflecting the
population ratio, was the Afro-Shirazi Party, of which Abeid

Karume was leader. When the British government decided to grant rapid independence to the protectorate on 9 December 1963, it negotiated primarily with the leaders of the ZNP. Given Zanzibar's history over the last 100 years, this was hardly surprising because it was they who represented the island's ruling class, the Establishment with whom British Residents had dealt since the start of the protectorate.

A strange electoral system gave the Afro-Shirazi Party a majority of votes but a minority of seats in parliament. This was a recipe for disaster, if ever there was one. Thus, on 9 December 1963, the sultanate of Zanzibar became fully independent under a government dominated by the ZNP and led by Ali Muhsin.

Within five weeks of independence, however, while leaders of the Afro-Shirazi and Umma parties were doubtless contemplating revolutions of their own, the government was violently overthrown. It took only a few days and was achieved through a surprise peasant revolt led by an unknown Ugandan labourer called John Okello, soon to be known as the Field Marshal.

The rising started with a successful raid on the main police armoury, swiftly followed by the seizure of the radio station. There was little resistance after that as the heavily outnumbered police were not prepared to fire on their own brothers and some even joined in the uprising. A series of extraordinary broadcasts followed from Zanzibar radio, some of which I listened to and found of compelling interest. They gave a 'ball by ball' commentary on the progress of the rising, including detailed orders to revolutionary units and occasional extraordinary quasi-religious speeches by the Field Marshal himself. I found it hard to tear myself away from the set, for I realized that this was history in the making.

Before the rebels had time to secure the whole island, the British high commissioner and his staff, with the help of the Royal Navy, managed to get the Sultan and his family and most of the small British and European population safely to Dar es Salaam. The full ferocity of the rebel assault, however, was reserved for revenge on their hated Arab masters, who were mercilessly hunted down, murdered and raped; their homes were looted and pillaged in a frenzy of destruction that shocked and alarmed their mainland neighbours. Women and children were included in the massacre to the refrain of *mtoto wa simba ni simba tu* (the child of a lion will be a lion one day). Various estimates agreed that at least 10,000 people were killed.

After this murderous interlude had ended, Okello installed a Revolutionary Council under the leadership of Abeid Karume, the Afro-Shirazi leader, which included Babu and the communist Abdulla Kassim Hanga.

Strangely enough, Father Neil Russell, who was on a visit to Zanzibar at the time, met John Okello on the boat sailing to Pemba and found him, so he later told us, 'very polite and respectful'. Shortly afterwards, his mission accomplished, Okello returned home to his native Uganda, as quickly and mysteriously as he had arrived and was rarely heard of again.

* * *

No sooner had the Zanzibar revolution, which had deposed the Sultan on 12 January, burned itself out, than the Tanganyika Rifles mutinied in the small hours of Monday 20 January 1964, the timing doubtless influenced by events across the sea. The mutiny was organized by about 20 men headed by a Sergeant Ilogi, who called himself 'Major Hingo', and was conducted with considerable efficiency and, with one or two unfortunate exceptions, with reasonable humanity. Deceived by a bogus fire alarm, all the British officers at Colito barracks near Dar es Salaam were quickly rounded up at bayonet point and locked in the guardroom.

The mutineers also quickly seized the airport, the railway station, the broadcasting station, the post office and other strategic targets. The British officers were taken to the airport and flown to Nairobi. The second battalion, in which Sam Sarakikya was a young captain, also mutinied at Tabora where the mutineers beat up a number of European and Asian civilians and pretended to shoot a British woman teacher. The mutineers' demands were simple — remove all British officers and replace them with Africans and improve pay and conditions.

The next five days were surreal. No one seemed to know what was going on or who was in charge of the country. The mutineers had seized Selander Bridge, cutting off Oyster Bay, so no one could go to work in their offices and the government virtually ground to a halt. At breakfast time on the Monday morning, I was startled to see an army vehicle drive past our house down Mzinga Way with a neighbour of mine, a British army officer who lived up the road, crouched in his pyjamas with a gun at his back.

Crowds of frightened people thronged the nearby shopping centre to lay in supplies for a siege. The President and Prime Minister appeared to have disappeared overnight and Oscar Kambona seemed to be in charge. He broadcast to the country in Swahili that evening and tried to negotiate with the mutineers and persuade them to return to barracks. It later transpired that Nyerere and Kawana had been advised by their ministers to go into temporary hiding, both for their own safety and, I think, to spare the state further humiliation. It was obviously preferable to negotiate with such desperate men at a lower level. Kambona himself and several other ministers were badly beaten up and Oscar had a black eye and swollen face. Joseph Nyerere and TANU treasurer Bokhe Munanka were also assaulted.

Drunken soldiers who had consumed all the beer in the New Africa Hotel now went on a rampage in Arab and African bazaars, looting shops, molesting passers-by and causing considerable damage, especially in Kariakoo and Magomeni.

Shooting broke out in the afternoon when an Arab in Magomeni shot dead two soldiers and two civilians in defence of his shop; he was then massacred with his entire family. In all, 17 people were killed and 20 seriously injured. We could hear the sound of firing from our house in Oyster Bay.

An ominous BBC news bulletin that evening told us that 'the situation in Dar es Salaam continues to deteriorate,' which was not very reassuring. Someone from the British high commission telephoned to tell us 'to pack a suitcase each of personal belongings' and be prepared to embark that night from Oyster Bay beach on the warship HMS *Rhyl*. It had just arrived off the coast from Zanzibar with men from the Staffordshire Regiment on board to rescue us should things get worse. Fortunately, this was not to prove necessary. Susan, always at her best in times of danger, slept peacefully while I kept watch all night with a loaded shotgun, which I determined not to use save as a last resort. My contingency plan was to invite any mutineers in, give them a drink, talk to them politely and, with luck, persuade them to leave. Fortunately, nobody appeared and we could breathe again.

On the surface, things seemed to be back to normal on Tuesday and we all warily drifted back to work to exchange stories about the amazing events. Nyerere returned to State House that night and made a sad broadcast appealing for calm. He referred to Monday 20 January as 'a most disgraceful day'. He was naturally shaken and distressed by the mutiny just two years after independence. Similar outbreaks in Kenya and Uganda had been speedily put down by British troops. The next day, Wednesday 22 January, he toured the city and greatly reassured the inhabitants.

At the nearby Karimjee Hall there was a meeting in honour of the late Dag Hammarskjöld, the Swedish former secretary-general of the United Nations. Nyerere himself chaired the meeting. He was fresh from holding a press conference at which, in view of the government's utter powerlessness, he had adopted an equivocal attitude towards the mutineers.

Ironically, at much the same time, the trade union dissidents Mkello and Tumbo were plotting against him in Morogoro and wondering how best to exploit the mutiny to obtain power for themselves. It seemed clear that the plotters had made contact with the mutineers and were planning to take over the state. The police could no longer be relied on and several had already joined the mutineers.

Faced with this deteriorating situation, on the evening of Friday 24 January Nyerere reluctantly agreed to request British help. Kambona delivered his letter personally to Stephen Miles, the acting high commissioner, at about 7.00 p.m.

At dawn the next morning, Saturday 25 January, we awoke to the sound of heavy gunfire from the sea. I drove to the beach and saw the cheering sight of eight helicopters with jeeps slung below them ferrying Royal Marine commandos from the deck of the aircraft carrier HMS *Centaur* to Colito barracks, which was being bombarded with airbursts by HMS *Cambrian* to avoid loss of life. It was about 6.30 a.m. and the sun was just rising.

We later heard that after a single rocket had killed three *askari* in the guardroom and wounded several others, the mutineers began to surrender and a few ran away. The brief action was over in half an hour and the mutiny ended.

Later that morning, I witnessed some extraordinary scenes in the centre of the city. Thousands of cheering Africans, Asians and Europeans were giving the commandos and an armoured-car squadron from the 16/5th Lancers an emotional welcome, greeting their 'rescuers' like conquering heroes. The British were in fact asked to hold the city for a week, during which a humiliated government carried out a draconian purge of mutineers, plotters, traitors and all other questionable elements with suspect loyalties.

The president promptly wrote a letter of thanks to the British government, which Secretary of State for Commonwealth Relations Duncan Sandys read to the House of Commons a few days later. British officers and men were fêted wherever they went and many parties given for them. We had three young Royal Marines to dinner one evening and enjoyed their refreshing company.

For the government, however, their presence was obviously a necessary evil and a humiliating and mortifying ordeal. After three months or so, therefore, they were replaced in May 1964 by a splendid Nigerian battalion under Colonel Pam, who was later murdered in his own country during a revolution there.

Nyerere disbanded the Tanganyika Rifles in disgust; the soldiers were sent home to their villages in disgrace, though many were later forgiven and recruited again to form the necessary nucleus of the new Tanzania People's Defence Force (TPDF), which, untainted by any colonial connection, was formed some time later. The ringleaders were severely dealt with and received long prison sentences.

Shortly afterwards, a squadron of the Imperial Ethiopian Air Force arrived in Dar es Salaam and was stationed for some months a few miles west of the capital near the Ukonga prison. So far as I know, they did not instruct the local embryo air force, or fly much, but acted merely as a political presence to assist the government regain some kind of stability, presumably sent by the OAU whose headquarters were in Addis Ababa.

For some months before the mutiny, the government had been considering plans to confer local honours and awards on Tanganyika citizens and others judged to have rendered outstanding service to the new nation. They would replace the traditional orders and decorations conferred in the past by the British sovereign on her subjects throughout the British Empire in the traditional New Year's and Queen's Birthday honours lists. Indeed, the local investitures by the British governors had been a feature of the Dar es Salaam 'season'. Proposals had already been drawn up for the institution of two Tanganyikan orders of chivalry, the Order of Kilimanjaro and the Order of the Star of Africa, each of which would have three classes on the lines of the orders formerly issued by the sultans of Zanzibar.

However, so shocked and disgusted was President Nyerere by the shameful disloyalty of his soldiers that rumour had it that he said that such people did not deserve any decorations and he cancelled the proposals on the spot. This was an inglorious end to a tragic episode in Tanganyika's short history.

The mutiny did, however, concentrate people's minds and bring them down to earth in no uncertain manner. The Tanganyika Rifles had after all been a very hastily improvised form of the old imperial King's African Rifles, whose very title showed where its main loyalties lay. Its hastily camouflaged nationalist successor still had British commanding officers and over 90 per cent of its officers were British two years after independence. It was hardly surprising that something snapped.

The government was now quietly determined to cut all military ties with the former colonial power and build a new people's army almost from scratch. Its officers and men would be trained by a variety of smaller states, such as Israel and Canada, with no conceivable political axe to grind in East Africa. Recruitment too would be extended to all tribes and not merely confined to the so-called warrior tribes like the Hehe, Ngoni and Nyamwezi who had originally been arbitrarily selected by the Germans and confirmed by the KAR. This perhaps was the 'silver lining'.

24

Union with Zanzibar and the Birth of Tanzania, 1964

While mainland Tanganyika was in the throes of mutiny and mayhem, the island of Zanzibar was waking up to a new post-Red revolution communist dawn. It soon attracted attention worldwide and provided an ideal opportunity for communist states, which were hitherto largely unwelcome in independent African countries, to recognize the new regime and, in some cases, buy themselves in with interest-free loans and gifts of money and goods.

Thus, China gave a large interest-free loan, the Soviet Union bought a lot of cloves and began to train the new army and East Germany took over the hospitals and gave a new radio transmitter. Countries hitherto virtually unknown in the region, such as Cuba, North Vietnam, North Korea, Bulgaria and even Albania, managed to get some kind of foothold on the island.

Ironically, this miniature communist state ruled by its Revolutionary Council just 22 miles off the mainland became almost like an African Cuba. Festooned in the unfamiliar flags of hitherto unknown lands, it bristled with the strange calibre weapons which, under the supervision of officers from Moscow and Havana, had been supplied by arsenals from Brno to Pyongyang.

While not actually pointing a pistol at the heart of Tanganyika* in Dar es Salaam, our democratic government and the rest of us

---

* A reference to Napoleon's remark: 'Give me Antwerp — it will be a pistol pointing to the heart of England.'

too, for that matter, felt a certain disquiet and a strange sense of foreboding. Zanzibari refugees began to arrive in Dar es Salaam with terrible tales of the new order — some doubtless exaggerated. The *Tanganyika Standard* began to print photographs of a bizarre collection of foreigners, nearly all in some kind of quasi-military uniform, supervising the erection of hideous blocks of workers' high-rise flats, driving tractors on 'collective' farms, and training men and women soldiers.

The Tanganyika government had good cause to fear that its hitherto harmless little neighbour might become an offshore centre of communist subversion directed towards the mainland governments. Quite apart from that, however, there had for centuries been close traditional links between the mainland Africans and the African majority on the islands of Zanzibar and Pemba, while TANU and the Afro-Shirazi Party were also closely linked.

The failure to achieve an East African federation the previous year, which Nyerere had always warned 'if not done before *uhuru*, could never be done after it', had left Tanganyika isolated, especially given the instability of the Congo on its western border. Above all, the army mutiny had seriously weakened the government's position leaving it ashamed, humiliated, powerless and reliant on foreigners, albeit Africans, for its defence.

February and March 1964 passed uneasily with the country slowly recovering from the surprise blow that had so nearly strangled it at birth. Then, at Nyerere's express invitation, the OAU met in Dar es Salaam in February to hear a first-hand explanation of why the British had been asked to intervene and to receive an appeal for African troops to replace British soldiers until a new local force could be trained.

Then suddenly, at the nadir of his fortunes, Nyerere pulled off one of his most dazzling political coups. Towards the end of April, he and Karume announced out of the blue that they had signed an agreement of union between the two countries, which the National Assembly of Tanganyika ratified on 24 April. It resulted from negotiations between Karume and Hanga on the one side and Kambona and the trusted British attorney general Roland Brown on the other.

ιore extreme left opposed the union, which the
tionary Council apparently ratified while Babu
communists regarded it as a setback; Nyerere had
the red card. The Act of Union was formally
passeᴄ   ιpril 1964 and it has been celebrated ever since as
Union Day. ∠anzibar retained considerable autonomy under a
constitution for the United Republic of Tanganyika and Zanzibar,
which was said to be modelled on that of Northern Ireland — not
perhaps the happiest of precedents.

President Karume of Zanzibar became the first of two vice-
presidents in the united republic, Kawawa being the second — a
courteous gesture by the mainland. Indeed, substantial concessions
were made to Zanzibar in the negotiations preceding the union
and they achieved political representation in it out of all proportion to their modest population. Five of their political leaders
became ministers in the government of the united republic, while
52 Zanzibaris became members of the National Assembly,
including 32 members of the Revolutionary Council and 20
Zanzibaris nominated by Nyerere.

Zanzibar retained control not only over its own police, hospitals
and schools, but also over its own army and immigration department. All in all, Zanzibar got by far the best of the bargain,
though Nyerere doubtless felt that 'half a loaf of bread was better
than none'. Far from little Zanzibar being incorporated into a
union with big brother on the mainland, it almost succeeded in
swallowing up its bigger neighbour.

On Union Day, 26 April 1964, the Ministry of Cooperative and
Community Development ceased to exist and a new Ministry of
Commerce and Cooperatives was formed with the radical Zanzibar revolutionary leader Abdul Rahman Mohammed Babu as its
minister. This was part of the major cabinet reshuffle caused by
the union. We awaited the arrival of the now notorious
communist leader with considerable apprehension.

Fortunately, my fears were not realized. From the first day we
met, Babu and I got on very well; the chemistry seemed right. We
were much the same age — about 40 — the Anglo-Irish seemed to
have something in common with the Afro-Arab. His enchanting

smile, somewhat ravaged face, pallid skin, mischievous brown eyes and thick lips (the varied characteristics of his mixed ancestry) combined to produce a bewitchingly naughty look. In fact, he had the most attractively ugly face I had ever seen.

He had a bright intelligence deepened by curiosity, travel and wide reading, which was crowned by traditional Arab courtesy and a splendid sense of humour. He had a rare political honesty and always welcomed the truth, however unpalatable.

Ironically, he had been born into a well-known religious family whose ancestors had long ago migrated from the holy city of Mecca to Iraq. From there, they had gone to the Yemen before finally arriving in East Africa, where his father had lived and worked in Mozambique before moving to Zanzibar, and was for a time the Portuguese consul there.

Young Babu had lived in London for seven years from 1950 to 1957, where I suspect he first began to take a serious interest in journalism and radical politics. He was apparently an anarchist for a short time. He also worked with Fenner Brockway in the Movement for Colonial Freedom. He always told me how much he loved London and he spoke the most perfect idiomatic English.

A few days after the union on 1 May 1964, I was promoted, for the last time, to administrative officer Grade II as principal assistant secretary (Admin) in the new ministry. My duties were much the same as before save that my responsibilities included the commerce division in place of community development; my association with the cooperatives continued unchanged. One of my tasks was to arrange overseas scholarships and, in the honeymoon period of overseas aid from 1962 to 1967, we sent 500 students on overseas courses in 20 different countries.

Babu was always a great support and encouraged us in every way; he had no time for red tape and often removed obstacles placed in our path by bureaucratic officials. He had brought with him from Zanzibar a beautiful and charming Indian secretary, Shirin Hassanali, who sometimes typed my letters at great speed when the minister was away and my own secretary was overworked or away sick.

His wife Ashura was a great support politically and socially and gave delightful supper parties in their large German-built bungalow near the gates of State House, to which Susan and I were sometimes invited. Little did I think in those early days that Babu and I would remain fast friends in Africa and London until his death 32 years later, in 1996.

The next six months were extremely difficult for the fragile new union between the Republic of Tanganyika and the People's Democratic Republic of Zanzibar — to give them their full titles. The new United Republic of Tanganyika and Zanzibar (*Jamhuri ya Umoja wa Tanganyika na Unguja*) had not yet acquired a proper name or even a new flag.

Despite the many concessions made to the miniature newcomer — some almost absurd and the source of many a joke among my Tanganyikan friends — the Zanzibar government, while paying lip service to the union, carried on much as before. The precariously balanced union government seemed powerless to intervene or enforce its puny authority in any way. The old Swahili proverb: '*mpanda wa farasi wawili hupasuka msaamba*' (the rider of two horses splits his arse) was apposite.

The tough former boatman Abeid Karume and his cronies in the Revolutionary Council pressed on regardless with their own policies. They rapidly implemented a decree passed in March 1964 that enabled the President to acquire any property without the payment of compensation whenever it appeared to him that it was in the national interest to do so. A free for all ensued and members of the Revolutionary Council promptly helped themselves to the property of a great many Arab and Asian citizens. Such racially motivated highway robbery was totally contrary to the non-racial democratic policies of the mainland government.

There were also ugly rumours of 'liquidations' of political opponents, corruption and other abuses of power by those in authority. It was difficult for people on the mainland to visit the island, the tourist trade dried up and even Nyerere himself was advised by the mainland police to postpone his planned first official visit to the island.

My friend Babu, the senior Zanzibar minister with the union government, made his home in Dar es Salaam and decided against returning to the island for reasons of personal safety. As with all revolutions, today's hero is often tomorrow's traitor. The mainland-dominated union government failed to prevail upon the island authorities either to merge the Afro-Shirazi party with TANU or to cooperate in the five-year development plan. They even refused to agree to substitute the initial 'interim' constitution with a more permanent one, so it remained 'interim' for the foreseeable future.

Serious diplomatic problems arose over the status of communist embassies offshore and on the mainland, where quite different political ideologies reigned. West Germany, which had an ambassador in Dar es Salaam, was a major source of capital and technical assistance for the mainland. East Germany, on the other hand, was the first country to recognize the new People's Republic of Zanzibar and to open an embassy there. It had sent a considerable amount of aid to the island before union and had promised more. An extraordinary tug of war ensued with the Iron Curtain now coming down in the Azanian Sea.

Union was beginning to have major effects on the foreign policy of the united republic, which had now moved from its unexceptionable non-aligned policy to being in the front line of the cold war. On 27 May 1964, the union government's foreign minister Kambona announced after a visit to Bonn that all countries that had had missions before union in both Tanganyika and Zanzibar would now be permitted embassies in Dar es Salaam. However, they would only be allowed to have consulates in Zanzibar and this would have meant downgrading the East German embassy there. Both the East German government and the island authorities fiercely resented and defied this ruling; the seemingly intractable impasse it produced could well have brought all West German aid to a halt.

While the Zanzibar crises to the east threatened the stability of the new state, another crisis erupted again in the vast unstable Congo to the west, soon after the withdrawal of the last United Nations' peacekeeping troops in June 1964. Rebellions broke out in various parts of the country. The hated African quisling Moise Tshombe, ruler of breakaway Katanga Province, was appointed prime minister in July by President Kasavubu and at once started to re-recruit the motley collection of foreign mercenaries who had helped him seize power in Katanga several years earlier. Recruited mainly from Belgium and southern Africa, prominent among them were legendary characters like Mad Mike Hoare, whose courage and daring inspired his comrades.

Tshombe also turned to the US and Belgian governments for support in his struggle against the rebels and, to the fury of the OAU and the African states in general, it was freely given. Widely regarded as the murderer of Patrice Lumumba, Tshombe was regarded with hatred and loathing by ordinary Tanganyikans, and his white mercenaries known in Swahili as *askari malaya* (soldier prostitutes) were held in the utmost contempt.

* * *

Meanwhile, in Dar es Salaam a competition open to the public was in full swing to choose an appropriate name for the new nation, for which foreign journalists had already coined the coded word Tan-Zan from the prefixes of the two countries involved. A friend of mine, who was dealing with the papers, gave me a glimpse of the file, which contained more than 800 different suggestions. They included such exotic names as Azania (the Greek word for East Africa); African Democratic Republic; Kilimanjaria; Nyereria; Black Pearl and Tanzania, which the committee responsible finally selected. It was chosen as an amalgam of the historic Azania and the Tanzan coined by the media and hence rapidly coming into popular usage in press and radio reports. It proved to be a popular choice both inside and outside the country, though most foreigners persisted in pronouncing it as in 'Ruritania' rather than in the correct Swahili manner with the accent on the penultimate syllable.

The new name, the United Republic of Tanzania came into use in October 1964 and the new flag, incorporating a blue segment symbolic of the seas surrounding the spice islands and uniting them to the mainland, was flown for the first time. The national anthem remained unchanged.

Union with Zanzibar and the Birth of Tanzania, 1964

Tanganyika achieved independence on 9 December 1961 in the most peaceful manner possible. It was the envy of all Africa if not the entire British Commonwealth. However, its successor state, the United Republic of Tanzania, was born in the aftermath of a bloody revolution in Zanzibar and a shameful mutiny on the mainland. It was nurtured in infancy amid the internal intrigues of Africa and the chill blasts of the cold war.

25

Cold War in the Tropics, 1964–66

T he young restructured nation pulled hither and thither by both sides in the cold war now placed great emphasis on self-reliance. Thousands of people throughout the country built a wide range of public works through self-help schemes, for which they were paid nothing. The funds that were available were reserved to purchase the necessary materials.

A great upsurge of patriotic energy was effectively harnessed to implement the first five-year development plan the president launched in May 1964. It was a natural sequel to the centuries' old tradition of tribal turnouts that had built the dams and maintained the roads in the Handeni famine of 1953. The plan was the first major step in the war Nyerere declared on poverty, ignorance and disease. It sought to increase the national income by expanding agricultural production and thereby creating the funds needed to finance improved educational and medical facilities.

Without an efficient infrastructure, Third World countries tend to soak up foreign aid like blotting paper. Top priority was given to constructing good roads, railways and harbours and improving the telecommunications system. Since none of this was possible without trained personnel, as soon as possible crash training programmes were launched at home and abroad. The diversity of donors was not an unmixed blessing. Army officers were trained in countries as varied as Britain, Canada, China, Israel, North Korea and the USSR. Not only did the military systems of these countries vary, but also their basic drill, weapons and ammunition, not to speak of the various language problems this raised.

To a lesser extent, this problem obtained in all fields. One of the first Tanzanian dentists trained in Oslo had to learn Norwegian before he could be taught how to drill a tooth. The whole system of necessity operated under great handicaps, slowing down the plan. The old proverb of 'beggars can't be choosers', applied with a vengeance.

It was a topsy-turvy world. As the Tanzanian youth moved out, so the foreign youth moved in, fired with idealistic enthusiasm, but not always skill or tact. Peace Corps volunteers from the USA and Voluntary Service Overseas (VSO) recruits from the UK led the way helping village and urban self-help schemes to build hospitals, schools, dispensaries, roads, dams and wells across the land. West Germans, Australians, Canadians, Israelis and Scandinavians soon followed.

These volunteers literally worked for a pittance. They were quite separate from the well-paid helper category of professional doctors, dentists, professors, teachers and agriculturists from the UN and a host of other countries. They paid most, if not all, their own expenses and, generally speaking, replaced the vanishing British colonial service officers, whose vacant bungalows they occupied.

Different nations gradually built up their own 'spheres of influence'. By and large, the British, Americans, Australians and Indians provided the general academic courses in the arts and finance. The Chinese built the Friendship Textile Mill outside Dar es Salaam and later the great Tanzam Railway from Dar es Salaam to Ndola in Zambia. The Canadians trained the air wing pilots. Israelis trained the national service recruits and the Scandinavians concentrated on building up the cooperative movement and starting the first cooperative shops.

The Soviet Black Sea Fleet trained 50 midshipmen for the virtually non-existent Tanzanian navy, while the Emperor of Ethiopia gave us 50 scholarships to Addis Ababa University. I remember them particularly well because they simply appeared in a newspaper advertisement in the *Tanganyika Standard* and applications had to be submitted within a few days. We literally scoured the streets for suitable candidates and, having found the necessary quota arranged their passports. We then had to find guarantors who would stand surety for their good conduct on the course and undertake to refund the fees if they behaved badly.

I took them to the TANU office, which refused to guarantee them, whereupon I guaranteed the lot myself. None of them let me down. There was never a dull moment and we lived life at fever pitch during that exciting time.

To revert to self-reliance and the five-year plan, as a mood of self-sacrifice swept the country, fuelled by patriotic rallies, fiery speeches and slogans on the walls, so did a hate campaign develop against the 'baddies'. Capitalists, exploiters, parasites and blood-suckers were daily castigated in the media and on political platforms. The Swahili language, like Arabic, was rich in invective and soon new expressions flooded into circulation, including *makabaila* (capitalists), *wa nyonyaji (damu)* (bloodsuckers), *ma papasi* (ticks) and *mirija* (straws used to suck out blood or anything else); self help — help yourself — the cynics said.

The powers of hereditary African chiefs are clearly demarcated by centuries of tribal tradition and ritual balanced by correspond-ingly onerous responsibilities, together invested with deep spiritual significance. TANU's new Young Turks were bound by no such restraints; neither heredity nor training had prepared them for the heavy responsibilities and considerable power so suddenly thrust upon them. It was no wonder that the new regional and area com-missioners partook in a number of abuses of power. In one tragic case near Mwanza, capital of the new East Lake Region, about 30 minor offenders were imprisoned overnight in a tiny local court lockup designed to take one or two prisoners only, with the inevitable consequence that by the morning many had died of suffocation. The area commissioner responsible was dismissed at once by a distraught idealistic president who as I recall broadcast to the nation 'more in sorrow than in anger' that such callous and thoughtless acts should stain the fair name of the young state. So far as I can recollect, this tragic case arose more from inexperience and thoughtlessness than from deliberate cruelty.

Cold War in the Tropics, 1964–66

For me at that time, the epitome of the spirit of the capital city was the young man cycling to work on his bicycle in a brightly coloured shirt and dark slacks. He would acknowledge my passing greeting with a wave of the hand, a mischievous smile and a saucy shake of the head. I codenamed him 'Kalamazoo, shake your head' after a popular dance tune of the time. His cheerful greeting never failed to make my heart sing.

Our coral garden in Mzinga Way was a constant solace in the cool of the evening or the dew-dappled dawns. Our gardener Kondo had recruited a 14-year-old assistant soon after the Zanzibar revolution. We at once called him the Field Marshal, to his great delight. The name suited him so perfectly that I have long since forgotten his real name.

He and my 11-year-old son Gerald soon became fast friends and used to engage in strong-arm duels on the kitchen floor.

The children built a fine tree house in the scarlet acacia tree near the front lawn to which they often repaired during their holidays. One day we were surprised to see smoke pouring out of the coconut frond walls as Lucy and Gerald beat a rapid retreat and the secret of the popularity of their arboreal eyrie was revealed.

We grew flowers in the front and vegetables at the back where we also had a badminton court, which gave us all great pleasure and relaxation for many years. It was a special court, for the ground underfoot was rather rough and the shuttlecock behaved erratically when caught in the sea breeze. Nearly every evening after tea we would play for an hour or so until sundown. We would then bath and settle down in our pyjamas and dressing gowns for a glass of beer before dinner and bed soon after 9.00 p.m.

As there was as a rule no work at all on Sundays, the routine was slightly different on that day. After the morning service at St Albans, we often drove away for the day to lunch with friends. These included the Brycesons, whose house was next door to the president's lodge on Msasani beach. At other times, we would pack a picnic or have lunch at one of the new tourist hotels or lodges that were beginning to spring up along the coast.

We often spent the day with Susan's cousin Daudi Ricardo. He

285

had left his great demesne at Matanana in Iringa district in the Southern Highlands Province and moved to a beach hut near the Silversands Hotel at Kunduchi. He shared this with his faithful pair of teenagers Ali, who had managed to escape from Zanzibar after the revolution, and Saidi. We would spend the day swimming, sleeping, eating and having a cool freshwater shower under the Heath Robinson contraption he had fixed up under a tree.

A delightful Dane called Paul Bertelsen, who was in charge of UNESCO adult literacy schemes in Tanzania often stayed with him at his beach retreat. Paul had recently carried out a successful campaign, one of the largest ever undertaken by UNESCO, in the Lake Province. He spoke perfect English — as Danes often do — and had degrees from both Copenhagen and Cambridge universities. His new Adult Education Centre in Lumumba Street, Dar es Salaam, was part of University College. His young assistant Nicholas Kuhanga, who was soon to become an MP, eventually succeeded Paul as director of the Adult Education Centre.

Like most Africans, the Tanzanian students were intrepid travellers, excellent linguists and incredibly adaptable to every kind of climate, environment and political system. I never ceased to admire the manner in which they coped with the freezing cold winters of Russia, Canada and Scandinavia, the seductive temptations of Western capitalism, the rigid controls of communism, the caste system of India and the harsh alien contradictions of life in China.

I would receive dozens of letters from our students abroad and, on their return, would listen avidly to their fascinating accounts of their interesting experiences. Whenever I could, I would visit them personally as well in Britain, Ireland, Czechoslovakia, Yugoslavia, Israel and Sweden, which I visited in 1967. I took about 100 Tanzanians to Expo 70 in Japan and was able to observe at first hand their reactions to such an entirely different culture.

Meanwhile, on leave in Britain in early 1965, I visited five of our star cooperative students. They were taking the only three-year degree course in cooperative studies in the world. It was in the lovely old university town of Marburg-an-der-Lahn near Cologne in West Germany. Only Standard 14 boys who had passed their higher school certificates were eligible. We had skimmed the cream of the sixth form boys of St Francis College at Pugu, St Andrew's College at Minaki and the government boys' school at Tabora to find candidates of the necessary calibre. They had to pass a crash course in the German language before they could even begin to attend lectures.

I spent a long weekend with them there in May 1965, met their professors who spoke highly of them, went boating with them on the river and drinking with them and their German friends in a beer cellar, singing the famous '*Trink Bruderlein, Trink*'.

On my return to London in mid-May 1965, I gave a lecture to the English-speaking union, which I entitled 'Tanzania: African Phoenix'. It was an impressionist glimpse of Tanzania; I felt that the title symbolized the country taking off like a phoenix rising from the ashes of the fires of revolution and mutiny. It seemed to go down quite well and was reported in the *Tanganyika Standard*.

Back in Tanzania, the country was slowly recovering from a fit of xenophobia. This followed the dramatic discovery of an alleged US plot to overthrow the government at the end of the previous year, which sparked off the usual run of marches and demonstrations culminating in the burning of the Stars and Stripes outside the US embassy. Of course, this fear and suspicion of Western powers sprang from a long legacy of colonialism reinforced by recent military intervention in the Congo. Also, Western diplomats made no effort to conceal their disapproval of the Tanzanian policy of non-alignment, with its 'dangerous' alliances with China and Russia.

Following the unilateral declaration of independence by Ian Smith's Rhodesian regime on 11 November 1965, on 15 December Nyerere led a number of African states in breaking off diplomatic relations with Britain, and demonstrators burned the Union Jack outside the British high commission. We went to the airport to bid a sad farewell to the high commissioner Bob Fowler, who later became British ambassador in Khartoum. Having started his own career as a district officer in Burma, he had always been particularly sympathetic to us administrative officers.

The Canadian government then agreed to look after Britain's

interests and a 'British interests' section of the Canadian high commission was opened in due course. It was headed by a gallant British diplomat called Bill Wilson with a heart condition that had to be checked once a year in London and that later led to his premature death. He had once been HM Consul General in Jerusalem, which he described as the zenith of his career.

The October 1965 National Assembly election endorsed Nyerere's plan for a one-party democracy, which TANU's national executive committee had already overwhelmingly approved. He felt that the imported Westminster-style multiparty democracy did not now, and perhaps never would, suit a young African state like Tanzania. He felt that different parties would accentuate existing tribal, religious and class differences and bring disunity to the country.

On the other hand, individual members of the National Assembly were democratically elected by universal suffrage and the people used their power to remove seven MPs, including two ministers and six junior ministers. In addition to the 17 members of the National Assembly nominated directly by the president, all 20 regional commissioners were members, as were all 17 members of the Zanzibar Revolutionary Council.

There is little doubt, however, that after *uhuru* and still more so after the union, the National Assembly, though not merely a talking shop or rubber stamp, ceased to have sovereign power in the Western sense and more nearly resembled a Russian *duma*. Real power now rested with the TANU party on the mainland, the Revolutionary Council on the islands and, above all, in the person of the president and commander-in-chief. Virtually all the mainland share of cabinet posts and other key jobs in the parastatals and elsewhere were filled by top TANU leaders, with the result that the party bureaucracy itself was correspondingly weakened.

This in turn led to increasing inefficiency at the grass roots level, which, in the fullness of time, was to corrode the body politic. The country was therefore largely ruled by an idealistic if somewhat autocratic president, supported by a strong team of ministers and civil servants. The regional commissioners, at least in theory, were seen as the essential link between government and governed.

With the benefit of hindsight, it seemed that the new African broom tried to sweep too much too clean too quickly, but they had to act fast while the momentum of freedom carried all before it. It was hindered too by the sad fact that the cold war itself was reflected in the uneasy relations between mainland and island.

26

The Arusha Declaration, 1966–67

The Arusha Declaration (*Azimio la Arusha*) like the Holy Roman Empire was only incidentally connected with Arusha and was hardly a declaration in the usual sense of the word. Rather, it was the culmination of years of thought by the intelligent idealist philosopher President Julius Nyerere. It was expressed in a series of resolutions first presented to a meeting of TANU's national executive committee held at Arusha in January 1967, in which Nyerere sought to persuade his lukewarm colleagues that a policy of *ujamaa* (African socialism) was now right for the country.

He had become disillusioned by the increasing capitalist tendencies of many of the national leaders who sought to increase their personal wealth by abuse of their positions in a variety of ways; by using the *mirija* (straws) I mentioned earlier to suck the lifeblood of the people.

Some built houses for rent, others ran market gardens or invested their money by buying shares in foreign stock exchanges. Large numbers of expensive foreign cars were ordered for ministers and regional commissioners, especially the notorious Mercedes Benz. This gave rise to the coining by the Dar es Salaam workers of the delightful word *Wa-Benzi* to denote their arrogant new rulers who were all too often seen to drive through the streets reclining their heads on the headrests provided, often accompanied by smartly dressed wives or other ladies.

Nyerere also deplored the way in which his ministers seemed to spend their lives travelling around in search of foreign aid, pointing out that foreign governments were not charities.

Instead, he wished to instil a real spirit of self-reliance, not only into individuals but also into the whole national ethos.

Even the cream of Tanzanian youth, the relatively pampered young men and women who, admittedly by their own gifts and hard work were privileged to study at Dar es Salaam's magnificent new University College campus, became intellectually arrogant. They would speak English to each other in a superior way in front of their less fortunate compatriots. They soon formed themselves into an exclusive intelligentsia on their hill at Ubungo, increasingly cut off from the aspirations and needs of their parents and families who had struggled so long and so hard to pay for their school fees, books and uniforms.

They became so bigheaded that they refused to do the recently introduced compulsory national service. Emboldened by the courteous and considerate manner in which Prime Minister Kawawa received them, they even hinted at a student revolt and finally marched on State House on 22 October 1966.

This time, as they marched up the drive to State House in their academic gowns and English language protests and banners, they had gone too far. The president and his cabinet met them. The TBC broadcast the proceedings to the nation as armed troops and police were moved into position at the gates of State House to cut off their retreat. A convoy of buses and lorries had been assembled for their onward transport.

It was, as I recall, a weekend afternoon and I listened in at home. I had seldom heard Nyerere so angry and upset. He felt that he, their *mwalimu*, who had struggled so hard to win them their freedom and had built them their new university, had been cruelly betrayed by those in whom he had placed all his hopes for the future.

He was incensed by their insistence on speaking in a foreign language and proceeded to lambast them, as far as I can remember, in both languages. He would not spend a cent of public money on educating anyone who thought that national service was a prison.

He would cut his own salary by 20 per cent and that of his ministers. He concluded by letting them know that they would all be expelled and sent home immediately in the waiting transport, where they could reflect on their foolishness as they helped their parents till their fields.

This righteously indignant decision, which virtually closed the university for nearly six months and thereby delayed the whole nation-building process, was, Nyerere believed, a price worth paying to establish a clear bottom line for any future dissidents.

I feel certain too that it helped concentrate his mind on the vital need to introduce a new political philosophy for Tanzania as soon as possible. This would seek to build a new equal opportunity, self-reliant democratic socialist state based, not on imported Marxist doctrines, but on traditional African values.

Hence, the various principles first presented to TANU's national executive committee at Arusha, modified in various respects by cabinet, parliament and TANU during the first half of 1967 and soon to be dubbed by the Dar es Salaam media as the Arusha Declaration. The two main planks of the declaration were the leadership rules, which were not universally popular with those most affected, and the bringing of all the major means of production and exchange under public control, which were.

To convince the political and civil service élite that they needed to accept restrictions on their personal acquisition of wealth — the fruits of freedom — was a major task that took patience, time and compromise to achieve.

Nationalization, however, was welcomed with open arms and the TANU committee urged its immediate implementation. Within a few weeks, cabinet approval was obtained and within the next few days, amid demonstrations and popular rejoicing, all the private banks, the National Insurance Corporation and virtually all leading foreign export trading companies had been nationalized. Barclays, Grindlays and the Standard Bank became the National Bank of Commerce, while great household names like Smith Mackenzie and Gailey & Roberts later became the State Trading Corporation (STC). The government also stated its intention to acquire majority shareholdings in several large manufacturing companies and in the famous sisal industry. Like a rush of blood to the head, Nyerere rode on the tide of emotional chauvinism, which he sometimes found hard to control. Europeans and Asians were naturally most affected personally and this introduced a discordant racial element. Once the ball had started rolling, it was difficult to stop it and, within the next few years, almost all the remaining European and Asian farms in the country had also been compulsorily acquired.

The commercial nationalizations raised false hopes, with many people disappointed to discover that the vaults of the private banks were not in fact filled with millions of pounds worth of gold and cash. In fact, the immediate result for the ordinary customer was that it often took up to an hour to cash a cheque 'because the cashier had gone for lunch', while within a year or so supplies of butter, cheese, chocolate, toilet paper, toothpaste and imported soap had virtually run out. In time, Chinese supplies of consumer goods began to arrive and their sandalwood soap in particular was quite excellent. Kondo, our gardener, told me that the Chinese toothpaste must be good 'because Chairman Mao brushed his teeth with it'. Many years later, I read in his personal physician's biography of him that Chairman Mao never in fact brushed his teeth at all, which made me smile.

The most revolutionary change of all to flow from the Arusha Declaration, in that it directly affected the vast majority of the population, was the decision gradually to convince peasants throughout the country to move from their scattered isolated villages into large socialist villages (*ujamaa vijijini*). There, it would be so much easier to provide schools, dispensaries and all other necessary facilities for them such as water and electricity supplies. Better still, it was hoped that communal farms would lead to increased agricultural output through greater use of tractors, fertilizers, extension services, rotation of crops and more economic use of manpower. Coincidentally, it would also of course be far easier to count, tax, politically educate and even arrest people there.

As usual, however, the selfish human factor often rebels against the best intentioned bureaucratic systems encouraged or imposed from above without the overwhelming popular support needed to ensure success.

The ultra-conservative traditional peasant farmers of Tanzania were no exception. As we saw in Handeni district, people actually preferred to live in remote hamlets for fear of witchcraft, to avoid tax collectors, to practise shifting cultivation and just to be independent, isolated and free.

Nyerere doubtless felt that the greater good of the greater number far outweighed these outworn old-fashioned considerations. Like Zumbe Hemedi Sonyo, he thought that he must lead and not follow the people. At all events, he staked all in the next few years in implementing the policy of *ujamaa* villages as the top priority of his government and of TANU since 1967. He even acquiesced in some measure of moderate coercion, which some over-zealous underlings unfortunately abused on occasion by burning down people's homes to persuade them to move elsewhere.

It is ironic indeed that the very Arusha Declaration — Nyerere's pride and joy — designed to raise the living standards of millions of farmers and their families and to build a new modern united nation, would ultimately prove his Nemesis.

27

Films and Famine: From Stockholm to Kilwa, 1967

hile these exciting political events were gradually unfolding in Dar es Salaam, I was sent to Europe on a whirlwind tour in March 1967. The main object of my visit was to spend three weeks in Sweden — the Mecca of the cooperative world — and make a film there.

In Tanzania, Sweden was now the fourth biggest foreign aid donor after the UK, the USA and West Germany. It played a leading role in the splendid Nordic Centre at Kibaha — 25 miles west of Dar es Salaam on the road to Morogoro, which consisted of a combined secondary school, farmers' training centre and medical centre entirely built, staffed and financed by the four Nordic countries. The Swedish International Development Agency (SIDA) also funded a childcare training centre at Musoma and a rural water development programme. The Swedish Cooperative Union (*Kooperativa Forbundet* or KF), under the inspired leadership of Dr Mauritz Bonow, played a vital development and training role in the cooperative movement in general and in the opening of cooperative shops in particular. It also helped staff and fund the new Moshi cooperative college.

Denmark, too, gave assistance out of all proportion to its size, whereas Norway and Finland were less heavily involved. Being totally and traditionally neutral and non-aligned, Sweden was an ideal partner and mentor for Tanzania, torn as it was between left and right, east and west. Their peoples fair and dark, their climates cold and hot, combined to invest them with the attraction of opposites. Generally speaking, the Swedes and their fellow Scandinavians loved the sunshine, light and warmth of Africa, while the Africans were attracted by the cold snows of the north and always seemed really happy there.

The prosperous Nordic countries — seeking fulfilment and a role in the world — came to Africa with a crusading zeal, not always so apparent in other donors. They were extraordinarily dedicated, efficient and hard working. Their centre at Kibaha was a model of its kind and a joy to visit. They nearly all spoke excellent English, in itself a great advantage. With their cheerful dispositions, they got on very well with the local people and appreciated their sense of humour and joie de vivre.

A burly middle-aged Swede from the KF called Arne Holmberg led the whole Scandinavian cooperative team, which was to introduce the first consumer cooperatives to Tanzania.

To return to my Scandinavian safari, for some time we in the ministry had thought that the publicity armoury of our farmers cooperative movement — now by far the biggest and best in Africa — would be incomplete without a first-class documentary colour film in both English and Swahili. It needed to be suitable for showing both at home for educational purposes and abroad at the forthcoming Expo 67 in Montreal and in our overseas embassies.

Although we had our own excellent film unit in the ministry run by Danny Densham from the UK, Dave Giltrow from the USA and young Cyril Kaunga — the Tanzanian director designate — from Tabora, it was over-worked and under-funded. So, when the Swedish KF representatives Arne Holmberg and Rune Forsberg said that they were prepared to send out their own crack film team and shoot the film for us, we jumped at the generous offer.

The only conditions attached to it were that I myself should go to Sweden when the filming had been completed to work with the KF film team there. I wanted to help them edit, write the English script, translate it into Swahili and narrate in English a 40-minute coloured documentary film on the cooperative movement in Tanzania with the title, which I chose myself, of *Shoulder to Shoulder* (*Bega-kwa-Bega*). They would produce their own

Swedish version to show to cooperatives and schools inside Sweden for educational, fund-raising and publicity purposes.

I duly set off for Sweden, arriving in Stockholm early in March to a warm welcome from my friend Rune Forsberg, who drove me to the cooperative's own hotel Malmen where I stayed as their guest. The city looked beautiful under a white carpet of snow.

Next morning, we started work on the film at the KF film centre in the lovely eighteenth-century Maria Torget square, ten minutes' walk from my hotel. We worked until evening with a youthful team of mostly female technicians at the exacting task of editing a film. With eyes glued to the viewer for hour after hour, we slowly reduced more than three hours of film to the required 40 minutes.

The Swedes and I wrote the script together in Swedish and English, a creative and enjoyable task, and I later translated it into Swahili. Next came the exciting visit to the recording studios, where I duly narrated the English version.

Shortly before leaving Stockholm, I received a message through the Tanzanian embassy to return as soon as possible because the president wished to put me in charge of all famine relief measures in the country. The situation was apparently becoming extremely serious, especially in the Southern Region.

I spent a crowded day in Copenhagen on my way home and had a useful and friendly meeting with Danish cooperative leaders who promised to do all they could to send more experts to help our new consumer cooperative shops.

I returned to Dar es Salaam a few days later after brief stopovers in Paris and Rome to see my daughter and mother respectively.

* * *

I returned to my ministry the next morning. I had hardly had time to give Minister Babu a brief verbal report on my Scandinavian safari and hand over Swahili and English copies of my precious film, before I was told to report immediately to Second Vice-President Kawawa. I had been seconded to his office until further notice for special duty as famine executive officer, or *bwana njaa* in Swahili — literally Mr Hunger.

The second vice-president, whom the president had appointed famine supremo some time before, told me that he had just been telephoned by Mr Bungara, MP for Kilwa in the Southern Region. Mr Bungara had said that reports from upcountry inland villages were extremely disturbing and that matters there were going from bad to worse. He felt that local leaders were no longer able to cope and asked for immediate assistance from the government before people began to starve.

Pointing to a map, the vice-president added that there were serious food shortages in many parts of the country and that the situation was particularly grave in the Rufiji, Handeni and Bagamoyo areas. The rains had started and it was difficult to move relief supplies of food along flooded roads, especially to southernmost Kilwa, which was virtually cut off except by sea and air.

Kawawa told me that the president had decided to appoint me famine executive officer for the whole country. I was to be responsible only to him and, within reason, he would give me full powers as his special representative to take whatever steps were needed to solve the problem and feed the hungry as soon as possible. He confirmed that I could requisition government transport (including aircraft), commandeer surplus food supplies, take on extra staff, draw any extra cash needed and, so far as I could see, do almost anything in his name to fight the famine. Even the local Gauleiters — the regional commissioners and their at times difficult police commanders — were asked to give me all possible help. He suggested I fly to Kilwa as soon as possible because that was where the situation was most critical. I was to investigate the position with local leaders on the spot, take whatever immediate steps might be necessary and report back to him as soon as I could in person, sending interim reports if necessary by telephone.

I was thrilled at the time to have been entrusted with such a challenging task, my first frontline assignment in the bush since the Handeni famine 14 years before. I had always felt that a famine was to a district officer what a battle was to an army officer, the supreme test of his efficiency, leadership and dedication.

In retrospect, I feel this was the greatest compliment ever paid to me as an expatriate officer, and indeed the most rewarding and worthwhile job I ever did in my 30 years' service in East Africa. What a contrast it was too from my previous task — interesting though it was — of making a film in Sweden.

I flew south to Kilwa the next morning in a small government Cessna aircraft. I called on the area commissioner to discuss the situation with him and on the regional commissioner who had come up from his headquarters in Mtwara to meet us. Mr Bungara, the local MP who had alerted Kawawa, was also present, as were the local police officer and some TANU officials. There was no sign of famine in Kilwa itself; being a seaport on the Indian Ocean, there was a plentiful supply of fish and coconuts to supplement the people's diet.

Our meeting at the *boma* lasted for several hours and I was surprised at how little most of them seemed to know about the situation in the upcountry villages in the west of the district. I thought to myself that, in this respect at least, things had changed for the worse since *uhuru*, for, whatever the shortcomings of British rule, failure to deal promptly with crop failures and food shortages was certainly not one of them. At Mr Bungara's suggestion, it was decided that he, I, the area commissioner and the TANU chairman would drive to the western villages the next morning and find out exactly what was going on.

After a night in the local resthouse, we set off in the area commissioner's Land Rover early the next day. After a few hours on a reasonable road — the best in the district — we reached our destination, Njinjo. Just before we arrived at Njinjo, we were stopped by a young boy who brought us to see his aged grandparents who were in a very weak state and reduced to eating grass and *mabiba* — very hard nuts normally only eaten by lions and other wild animals. We were all shocked by this sight and gave the boy a few kilos of the flour we were carrying for an emergency.

We spent several hours driving from village to village in the vicinity. It was the same sad story everywhere — older people and small children were lying down emaciated with hunger and unable to walk — hardly able even to talk. We were shown the grave of a man said to have just died of hunger; the situation was far, far worse than anything I had seen during the Handeni famine.

299

We could not even consider stopping to eat ourselves; it would have seemed obscene in the circumstances. If the area commissioner was ashamed, he did not look it — it appeared to be his first visit to the place, which looked completely abandoned by the government. The listless inhabitants seemed to have given up. Only the strong young teenagers seemed to have any spirit left. They wore brightly coloured shirts and shorts and many of them had bicycles, which they rode with great élan. They told us that several of the shops near the chief's headquarters at nearby Njinjo, where we were planning to spend the night in the resthouse, had hoarded bags of maize flour in the hope that the price would rise as the famine worsened. This was the usual wicked ploy of exploiters since time immemorial.

We decided to go there at once with a small police escort and demand to inspect all the shop stores. These were found to contain about 50 bags of maize flour, which I commandeered at once in the name of the vice-president, despite the Indian shopkeepers' angry protests. I gave them a letter, signed on behalf of Second Vice-President Kawawa, promising to buy them at the correct market price as soon as I returned to Dar es Salaam. We then worked till 10.00 p.m. that day and all the next day distributing food to people. If they could not walk, we took it to their own homes; if they could walk, they came to collect the 30 or so remaining bags from outside the *baraza*.

Unfortunately, however, a few remote villages about 15 miles further west off the nearest road were still without supplies. These had been completely cut off by floods following the recent heavy *masika* rains in March and early April. Then, I remembered those cheerful boys on their bicycles and asked them if they thought they would be able to take between five and ten kilos each on their carriers and somehow get through to relieve the starving people. I need not have worried; they were real rural Kalamazoo shake your head types and with a loud cheer promised to go at once.

Under a 19-year-old leader, they formed a 'bicycle brigade' of about 20 cyclists, which enabled them to deliver at least 100 kilos of flour per trip. They quickly loaded up their bikes with flour and, within the hour, they were off down the muddy footpaths and tracks, singing as they went. They got through in a few hours and made several round trips in the next couple of days, delivering several hundred kilos of food by their splendid efforts and undoubtedly saving some lives. Even now, 30 years later, I still feel moved as I recall their high spirits and smiling faces, which inspired us all in those gloomy days of deprivation and despair.

The area commissioner, the TANU chairman, Mr Bungara MP, and I spent the night in the Njinjo resthouse. The chairman was a devout coastal Muslim sheikh who spent a good deal of his time setting his prayer mat northwards in the direction of Mecca and waking us all up with his orisons at sunrise.

The area commissioner convened a big *baraza* the next morning to hold a postmortem on the reasons for the famine and to decide what immediate action was needed now and what steps should be taken to ensure that it could never happen again. Hundreds of people turned up. Food was handed out to households according to the numbers in the family and careful records were kept.

Furious, hungry peasants hurled abuse at the government in general and at the local leaders in particular. One ended his diatribe by pointing at me and shouting dramatically, 'It was better under them. What use has *uhuru* been to us?' His outburst was greeted by shocked silence, followed by a murmur of agreement. Before any dissent could gain ground, the area commissioner turned to me and said, 'As you can see, Sir, this poor man is completely crazy. I will get the police to arrest him at once; he needs looking after.' I nodded assent and managed to suppress a smile.

While an outburst by an old man angered by the poor leadership of the lower ranks of a new, naturally inexperienced regime was understandable in the circumstances, the clock cannot be put back. The only positive answer was to press ahead with educating and improving the new rulers. At least that was what I always said when such sentiments were voiced to me privately, as they occasionally were during my remaining years in Africa. As far as I know, the public outburst was unprecedented and was 'hushed up' at the time.

We all returned to Kilwa the following day. After a night's sleep under the stars in the courtyard of a kind person's house under the palm trees near the sea, I flew back to Dar es Salaam. I went straight to the second vice-president's office to make a personal report to Mr Kawawa. He was visibly moved by my account of the sufferings of his people and angered by both the local officers' incompetence and the traders' hoarding. He approved all my actions, which was a comfort, and promised to get a few hundred tons of food shipped down to Kilwa as soon as possible. I asked him for a cargo plane as well, so that the 50 or so tons of maize flour CAFOD (Catholic Fund for Overseas Development) had donated the previous week could be flown down in two or three round trips the next day. It was stored in a hangar at the airport.

By the time I got home and had had a bath an hour or so later, he had telephoned me to say that 'the plane awaited my orders'. We had great fun next morning loading up the aeroplane and seeing it safely off to Kilwa. It was a moment of pure joy.

Later, we also dispatched relief supplies from Oxfam by dhow and coastal steamer. However, the instant airlift ordered by Kawawa, who was so decisive and supportive, was the key factor in feeding people and, almost as important, in restoring their morale by making them feel that they were no longer abandoned and forgotten.

Throughout April and May 1967, I rushed around the famine areas of Bagamoyo, Handeni and Rufiji and we soon had the whole situation under control and relief supplies moving freely to where they were most needed. It was fun visiting Handeni again and getting a wonderful welcome from all my old friends throughout the whole of Uzigua, especially from Zumbe Hemedi Sonyo at Magamba and the mission ladies at Kideleko. I was particularly pleased to meet a young man of about 30 who not only remembered my having given him a one-shilling prize for answering a question correctly in a quiz during the 1953 famine, but even the question itself.

Being only a couple of hours' drive north of Dar es Salaam, Bagamoyo presented few problems, especially as I also knew the northern Uzigua areas well from my Handeni days.

Rufiji, however, was different. The *boma* at Utete on the croco-dile and hippo infested river about 100 miles due south of Dar es Salaam on the appalling 'main' road to Kilwa was more or less inaccessible in the rainy season. I had, in fact, once managed to get there in my secondhand Mini Minor, but during a much drier spell in 1955. This time, at the end of April when the rains were at their height and thunderstorms frequent and when speed was of the essence, I decided to go by air for a short visit to Utete.

A fortnight later, on 1 July 1967, the Ministry of Commerce and Cooperatives was abolished. After an uneasy fortnight in the Agri-culture Ministry, then headed by my friend Derek Bryceson, while they tried to decide what to do with me, I was posted to the newly formed Ministry of Commerce and Industries as principal assistant secretary (Publicity). This finally ended my long and happy association with the cooperative movement. I was about to enter a new world of international trade fairs and world exhibitions — a far cry from counting cash at the Nzega *boma* in 1948.

28
Snakes to Osaka, 1967–70

efore we could contemplate taking snakes to Osaka, however, we had to take stilts to Ndola. We had been invited to participate in the twelfth Zambian international trade fair to be held in the Copperbelt town of Ndola at the end of June 1968 — the biggest fair in Africa with a permanent exhibition site of 110 acres.

The new minister Aboud Maalim, another Zanzibari, placed me in charge of the Tanzanian pavilion and told me I had just a year to make it a success. Our pavilion at Expo 67 in Montreal, entered at the last minute on a shoestring budget, had not been a success and the government had now decided to take its appearances on the international stage more seriously. These world exhibitions and international trade fairs were not merely prestige and publicity stunts as some people thought, but rare opportunities to promote exports in general and tourism in particular.

The government had already decided that our participation in the next world exhibition to be held in Osaka in Japan in 1970 would be on a much bigger scale. It was decided that we should use the Ndola fair as a dress rehearsal for it, though our formal invitation did not in fact arrive until September 1967.

There were other reasons too for the importance of our Ndola exhibit. Zambia was our great ally; Nyerere and Kaunda were close friends and allies who shared a similar political philosophy. They were frontline states in the general struggle against white-dominated southern Africa with Zambia sharing a border on the Zambezi River with Smith's rebel regime in Southern Rhodesia.

Landlocked Zambia, whose outlet to the sea at Beira had been effectively cut off by the Rhodesian rebellion, now longed for a rail link with Dar es Salaam so that its valuable copper exports in particular could be safely exported.

For some years, Zambia and Tanzania had dreamed of this great railway that would at once link the two countries and relieve Zambia of unwelcome, humiliating reliance on its southern neighbours. In early 1965, the Chinese had offered to build the railway — a project Kaunda viewed with considerable suspicion, though Nyerere was more in favour of it. An Anglo–Canadian survey conducted in 1966, which concluded that it should prove economically viable, clinched the deal. By September 1967, under a tripartite agreement signed in Beijing by China, Tanzania and Zambia, China agreed to construct a railway from Dar es Salaam to Ndola, a distance of 1858 kilometres (1200 miles). Its cost of £175 million would be divided equally between the two countries. Chinese loans would help finance it and the sale of Chinese goods in the two countries would help service the loans — thus was the Tazara railway born.

Tanzania hoped too that the railway would open up remote areas of the Southern Highlands and the Kilombero valley for development. This would facilitate the marketing of sugar, coffee, tea and coal from the south of the country, in addition to the usual basic agricultural crops. The port of Dar es Salaam would also benefit from the increased shipping involved. Railways also usually have an unspoken strategic importance.

Our new ministry remained in the splendid new cooperative centre in Lumumba Street, into which we had moved from Independence Avenue in September 1966. This 12-storey skyscraper, the highest building in Tanzania, housed the whole of the old ministry under one roof, with great savings on transport and telephone bills.

There was a sad interlude before I flew to Ndola. Lord Twining had died in London on 21 July 1967 and a thanksgiving service was being held for his life on 19 September in his father's old church, St Stephen's in Rochester Row. Lady Twining wrote me a charming letter in which she asked if I could possibly get hold of the musical score for *Ngoma*, the KAR's regimental march, which her husband had specially requested be played as the organ voluntary at the end of the service. With the help of the police bandmaster, I managed to get hold of a copy, which was rushed to London in time for the service. I heard later that it had provided a moving finale to a beautiful service. Father Dick Walsh of the White Fathers read some of the prayers and Twining's old friend and chief Alan Lennox-Boyd (by now Lord Boyd) gave a moving address. The church was packed with his old administrative officers. My mother represented me and kept the service sheet, which I have in front of me. Surprisingly, it contains a passage from Pericles's speech after the Battle of Thermopylae:

> For the whole earth is the sepulchre of famous men; and their story is not graven only on stone over their native earth, but lives on in other lands without visible symbol, woven into the stuff of other men's lives.
>
> For us now it remains to rival what they have done; knowing that the secret of happiness is freedom, and the secret of freedom a brave heart.

I found these noble words inspiring, for I too mourned the man who had not only inspired me when I had served the British Crown directly in the colonial era but had also had the vision, insight and sympathy to encourage me to serve a free Tanzania.

* * *

Back in the ministry, we had now received the official invitation to participate in Expo 70 at Osaka. The Japanese had determined that this was going to be the biggest and best exhibition of all time and we were determined that Tanzania would be well to the fore in both events. Besides our increasing range of commercial exports such as furniture, fishnets, shoes, socks, shirts, blankets, sweets, meerschaum pipes, honey, wine and beer, and our art displays of ebony carvings and paintings, we planned to send the renowned Makonde stilt dancers to perform in the main arena. They came from the Newala district in the extreme south of the country and were famed for their stilt dancing and ebony carvings.

My Polish friend Bernard Kunicki had just produced a beautiful film on our wildlife entitled *Tanzania: Safari into Splendour.* He planned to screen it in the openair cinema at the trade fair and also, if possible, persuade Zambian Television to show it at the same time. I was determined to include Bernard in our team to Ndola so that he could film our exhibit and, if all went well, I would also try to persuade him to come to Japan. My old colleagues in the public relations photographic unit, John Mitchell-Hedges and Mohinder Singh, would of course be taking the still photographs.

The pavilion itself, the biggest and best yet built, would be designed by the government architect Mike Shanahan and built by the colourful Italian builder Corrado Tognetti's Dar es Salaam-based company Messrs Italframe Ltd. I envisaged our exhibit at Ndola being more than just the usual collection of colourful arte-facts neatly arranged in a picturesque display. I wanted a micro-cosm of the whole nation, a living entity of artefacts, products and above all people, who breathe the spirit of Tanzania with them wherever they go.

* * *

On 1 July 1968, all expatriate administrative officers were removed from their administrative posts and 16 of the 17 British officers were retired, I being the sole survivor. I was then placed on special duty as project leader of the Tanzanian pavilion at Expo 70 Osaka Japan.

This was a wonderful job with almost unlimited scope for creativity, enthusiasm and imagination, not to speak of the oppor-tunity to visit the mysterious Far East. It was also an ideal job for the last British district officer, who could be safely tucked away for a couple of years out of the public eye. I was the epitome of a back-room boy, but was lucky to be there at all because rumour had it that I too would have gone had my old friend the president not mislaid my file at State House.

I was flattered by this apocryphal story; Africans naturally held

307

all the key jobs. His Excellency Sebastian Chale, Tanzanian high commissioner in New Delhi, was appointed our commissioner-general and Frank Etuttu, a tall friendly commercial officer from Musoma, was deputy commissioner-general and made executive officer in charge of the pavilion.

We set the architect, builders and designers the challenging task of producing a prefabricated wooden structure. Made from our finest forest timbers, it could be shipped to Japan and reassembled on site by the Tokyo firm of Maeda Construction Ltd.

The pavilion symbolized a traditional African village of four circular houses crowned by a 36-foot-high canopy of four stylized scarlet flamboyant trees. It sought to express the national philosphy of *ujamaa* and to bring the spirit of Africa to the spectacular world stage of Osaka. The four houses represented the four halls of nature, people, culture and progress, in which we would display our unique treasures of scenery, wildlife, Makonde carvings, paintings, the replica of the *Homo Zinjanthropus* skull and a dazzling display of gems, including the recently discovered blue tanzanite. The central 'Plaza of Unity' under the flamboyant trees featured a sculpture park of large Makonde statues.

The pavilion would be surrounded by running water and a garden featuring African violets, our national flower that is indigenous to the Usambara mountains. The young Chagga artist Elimo Njau, whom I had met with Sam Ntiro at Makerere, designed an unusual Expo 70 poster, which he described as: 'Showing Africa in flames of progress. The circles represent racial harmony and peace between black and white. Mount Kilimanjaro symbolizes our struggle to achieve nobler ends. Bands represent African unity. And South Africa is all white and is isolated.' I liked the last sentence.

We used the poster as part of a campaign to involve the entire country in our Expo adventure. We also ran essay competitions with valuable prizes such as radios, which Japanese companies donated. We decided to send Deputy Commissioner-General Frank Etuttu to Osaka a year before the exhibition began as government liaison officer in Japan. His main job was to pave the way for our smooth participation by coordinating the exhibition work in progress there and in Tanzania. The lack of an embassy in Tokyo was a considerable disadvantage at that time, though it was corrected soon afterwards with the appointment of our first ambassador Mr G. Rusimbi. His appointment was a direct consequence of our large-scale participation in the world fair and subsequent expansion of our trade with Japan.

The next year and a half flew by in a kind of kaleidoscopic vista of architects and artists, conferences, confusion and crises, dancers and designers, films, financial worries, Japanese translations, quarrels, photos, snakes, stilts, stress, telephone calls and welcome weariness.

The year 1969 seemed to come and go in a flash. I was only dimly aware of events outside our closed world of exhibition planning through glancing at the morning newspaper ('the two-minute silence' as Twining had once dubbed it) at breakfast or listening half asleep to the BBC news at 9.00 p.m.

After hearing a loud explosion north of our home one day, I learned with great sorrow that my old friend Dr Eduardo Mondlane, leader of Frelimo (Mozambique Liberation Front) had been killed in a friend's home at Msasani by a parcel bomb sent to him by the Portuguese secret police, PIDE. Many a time I had gone for an early morning swim before breakfast at Oyster Bay beach with him and his beloved dog. We had hardly ever discussed politics. All hearts went out to his stricken American widow at his funeral at Kinondoni cemetery a day or two later.

I suppose political assassinations were an occupational hazard in Dar es Salaam at that time. The dingy offices of virtually all the exiled freedom movements of southern Africa were scattered along the south side of Mnazi Mmoja. These ranged from Frelimo (Mozambique), the MPLA, FNLA and Unita (Angola) to Zanu and Zapu (Rhodesia), Swapo (South West Africa or Namibia) and the ANC and PAC (South Africa).

Tanzania was a real haven for African nationalist movements. It gave them active financial and in some cases military support, as well as the use of its powerful radio transmitters to broadcast propaganda to the various homelands, Mozambique in particular. President Nyerere himself did what he could to promote cooperation between rival movements and to settle differences for the sake of the common cause.

It was difficult to know who exactly funded these organizations, but China, Russia, Sweden and various Western sources, including the World Council of Churches, all contributed in one way or another. The Americans ran an excellent international college for their students at Kurasini at which David Giltrow's wife Peggy was a teacher. He had been my colleague in the public relations department (film unit) several years before and I had a certain admiration for them. This was because, unlike the vast majority of expatriates, they lived modestly at Magomeni in the African area of the city and eschewed such luxuries as a motorcar, cycling everywhere through the hot crowded streets.

I was one of the lucky 12,000 guests invited to the opening ceremony at noon on Saturday 14 March when His Imperial Majesty Emperor Hirohito formally opened the exhibition. This took place in the archaic Court Japanese, used only by the royal family and incomprehensible to practically all his subjects.

Shortly before, an anxious looking Mohinder Singh rushed up to me spluttering, 'I've forgotten the bloody film, man!' Fortunately, Japan being a photo crazy country, he managed to buy some films at a nearby Kodak boutique and once more the situation was saved at the eleventh hour.

The formal opening was followed by a procession of the 77 nations present at the inaugural ceremony into the Festival Plaza. Our four hostesses were loudly applauded as they moved with grace and dignity to the rostrum, where they bowed to the royal box and the assembled multitude. They then declared, in clear voices, 'Tanzania: *Habari za Asubuhi*' (good morning). Preceded by the national flag, their pink and blue national dresses looked outstanding in the gorgeous array.

Expo 70 opened to the public the next day, Sunday 15 March, and more than 250,000 people visited it on the first day alone. The four-man contingent of Tanzanian traffic police took part in the impressive opening parade of the world's police at Festival Plaza. Watched by more than 10,000 people, they were later mobbed by hundreds of photographers and autograph hunters as

310

they visited the nearby Tanzanian pavilion. From morning to night, thousands upon thousands of people — mostly Japanese — poured into the pavilion in an endless throng. Thrilled by the sights and sounds of previously unknown animals, they stroked the lion and leopard skins and beat the drums. They found the Zanzibar door and Makonde carvings fascinating, the skull intriguing and the jewels enchanting.

Meanwhile, it was great to come home again to Mzinga Way. I found Susan refreshed after a restful visit to a coffee farm in the cool Southern Highlands and thrilled with the blue Thai rough silk dress I brought her from the factory in Bangkok. On my arrival at Dar es Salaam airport on 6 April, I was warmly greeted by Babu, who had again taken over from Maalim as our minister the previous year, and by Michiaka Suma, the Japanese ambassador. They then proceeded to hold a press conference at which I was billed the main speaker. I gave an upbeat account of our pavilion. I told them that it was being visited by about 6000 people an hour and that, by the time I left Osaka just over a fortnight after the opening, 500,000 people had seen it. I also announced that we had sold £7000 worth of cashew nuts, that wood carvings had had to be rationed to stop them running out and that the police band would be playing at our pavilion during Tanzania Week from 10 to 17 June. Our national day was confirmed as 15 June when, as the president was unfortunately unable to attend, the second vice-president, Rashidi Kawawa, would be the Expo guest of honour and deliver the keynote speech at the Festival Plaza. I concluded loyally by giving my own opinion 'that the Tanzanian pavilion at Expo 70 was among the best 30 in design and exhibits'.

Life continued to be pretty hectic for the next two months, for it was quite a tough administrative — and at times diplomatic — task to arrange the movement, accommodation and performances for such a large contingent of bands, dancers, drums, snakes and stilts over such great distances.

I was back in the Tower Hotel in Kyoto for the warm summer sunshine of early June to finalize the many last minute details for the dance company's impending arrival.

311

The exhibition was now at its peak with more visitors than ever and our pavilion and boutique continued to do a roaring trade. Our films too, led by Bernard Kunicki's award-winning *Tanzania: Safari into Splendour*, also drew large crowds daily in the auditorium at the Expo Club. While in Kyoto in March for the opening ceremony, Bernard made an excellent film, since distributed in its Swahili and English versions, on Tanzania at Expo 70.

We were centre stage at the Festival Plaza for our great day, 15 June, getting excellent nationwide television, radio and press publicity. Our dancers, drummers and singers performed splendidly, none more so than the blind drummer Morris Nyunyusa who became an instant celebrity. Second Vice-President Kawawa started his speech by telling the audience that 'the spirit of man first breathed two million years ago in the Olduvai Gorge in northern Tanzania' and his words too were well received, spoken in English and translated into Japanese. All told, there must have been more than a hundred Tanzanians there that day, including the police band and the vice-president's 17-man delegation. Minister Babu was there of course, obviously enjoying himself and cheering us all on.

On his return to Dar es Salaam on 20 June, Mr Kawawa said that part of Japan's interest in developing more trade ties with Tanzania was because of the country's successful pavilion at Expo 70. He added, 'We have benefited a great deal from our participation.' He hailed the performances of the 25 traditional dancers, the police band, the Morogoro jazz band and the blind drummer Morris Nyunyusa, who he said had thrilled the audience at Expo 70.

Minister Babu and I returned home two days later with Oliver Maruma and the dance company, all of whom were tired but happy that everything had gone so well. In a characteristic gesture, Babu had ordered beer for the whole party on the flight home, only to be told that it had run out. 'That's all right,' he said, 'get them champagne!' Many years later, when he came to dinner with us in our London flat, we opened a bottle of champagne for him and reminded him of the story. He was delighted.

29
Last Man Out, 1970–72

Life inevitably seemed dull after the exhibition adventure, but we were left very busy until September 1970 when it came to an end. Indeed, we were still winding it up almost until the end of the year. The strains of our exhibition signature tune 'Tazama Ramani' (Look at the Map) were still ringing in my ears, and the memory of our lovely timber pavilion has remained with me ever since. It was included in a special souvenir edition of Japanese postcards of the 12 best pavilions at Expo 70.

As I gazed on the pavilion on my last day at the exhibition that had played so big a part in my life over the last few years, I thought about my own divided loyalties. The constant tension engendered by my Anglo–Irish identity perhaps helped explain the British–Tanzanian aspect of my personality, which transcended at once my traditional loyalty to the British crown and my fierce love of Tanzania. Taken aback by the intensity of my own feelings, I felt my heart swell with pride as I bade farewell to the pavilion and saw its fluttering blue, black, green and gold standard fade slowly into the vanishing haze. That these at times conflicting loyalties had survived the burning of the Union Jack, the freezing of British loans, the breaking of diplomatic relations, the seizing of British property and the exchange of insults, never ceased to surprise me.

Dar es Salaam's British residents sometimes accused me of being too pro-African and thus, by implication, anti-British, if not treacherous. On one memorable evening, I replied to my fellow guests at the Oyster Bay Hotel that I personally felt that Her

313

Majesty's interests in East Africa were best served by doing every-thing possible to assist, support and succour the young republic. It was, after all, a fellow member of the much-vaunted British Com-monwealth of Nations. As to my personal loyalty, I pointed out forcefully to my detractors that my family had served the British Crown almost continuously for over 450 years and that the patriotism I had taken for granted since birth was strong enough to include my adopted country. Silence ensued and the matter was never raised again in my presence.

A few ill-disposed Tanzanians, disgruntled at the continued presence in the government of a 'colonialist' officer, also ques-tioned my loyalty to their country. A thinly disguised attack on me in an article in one of the local English language newspapers referred to 'a trusted expatriate who doubtless used his expert knowledge of Swahili to spy for his own country'. I was momen-tarily upset, but heartened by African friends who told me that no one believed such rubbish.

Torn thus between the Scylla of my past imperial homeland and the Charybdis of my newly found republican allegiance, I had to tread warily and trust my own destiny. Even my own mother, after staying with settlers in Kenya, confided that her friends had told her that 'no gentleman now worked in Tanzania', while my future stepfather told her to get me out at once. I must have been a bit shaken by such comments because I took the precaution of asking the British high commissioner Sir Horace Phillips and his successor Arthur Kellas if they felt that my present work was in Britain's best interests. To my great relief, they both unhesitatingly replied in the affirmative.

Soon, however, my direct involvement with the government per se came to an end with my official retirement after 23 years' service from Her Majesty's Overseas Civil Service (HMOCS) on 20 December 1970. I had lasted for two-and-a-half years after the purge of British administrative officers on 1 July 1968, being 'hidden' on special duty at the distant Expo 70 project, which essentially became my swan song.

I did not feel sad, however, because on 5 May Babu had offered me a further three-year contract as public relations consultant to the newly formed State Trading Corporation (STC). He had little difficulty persuading me to accept what seemed to be a challenge that was totally different from anything I had hitherto attempted. Babu himself was also soon dropped from the government by Nyerere and succeeded as minister early in 1971 first by Paul Bomani and later by the former finance minister Amir Jamal.

The STC, a child of the Arusha Declaration, came into being on 11 February 1967, a few days after the government took over the private foreign trading companies. Its Swahili motto, *Saidia Tujenge Chetu* (help us to build ourselves up), carries the same capital initials as its English title. It had perhaps been given the hardest task of all in the national struggle to bring the economy into the hands of the people themselves. During the previous two years, it had completed its critical expansion phase. Having integrated the former foreign trading companies and opened branches throughout all 18 regions, its shipping agencies and port services were now acting as agents for leading shipping lines to and from most destinations in the world. The process of welding STC into one effective organization had been going on for more than four years, in fact ever since it had first inherited the diverse legacies of the former trading companies.

Before reporting for duty with the STC, however, on 21 December 1970, the day after my official retirement from HMOCS, Susan and I proceeded to Britain on four months' retirement leave from August to December 1970, leaving colleagues in the ministry to 'mop up' the Expo 70 work.

As my three-year contract with STC began on 1 November 1970, for seven glorious weeks both my old and my new employers paid me — a highly satisfactory but sadly rare state of affairs. While on leave in London, we visited Susan's parents in their new home in the Sussex village of Fletching where they had recently celebrated their golden wedding. Sadly, it was to be the last time we would see Susan's mother Stella, with whom I had always enjoyed a very special rapport.

TANU Guidelines 1971 set the scene and became at once the Bible and instruction manual for party workers, political activists, local leaders and young patriots everywhere. Like all Bibles, it was

315

liable to differing interpretations by zealots of varying creeds. Soon it was being cited to regulate the length of young men's hair and of young women's dresses. The popular miniskirt was thought to be un-African, decadent and Western. In no time, policemen were going round the streets with tape measures, stopping young women on the street and measuring their dresses to ensure they were 'knee length', failing which they were allegedly taken down to the station for further inspection.

Men too had to conform to the strict dress code. Soon, students returning from the West were having their long hair cut at the airport on landing and being returned to their families looking like prisoners. The previously fashionable *suruali za mchinjo* (butcher boy's trousers), so tight that it was jokingly said that two girls were needed to pull them off (one for each leg), and the wide flared *bugalo* trousers, were both severely frowned upon and replaced in the main by more sober apparel.

The bulk of the population, peasant farmers living in traditional style in upcountry villages, had never been fashionable, so were entirely unaffected by these modern urban admonitions.

Up until the time I left the country a couple of years later, corruption was rare and confined mainly to junior policemen asking a cyclist without a lamp for a shilling or so in the few days before pay day — *siku za mwambo* (days when one is stretched). It was still virtually unknown among ministers and senior officers, who were still inspired by Nyerere's wonderful example.

Bernard Kunicki would drive down from Nairobi with his faithful 'padlocks'* bringing much needed supplies of butter, cheese and chocolate. He gave us excellent dinners and lunches at the fashionable Motel Agip, where the dark dashing young headwaiter doubled as the Spanish consul.

By July 1971, Amir Jamal had succeeded Paul Bomani as minister for commerce and industries and he escorted President Nyerere around our STC pavilion at the annual *Saba Saba* trade fair when we won the cup for the best pavilion. My nephew and godson Jonathan Shackleton was staying with us, and Susan had

---

* Trusted retainers.

taken him on safari to the Northern Province to see the famous game parks there. While they were away, I received a telegram for Susan telling her that her mother Stella had been killed and her father badly injured in a car crash on 7 July — *Saba Saba* day itself. I had to break the news to Susan and to Stella's grandson when they returned a few days later. Her tragic death also cast a cloud over our daughter Lucy's wedding, which was planned to take place at the local village church of Fletching at the end of September, a couple of months later. Fortunately, the family felt that Stella would have wished her granddaughter's wedding to go ahead as planned. Her youngest daughter Sarah, who had been our bridesmaid aged 14, and her naval husband Commander Jim Swinley, who had a lovely old house and garden nearby, kindly agreed to host the wedding reception.

Susan and I, who had been on our retirement leave only nine months before, managed to get three weeks' compassionate leave to attend Lucy's wedding on 25 September to Peter Fisher. He was the elder son of a distinguished admiral who had commanded the battleship *Warspite* at the decisive battle of Cape Matapan in the Second World War and later became Fourth Sea Lord.

We returned to Tanzania in October 1971 in time to join the planning for the highlight of the year — the celebrations to mark the tenth anniversary of *uhuru* planned to last for 12 days starting on 1 December and reaching a climax on Uhuru Day itself, 9 December. Here, Nyerere again broke new ground by inviting many of the former colonial administrative officers who had left the country, at or soon after independence, to return as his government's honoured guests, to see for themselves what progress and development had taken place under an independent government. Their wives were also invited and, in the fortnight or so they spent in the country, every effort was made to ensure that they were taken to visit at least one of their former upcountry districts.

Many of them were considerably impressed by progress made in the country since their own departure, though naturally some of them also expressed strong reservations. After a week or so visiting their old 'stamping grounds', they returned to Dar es

Salaam for a round of celebrations, parades and parties, culminating in a glittering state banquet at which the president paid tribute to their past service in laying the foundations of the modern Tanzania.

Some 50 former district officers and their wives attended and the government met all their travelling and hotel expenses. This unprecedented gesture of goodwill and reconciliation was typical of Nyerere's imaginative vision and magnanimity, which set the scene for the excellent personal relations between the people of Britain and Tanzania that have continued ever since. The formation of the Britain–Tanzania Society in 1975 strengthened them further. The late Archbishop Trevor Huddleston, former Bishop of Masasi, was its first patron.

Meanwhile, construction of the great railway from Dar es Salaam to Ndola on the Zambian Copperbelt, begun in 1970, proceeded apace. It would, when completed in 1974, be the final plank in the great 'land bridge' joining Zambia to Tanzania. The others were the underground oil pipeline and the fleets of enormous lorries moving up and down the Great North Road, which between them gradually prised Zambia away from its previous forced dependence on South Africa. The Great Tazara Railway was Nyerere and Kaunda's trump card in gaining economic independence; and also the international status symbol for which both young nations yearned.

Who could have foreseen then that, 25 years later, a luxury passenger train would carry tourists along that line from Cape Town, capital of a free democratic Republic of South Africa, to Dar es Salaam? This was perhaps not quite the dream Cecil Rhodes had in mind at the turn of the century.

About this time, too, plans were going ahead for building a new capital at Dodoma, the rather dry and dusty capital of the Central Region, notorious for its aridity, famines and food and water shortages. It seemed at first sight a strange place for a capital, but strategically it was ideally situated in a central position on both the main East-West railway line and the Great North Road.

At one time, I believe, even the Germans toyed with the idea and had ambitious plans for a large canal that would bring the waters of Lake Victoria to irrigate the parched soil of the Central Region. The British also briefly considered this idea, but both governments rejected it because of the enormous expense involved.

This was the classic syndrome of governments feeling exposed and isolated on the seacoast. The commercial capital would always be Dar es Salaam, and up to the time we left at the end of 1973, only the second vice-president's (Kawawa's) office had in fact been moved to the new capital; even now — 25 years later — the transfer has not been fully completed.

In January 1972, Gerald, who was home from Oxford for his Christmas vacation, paid a visit to our old station, Handeni. He received a heart-warming welcome from many old friends nearly 20 years after we had left, with Zumbe Hemedi Sonyo, the former Chief of Magamba, and my old office messenger Juma sending especially affectionate messages. I was particularly touched by the kind reception he received from the area commissioner, who also sent Susan and me an invitation to come and stay. Such were the excellent personal relations in Tanzania between the representatives of the old and new regimes ten years after *uhuru* — a tribute perhaps to them both.

Indeed, race relations as a whole in Tanzania between Africans, Asians and Europeans were excellent, with only the *kaburu* (ugly Boer) from the 'unmentionable' having anything to fear in the unlikely event of putting in an appearance.

Early in April 1972, Sheikh Abeid Karume, the first vice-president and president of Zanzibar, was assassinated by a young officer of his bodyguard, who shot him several times at point blank range as he was relaxing outside his house playing the traditional game of *bao* (board), vaguely similar to draughts. His murder sent shock waves across the land and gravely threatened the stability of the country and even the fragile union itself.

Babu, although protesting that he had been out fishing in the Indian Ocean with the mysterious Misha, the Romanian owner of Silversands Hotel, at the time of the murder, was none the less widely believed to be the ringleader of the plot to kill Karume. He was promptly arrested by Nyerere and detained without trial at Ukonga gaol — for his own protection.

319

Soon afterwards, he was sentenced to death in absentia by a court in Zanzibar. He was destined to remain in detention, first in Ukonga and then in Tabora, for six years until Nyerere pardoned him in 1978. He then went into a kind of exile in Britain and the USA where he worked as an academic and journalist.

It was popularly rumoured that Babu and his associates, who included the Romanian, had plotted Karume's downfall in the bar of the Sea View Hotel. I met its Greek manager George, who had been a good friend of ours, a few years ago in Mr Patel's newsagent's shop in Gloucester Road, South Kensington, where Swahili is commonly spoken.

On 8 April, a week's national mourning for Karume was decreed and the STC band's performance at Dodoma was cancelled. Sheikh Aboud Jumbe, a gentler and less controversial figure, succeeded Karume as first vice-president of the (still) united republic and president of Zanzibar. Life, at least on the mainland, slowly began to return to normal.

Babu, whom I often met in London after his release in 1978, was remarkably philosophical about his long detention, which had seriously affected his health, leaving him nearly blind at one time and with poor circulation in his legs. Indeed, he often spoke of the great kindness of the warders, especially at Tabora prison and the many good friends he made 'inside'. He appeared to harbour no grievance whatsoever against the governments of either the United Republic or Zanzibar, though not unnaturally his relations with President Nyerere remained strained for the rest of his life.

30

'Kwa Heri' (Farewell),
1972–73

The milieu in which we live has become increasingly African, with half the office correspondence conducted in Swahili. Apart from diplomats, Europeans are few and far between; our visitors' book fills up with mainly African names. Cyril Okido, a Chagga from Kibosho, who first appears in 1965 as a trainee teacher at Morogoro Teachers' Training Centre, proudly signs himself 2/Lt C. J. Okido in the TPDF in January 1971. Sent to China for training in 1972/3, he later distinguished himself as a colonel in the Uganda campaign that toppled General Amin, who had unwisely invaded the West Lake Region of Tanzania.

Gerald, who had been on an adventurous journey in a Land Rover from London, arrived in September 1972 via Gibraltar and the Sahara desert. He was with his great friend Alan Gibbs, a contemporary of his at Christ Church, Oxford, and three other members of their expedition led by a young Frenchman, Pierre Jaunet. He sent a mysterious telegram from Beni in Zaire, which read: 'ideology has forced change of route now arriving 14 September.'

I was completely baffled by this cryptic message, but suddenly realized in the middle of the night that the unusual first word referred to Idi Amin, the evil dictator wreaking havoc in Uganda, through which they had intended to travel. They now came instead straight to the West Lake Region of Tanzania, where he had a bad attack of malaria in a mission hospital at Kibondo in our old Buha district — shades of Napier's immortal telegram, 'PECCAVI (I HAVE SIN[NE]D).'

Alan stayed on for a fortnight or so until the end of September. No sooner had Pierre and his friends left than Jeremy Ferguson arrived for a couple of nights; he too organized trans-Saharan tours and Gerald had met him on their journey. He greatly impressed us by walking barefoot the five miles from Dar es Salaam to our home. We impressed him by asking him to leave after only two days, for Susan felt that our ménage was about to be overwhelmed by the deluge of young visitors. Jeremy, or 'Fergie' as he is popularly known, has been drawing my attention to this incident at regular intervals for the past 25 years.

My mundane duties at the STC continued throughout 1972, with the usual round of tours by the band, opening new branches and shops, arranging press conferences, press releases, broadcasts, magazines, *Saba Saba* exhibition stands, parades and floats to mark the tenth anniversary of the republic and so on ad nauseam. We seemed to be living on past capital, endlessly celebrating anniversaries and doing nothing. The constant high-flown rhetoric no longer matched the facts. It was a frustrating time, for most of the skilled and experienced expatriate staff had left the country and their replacements were of necessity largely inexperienced and inadequately prepared and trained for their new responsibilities. Some were plain inefficient, others lazy and a few corrupt.

The whole vast hastily assembled enterprise began to disintegrate; auditors' reports became ever more censorious, expenditure ever more nugatory. Shortages of essential household goods occurred without warning with increasing regularity. With the STC rapidly becoming an object of contempt and ridicule, its decline towards the end of the year threatened the very credibility of the government itself. Ruthless action had reluctantly to be taken to dismantle it in the hope that, with the new philosophy of 'small is beautiful' it could be managed more efficiently in smaller units.

Writing to my mother for her birthday on 22 November 1972, I added a postscript: 'STC comes to an end and is being reorganized into 24 small companies, hence my job also ends! Still no news re tourist job.' I need not have worried. Apart from the fact that my three-year contract still had a year to run, nothing moved very fast. The old adage, 'There's plenty of time in Africa', applied with a vengeance, and it was not until 14 March 1973 that I started work as director of public relations for the Tanzania Tourist Corporation (TTC).

At first, as I moved around the country from one luxury safari lodge to another, or visited idyllic coastal resorts north of Dar es Salaam and a deep-sea fishing lodge on Mafia Island, I thought that tourism would be one long holiday. I was rapidly disillusioned, however, and soon realized that tourism was a cut-throat international industry, extremely sensitive to the slightest political change or security risk. It was of course potentially a great foreign exchange earner and had been the leading export of countries like Italy, Greece and Switzerland for many years.

It does not matter how beautiful the scenery, how unspoiled the beaches, or how unique the wildlife if the hotels are uncomfortable, the food poor, the staff rude, or the guests robbed. Tanzania soon realized that tourists seeking sunshine, beaches and excitement can also find them in the West Indies, India, Malaysia and Thailand and nearer to home in Morocco, Tunisia and the Gambia, most of which have had a few years' start and a more sophisticated background.

A riot or two and the odd murder can also empty hotels almost overnight and, unless a hotel can maintain an average of 50 per cent 'bed-occupancy', it simply cannot break even. Unless the hotels and ancillary services, such as the arrangements for meeting people at airports, are efficiently run, the best publicity films and the glossiest brochures are of little avail. The old Swahili proverb as usual applies again: *'chema chajiuza, kibaya chajitembeza'* (good things sell themselves, bad things parade themselves).

In Third World countries, there is the additional danger of exposing poor villagers living in the vicinity to hordes of apparently very rich, spoiled foreigners with nothing to do but idle the hours away pointlessly lying on beaches or gazing at wild animals. This situation is undesirable because it tends to corrupt poor people and tempt them into begging, or becoming touts and even robbers. Is it a price worth paying? This question was frequently posed as we planned the early stages of the new tourist industry.

Tanzania: Journey to Republic

In May 1972, our daughter Lucy brought her husband Peter to visit us — her first visit as a married woman and his first visit to Africa. They could only stay for just under three weeks, but managed to visit the game parks in the north and to spend a day in Zanzibar, where I had not been since the revolution in 1964.

As a reward for these exertions and the completion, with Bernard Kunicki's help, of a beautiful STC 1974 calendar, kind Gabriel Mawalla gave me a very, very long weekend off. Susan and I went to Mafia Island Lodge from Saturday 13 to Friday 19 October, where we stayed in the presidential suite and 'inspected' the lodge.

This proved to be our last holiday together in Tanzania and we had a restful time strolling along the beach, swimming and sunbathing. On one memorable afternoon, we went out deep-sea fishing in a choppy sea, and caught several very strong barracuda and swordfish after 'playing' them for about twenty minutes. I had no idea how powerful they were and had to hang on for dear life to avoid being dragged overboard; I was glad to catch them before they caught me. At least they proved a useful addition to the Mafia Island Lodge cuisine, for I had landed over 150 pounds of fish in the afternoon.

We had just two months left, for it had now been arranged that I would leave on 19 December. Susan would fly home ten days earlier — appropriately on 9 December, Uhuru Day — to avoid the nightmare of the final packing up when the house would inevitably become extremely uncomfortable.

I was to do one last safari before then to my beloved Northern Region to carry out a troubleshooting inspection of Tanzania Tours Ltd (TTL), which had signally failed in its key role of transporting tourists efficiently around the country.

There were disquieting reports of aeroplane loads of tourists being stranded at Dar es Salaam airport on arrival from Europe because someone had blundered. If such a state of affairs were allowed to continue, it would spell the death-knell of our tourist industry, even before it had been christened.

I duly returned to my old station Arusha for the first week of November for my last safari, during which I also visited Lake Manyara and Ngorongoro crater. To get the flavour as it were of the business and to see the problems confronting it for myself, I drove everywhere in a TTL Land Rover. Having made it my business to study stock control in the STC and bed-occupancy rates in the TTC, I now immersed myself in the details of expanding safari and maintenance facilities, constructing a 5000-gallon underground fuel tank and providing more tools and spare parts.

Somewhat to my surprise, I found it all fascinating; it reminded me a little of my early days in Africa as a soldier. The drivers and mechanics were splendid men, but badly led and sometimes left in the bush with no proper food or accommodation.

I was so upset by the inefficiency of our vitally important tourist industry that I drew up proposals for a complete overhaul of the TTL on my return to Dar es Salaam. I put this to Gabriel Mawalla with such conviction that he more or less asked me to stay on for yet another year or two and run the company myself.

I must confess to having been sorely tempted for an hour or two, flattered doubtless by the offer of such a challenging frontline job to postpone, yet again, the 'evil day'. In any case, it was extremely doubtful if the government would have accepted Mawalla's proposal, which politically — 12 years after *uhuru* — was obviously a retrograde step.

Gerald had written to me some months earlier urging me to 'take a Disraelian leap in the dark' and return home before it was too late. I took his advice, the more so since, aged 49, time was running out to have any realistic chance of getting another job on returning to Britain. I had applied for a job at the United Nations, but failed to get it because the United Kingdom quota had been filled, although I was supported by Sir Richard Turnbull from the colonial regime and ministers Babu, Bomani and Nsilo Swai from its successor.

I was touched by a beautiful painting of a Kilimanjaro homestead in the banana trees, handed to me the day before I left by Sam Ntiro, Tanzania's leading artist, with the request that I 'should look at it, until one day I would return'.

Soon Susan too was gone. I started the final bleak task of selling the car to a Dar es Salaam taxi-driver, who kept it on the road for at least another ten years, crating our belongings for the Express

Transport Company to ship to London and saying goodbye to a host of friends.

The faithful Shabani Sultan Seffu, usually known as Shab, came to stay to help me pack up and generally survive the last ten days. A Zigua student at the Aga Khan Secondary School whom we had got to know some years before, he had often stayed with us and joined enthusiastically in the badminton and swimming. I had taught him to drive and now he drove me everywhere. Almost too exhausted to think, I seemed to crowd a month's work into a week. I rushed from shipping and airways offices to banks and embassies as I tried to extricate myself from the silken bonds of 25 years' residence in Tanzania and prepare to venture into a known yet unknown land.

Shabani, who celebrated his twenty-first birthday the day before I left (18 December) was soon to marry his sweetheart Pascalia and call his first child Susan. We have kept in touch ever since. David Ricardo and Shab saw me off at the airport the next day, Wednesday 19 December 1973, on Super VC 10 Flight EC 634 exactly 30 years and one week since I had sailed into Kilindini harbour, Mombasa as a teenage soldier in another world.

Conclusion

In this memoir I have tried to portray something of the minor part I was privileged to play in the last 12 years of British colonial rule in Tanganyika and the first 12 years of independence there. I have sought also to give a glimpse of the last years of the British Empire in India, Ceylon, Aden, Kenya, British Somaliland and Sudan. I have tried, too, to convey to posterity something of the spirit of the times — of the high endeavour that infused the youth of postwar Britain, enabling them to transform in a few years the old autocratic empire to the new democratic Commonwealth of independent nations. I have also stressed the deep underlying friendship between the races throughout this period, without which such a smooth transfer of power would have been impossible.

I had the added advantage of having been born in the Irish Free State, two years after its creation in 1922 after 750 years of British rule — arguably its first overseas possession.

My own forebears had been 'colonists' themselves for 300 years, members of the Anglo–Irish whose unique dichotomy I considered at the beginning of the book. At all events, this ancestry gave me a definite empathy with the African people with whom I have always felt the closest rapport.

Britain, with no written constitution of its own, has had a genius for evolving systems of government best suited to a bewildering variety of local conditions. It has included dominions, crown colonies, protectorates' mandates (later to become UN trusteeship territories) such as Tanganyika itself, condominiums, Indian states, a self-governing colony and high commission territories within its imperial embrace. Its own destiny had been shaped by centuries of Roman rule and Norman conquest. By any standards,

327

its achievements have been extraordinary and its contribution to mankind unequalled.

Tanzania itself got off to a flying start with three constitutions in its first three years: a self-governing dominion with a governor-general from 1961 to 1962, a republic in 1962 and a united republic in 1964.

The global postwar revolution, which in a few decades transformed the British Empire into a self-governing Commonwealth of Nations, was not achieved without tragic loss of life. This was especially true of the birth pangs of India and Pakistan, ironically the oldest and most cherished children of the Raj. We, who served Tanzania, black and white alike, can take some pride from one of the smoothest transitions in the entire empire, a fact that has undoubtedly played no small part in the recent relatively trouble-free history of the country.

The empire, which as late as 1940 Churchill had dreamed would be 'lasting for a thousand years', albeit somewhat metaphorically, had by June 1997 virtually ceased to exist. The small but dedicated colonial and overseas civil services, which served it so well for 160 years, have also come to an end, an event appropriately celebrated in Westminster Abbey on 25 May 1999.

I was proud to have played a small part in the unfolding of this drama and was lucky to be a pawn on both sides of the chess board, joyfully undertaking the necessary somersault that marked the sudden role reversal from ruler to partner. I have no regrets and feel nothing but gratitude to the land that gave me such a feeling of fulfilment and has left me with such happy memories.

Index

Index

Index

Index

Index

Index

Index

Index

Index

Index

Index